**WITHDRAWN**
UTSA LIBRARIES

# Reflexive Practice

# Reflexive Practice

## Professional Thinking for a Turbulent World

Kent C. Myers

With contributions from

David L. Hawk
Thomas W. Cuddy
Eleanor Criswell
Kim Forss
James T. Ziegenfuss, Jr.
Margaret M. Nicholson

REFLEXIVE PRACTICE
Copyright © Kent C. Myers, 2010.

All rights reserved.

First published in 2010 by
PALGRAVE MACMILLAN®
in the United States—a division of St. Martin's Press LLC,
175 Fifth Avenue, New York, NY 10010.

Where this book is distributed in the UK, Europe and the rest of the world, this is by Palgrave Macmillan, a division of Macmillan Publishers Limited, registered in England, company number 785998, of Houndmills, Basingstoke, Hampshire RG21 6XS.

Palgrave Macmillan is the global academic imprint of the above companies and has companies and representatives throughout the world.

Palgrave® and Macmillan® are registered trademarks in the United States, the United Kingdom, Europe and other countries.

ISBN: 978–0–230–10394–8

Library of Congress Cataloging-in-Publication Data

    Reflexive practice : professional thinking for a turbulent world / Kent C. Myers.
      p. cm.
    Includes bibliographical references and index.
    ISBN 978–0–230–10394–8
      1. Organizational change. 2. Organizational effectiveness.
    3. Organizational behavior. I. Myers, Kent C.

HD58.8.R3867 2010
658.4'06—dc22
                                                        2009053939

A catalogue record of the book is available from the British Library.

Design by Newgen Imaging Systems (P) Ltd., Chennai, India.

First edition: September 2010

10 9 8 7 6 5 4 3 2 1

Printed in the United States of America.

# Contents

*List of Tables and Figures* vii
*Notes on Contributors* ix
*Preface* xi

### I Kernel

1 The Turbulent Environment, Then and Now 3
2 Reflexive Practice for the Times We Live In 19
3 At-Risk Practices That No Longer Work 41

### II Facets

4 Intelligence for Security 67
5 Economy for Good 89
6 Economy, Environment, Energy: Worlds Apart, or Three Perspectives on the Same World 107
*David L. Hawk*
7 National Environmental Policy Act as a Reflexive Setting 125
*Thomas W. Cuddy*
8 Reflexive Personality 145
*Eleanor Criswell*
9 Reflexive Practice on the Global Scene 173
*Kim Forss*
10 Building Reflexive Practice in Graduate Education 189
*James T. Ziegenfuss, Jr.*
11 A Behind-the-Scenes Scenario with Reflexive Practitioners 199

Appendix: C-SPAN: Window on Practice 217
*Margaret M. Nicholson*

*Notes* 229

*Bibliography* 241

*Index* 247

# Tables and Figures

## Tables

| | | |
|---|---|---|
| 1.1 | Shift in individual morality | 5 |
| 1.2 | Shift in organizational behavior | 5 |
| 2.1 | Cognitive configuration for reflexive practice | 21 |
| 3.1 | Cognitive configuration for rational practice | 44 |
| 3.2 | Cognitive configuration for focused practice | 47 |
| 3.3 | Cognitive configuration for principled practice | 53 |
| 3.4 | Cognitive configuration for interested practice | 56 |
| 3.5 | Contrastive characteristics of practice types | 60 |
| 3.6 | Strategies for avoiding confrontation | 62 |
| 8.1 | Characteristics of reflexive versus at-risk personalities | 155 |
| 9.1 | Reflexive practice in the case of Concerned Parents Association | 176 |
| 9.2 | Characteristics of the China Council and the environment it works in | 179 |
| 9.3 | Characteristics of the SRIJAN Network and the environment it works in | 182 |
| 9.4 | Characteristics of the EPOPA and the environment it works in | 187 |

## Figures

| | | |
|---|---|---|
| 1.1 | Generic model of practitioner cognition | 17 |
| 2.1 | Two factors of robustness | 28 |
| 11.1 | First-round cognitive map | 203 |

# Contributors

KENT C. MYERS is a strategic management consultant to the U.S. government. He has worked with many intelligence, military, and other federal clients. He has a Ph.D. in Social Systems Sciences, Wharton School. Research interests include resilience strategy, interorganizational networks and alignment, and environmental scanning. Since 2006 he has conducted varied strategy and research tasks for the Office of Director of National Intelligence.

DAVID L. HAWK is Dean of the New Jersey Institute of Technology and professor of design. He holds a Ph.D. in Social Systems Sciences, Wharton School. He was instrumental in the U.S. government's Energy Star program and has served on policy panels, including a federal panel on business innovation. He runs professional education programs that introduce new practices in environmental management.

THOMAS W. CUDDY is Environmental Director with U.S. Federal Aviation Authority, responsible for environmental oversight of the new generation flight system. He holds a Ph.D. in Anthropology, Columbia University. He has published a book on Virginia's early industrial archeology and another on Central American archeology.

ELEANOR CRISWELL is a clinical psychologist in private practice and an applied research psychologist. She has worked on a wide variety of problems related to stressful work in national defense; technology for training, simulation, and decision support; vulnerability and preparedness at military and civilian locations, and on intelligence analysis with Kent Myers when both were employed at SAIC. In clinical practice, she works with stress in workplaces, career changes, and personality/intellectual characteristics. Her Ph.D. in psychology is from the University of Florida, and she completed postdoctoral work at Johns Hopkins University Medical School, George Washington University, and the Veterans Hospital in Richmond, Virginia.

KIM FORSS works out of his company Andante—tools for thinking AB, based in Strängnäs, Sweden. He holds a Ph.D. from the Stockholm School of Economics where he specialized in social systems sciences, with a particular emphasis on the design of evaluation systems. He takes evaluation assignments for international organizations, civil society organizations, and public agencies.

JIM T. ZIEGENFUSS, JR. is on the management faculty at Pennsylvania State University. He holds a Ph.D. in Social Systems Sciences, from the Wharton School. He is the author of several books on strategy, and recently examined youth service.

MARGARET M. NICHOLSON has over 30 years' experience in the planning and design of organizations. After earning her Ph.D. in Social Systems Sciences from the University of Pennsylvania, she taught and consulted with universities in the United States and Europe. She assisted in the development and internationalization of the MBA Program at Rotterdam School of Management, Erasmus University. She organized an international conference, *The Systems Approach: The New Generation,* focused on Russell L. Ackoff's influence on his students. She edited, with Kent Myers, selected papers from a follow-up conference that were published in a special edition of *Systems Practice and Action Research.*

# Preface

*Our world faces a crisis as yet unperceived by those possessing the power to make great decisions for good or evil. The unleashed power of the atom has changed everything save our modes of thinking, and we thus drift toward unparalleled catastrophe. We scientists who unleashed this immense power have an overwhelming responsibility in this world life-and-death struggle to harness the atom for the benefit of mankind and not for humanity's destruction.*[1]

This quotation from Albert Einstein is important for what it says about the times we live in, for reminding us how close we are to catastrophe, and for calling on the professional to do something. It is the professional's role to understand what has changed and to initiate an appropriate response. The professionals had a hand in making things the way they are, and that now requires a change in how professionals and everyone else thinks. It is an excellent example of a deeply reflexive situation, a major one that will not clear up on its own. Professional thinking has come to exert a surprisingly powerful influence on society. As long as professionals think as they always have, it will be very hard for the rest of society to avoid catastrophe or to adapt to the whole range of new powers that have been unleashed.

Yet it is damnably difficult to change one's mode of thinking. Professionals, like everyone else, are not inclined to change. The professional will avoid or discount evidence that he needs to change, or will simply not know how to change. We have no assurance that the approach we present in this work will help avoid catastrophe any more than any other, but we think we have something to add, and offer new ways of telling the story that might resonate.

Let's begin by looking at what happened over the years to the quotation from Einstein. The evolution of the quotation will itself says something about how professionals think. What began as a reflexive challenge was reduced, in its retelling, to something much more tame and palatable. One of the first steps toward reinterpretation was taken by Einstein himself. He wrote:

> Many persons have inquired concerning a recent message of mine that "a new type of thinking is essential if mankind is to survive and move to higher levels."... Today the atomic bomb has altered profoundly the nature of the world as we know it, and the human race consequently finds itself in a new habitat to which it must adapt its thinking.[2]

What he said originally, and subsequently misquoted himself as saying, certainly struck a chord, as evidenced by the frequent repetitions and revisions that followed. The next step in this process was to isolate the punchiest sentence from the original:

- "The unleashed power of the atom has changed everything save our modes of thinking, and we thus drift toward unparalleled catastrophe."

This eliminates explicit mention of two roles—the powerful decision maker and the responsible scientist. It becomes a free-floating statement about thinking and the atom, stripped of agency, context, and reflexivity. The reader easily identifies himself as the superior thinker who is separate from the inferior drifter. The original doesn't allow for such a complacent reading. It instead drives the indictment right back on the scientists who played a part in releasing what is now out of control. The scientists were perhaps not thinking or didn't at the time know how to think about what they released, but they now need to learn.

Several minor corruptions of the original quotation followed. One can see that the errors are not random; the meaning is deflected by the cognitive orientation of the person who is remembering the quotation.

- "The splitting of the atom has changed everything save our modes of thinking, and thus we drift toward unparalleled catastrophe." (Unleashed power becomes a ho-hum technical "splitting.")
- "Since the advent of the Nuclear Age, everything has changed save our modes of thinking and we thus drift toward unparalleled catastrophe." (A crisis event has been stretched into an "Age," suggesting that the emergency has passed. We now have plenty of time for conferences. This particular corruption is amusing because it got past Harvard's editors and into Graham Allison's book on the dangers of proliferation.[3]
- "The release of atom power has changed everything except our way of thinking...the solution to this problem lies in the heart of mankind." (This author applies the problem/solution frame. The problem is now attributed to ill will or emotion and Einstein's judgment on specifically professional thought is removed.)

A separate family of misquotations appeared, and these seem to derive from Einstein's revision. Here are three variants:[4]

- "The significant problems we face cannot be solved by the same level of thinking that created them."
- "Problems cannot be solved by the level of awareness that created them."
- "We can't solve problems by using the same kind of thinking we used when we created them."

This new family of misquotations has a viral quality. We know a writer who, while he suspected that this statement was not authentic, used it anyway because it was just too good to pass up! In this family, the specific connection to nuclear weapons is severed, as well as the connection to disruptive social conditions in general. Thought now becomes an abstraction about problem solving. Further, it is not just change in thinking that matters, but newer or higher thinking is now better than older or lower thinking. Einstein only said a change was required. Also, in his revision, he said that it was mankind that becomes higher, not specifically his thinking. Finally, the problem/solution frame is imposed. Einstein didn't suggest that there was a conventional solution to the nuclear threat, and certainly not a "technical" one, either in the sense of a straightforward political accommodation or an adjustment to the technology. He instead pointed to a change in people that would allow them to develop in a safer direction, essentially a cognitive as well as moral change in humans. The point is not to let novel conditions lead to catastrophe. A change in thinking, and more specifically a change in the thinking of privileged professionals, was necessary.

This reframing of a difficult challenge into a fixable abstraction is a favorite routine in management literature. To have Einstein apparently endorse the whole apparatus of managerial problem solving gives it prestige. This is how management theorists see themselves, as "high level" problem solvers applying "powerful" abstractions. It is evidence of a cognitive pattern at work, one that we will describe later as rational practice. It certainly has currency, but we will argue, as Einstein might have done, that such practitioners do not actually exhibit the change in thought that is required. They have not read the situation, have not read themselves, and have not engaged effectively. While they certainly do not intend to drift toward catastrophe, that may be the result.

Returning again to the authentic quotation, political psychologist Robert Holt explains further why Einstein's point is difficult to grasp:

> ...the best that one can demonstrate about the arms race mentality is that its premises are conventional and anachronistic, not that they

grossly violate ordinary standards of realism. Ironically, if one relies on the usual, standard definition of reality as established by general consensus, the burden tends to fall on those who want to argue, as I do, that this consensus needs drastic revision.[5]

Holt accepts that conventional thinking is very convincing and hard to differ with, given its premises. It's just that its premises are anachronistic. But that fact is obscured. The rational management theorists and many other like-minded professionals are enthralled by the consensus, to which their thinking then conforms, and the pattern is unshakable. The culture has even induced thought leaders to gradually rewrite and domesticate Einstein, as we have illustrated above, with the result that professionals are released from his critique and are able to incorporate him as one of their own.

It is difficult to resist "good" ways to do our work that generate snappy answers that everyone else will recognize and applaud. We fight that temptation in this work. What we have to say is not a final revelation; it is an inquiry into practice, an exploration of how to think and act differently. We invite the reader to explore as well, not just observe or contend with us under the same assumptions, then continue as before.

The sweep of the argument is as follows. We review what is different about today's environment, then sketch a pattern of practice that aligns with social adaptation within that environment. We contrast that response with four other more familiar patterns of thinking (e.g., principles, interests, rationality, and focus) that we argue are no longer adaptive. Then we apply the reflexive practice schema to several facets of the modern crisis, including intelligence, economics, energy, and environment. The reader may not be directly engaged in any of these domains, or may not recognize how we have delimited the subject matter, but the aim is to rapidly survey territory where we will certainly need new thinking in order to escape catastrophe. Then we explore additional perspectives—personal psychology, education, and global settings—that cut across all practice domains. We conclude with a scenario in which practitioners, while working in variety of institutions and domains, help each other to think and act differently.

Much is left out. We sample the landscape for illuminating experiences from which the readers may learn to think differently, toward generating the kind of professional practice that fits the times we live in and uses the power thus gained for good.

# I

# Kernel

# 1
# The Turbulent Environment, Then and Now

The point was made long ago that the rate of change in society is fast, however one may measure it, and that this condition is both dangerous and potentially beneficial. Consider the curious professional responses to this condition. Have professionals really understood the implications? More specifically, do practitioners now think and act differently? Were they perhaps befuddled by all the data and somehow missed the significance?

Eric Trist, an early observer of the change, presented an all-encompassing and relatively simple theoretical construct called turbulence.[1] He considered it a permanent and salient feature of postindustrial society. Yet postindustrial society has not fully arrived–it is "structurally present and culturally absent."[2] "Structure" means the turbulent economy for the most part, while culture is not well adapted to the new structure. Individuals and organizations suffer from this mismatch.

In developing the concept of turbulence, Trist describes different levels of social complexity. He asserts that we have passed into, and can expect to stay in, the fourth and most intense level of complexity. At this level change is occurring continuously, quickly, and deeply to the point of eroding any fixed cultural arrangements. The ground continues to change, not simply activities in the forefront. Nothing in the social environment is completely given that would allow one to calculate a local solution with confidence, both because of current uncertainty about what forces are in play today, and because further changes are likely to occur soon and cannot be predicted reliably. To be adaptive within such an environment, one must continue to find and converge on new opportunities and not expect to achieve stability, only to stay afloat in the rapids. No life configuration is guaranteed to be safe and satisfying, other than to develop a skill and taste for change itself. All institutions, including families as well as jobs, are forced to be more fluid than they once were.

Coupled with postindustrial structure, there must be a matching culture of some kind. Trist's point is that the culture that would be appropriate for the times is absent, though under the pressure of continued turbulence, it has been emerging. In the meantime, there are many attempts to fill the "cultural absence" with solutions that are ill-fitting, in the sense that they are not well matched to the turbulent conditions, however well justified they may be in other respects.

Cultures, almost by definition, seek and reinforce stability, the very result that would not be adaptive in a turbulent environment. When challenged by change, the first cultural response may be to not move at all. One can look away from the challenge or deny it. Some hope to find a niche that changes less and that offers protections and advantages. Others attempt, and fail, to return to the way things once were, or to the way things were thought to exist, all of it relatively stable of course. Reversion to industrial culture is an attractive option. Many people find it familiar, relatively comforting, and seek to maintain it. But the mismatch of culture to actual conditions is quite visible. For example, a labor union may extract a wage concession. This follows a satisfying industrial narrative, but the workers may have failed to perceive that their business is obsolete and that radical changes in strategy that might have saved the company and the workforce are too little and too late.

Trist describes an emerging ethos that gives people a way to thrive in a high-change environment. In the Table 1.1 he paints how individual morality might be shifting. In Table 1.2 he describes a new pattern emerging in organizational behavior.

We need not dwell on the particulars but simply observe that since 1973 when these tables were first published, many of these postindustrial characteristics have indeed become more common, at least as aspirations. Book after book emphasizes collaboration. Some, for instance re-conceive business competition in terms of "co-opetition," or adaptation through co-evolution.[3]

But we are getting ahead of ourselves. There is more to say about turbulence. Trist added a note to his book just before publication: "Two books have recently appeared whose approach is closely related to our line of thought but which were not available when this was being developed. They are *Future Shock* by Alvin Toffler and *Beyond the Stable State* by Donald Schon."[4] Both these works caused a

Table 1.1  Shift in individual morality

| Industrial Morality | Gaining in Relevance and Centrality |
|---|---|
| Achievement | Self-actualization |
| Self-control | Self-expression |
| Independence | Interdependence |
| Endurance of distress | Capacity for joy |

Table 1.2  Shift in organizational behavior

| Prevailing Practice | Emerging Ethos |
|---|---|
| Mechanistic forms | Organic forms |
| Competitive relations | Collaborative relations |
| Separate objectives | Linked objectives |
| Own resources regarded as owned absolutely | Own resources regarded also as society's |

sensation when they first appeared. Memory of these works may have faded, but their themes remain fresh.

Toffler's original and more accurate title for his work was "change shock."[5] His notion was that people are experiencing culture shock, not because they have suddenly moved to a different culture, but because their home environment dropped out from under them. The culture that they took such great pains to master is no longer well matched to their situation. Moreover, they will never be able to feel "at home" in the same way again, because the world continues to change. The problem becomes one of finding a way to be at home with change itself. No conventional notion of culture offers an answer. Schon dwelt less on the shock and more on the difficulty of developing social learning processes adequate to the challenge. We will discuss later how these authors explored the implications of their initial concepts, but first let's consider some objections.

## Doubts about Turbulence

Is turbulence (or change, or instability) as salient and ubiquitous as these three writers say? For many people, day to day, there may be anxiety, but no emergency. Turbulence is not experienced as a constant condition by the individual, who tends to lurch from one placid condition to another. The difference is rather that transitions are more frequent to the point of being anticipated. People can expect to have many jobs, and increasingly the jobs consist of a rapid succession of quite different projects involving new teams and problems. Unfortunately, we have to include the family as one of those institutions that has a tendency to reconfigure more frequently, even though tradition and incentives work to keep the family "intact" according to a particular formula. One can succeed in one's career and family, and it is possible to create temporary enclaves of stability. What we are drawing attention to, however, is the need for readiness to move on. This is in preference to, not a stable state that is no longer available, but a series of drawn out crises as one hangs on too long when things turn bad, ending with too-late, shocking, painful, forced adaptations in one's career, family, institution, or society. Repeated adaptations appear to be "normal" for the foreseeable future.

How long will turbulence continue? Is it only our current transition period that is difficult, and are we headed to a new stability? We are in the middle of it and there is no way to know. Trist quotes Levi-Strauss who toys with the possibility that civilization may pass quickly through these troubled times and reorder into something resembling a "pre-civilizational cold culture," where there is little human exploitation or growth, made possible by material sufficiency due to technology. That would constitute the end of the epoch of civilization as we know it (though perhaps not "the end of history"). Trist adds that this would be a return to a lower level of complexity, what he called a placid clustered level. Taichi Sakaiya offers a similar speculation, that culture will return to a subjective era, last seen in the Middle Ages, when material wealth will lose its appeal.[6] The values that Trist outlines are somewhat consistent with what Sakaiya sees. These speculations are interesting and may be correct, but regardless of what we might end up with, there is little reason to believe that turbulence will subside in anybody's lifetime (though a collapse for various reasons and a return to barbarism is not out of the question).

## The Texture of Change

Schon named three "distinct but intersecting currents of social change":[7]

- Intolerance over the emphasis on consumer goods and production and neglect of public problems and systems

- Dissatisfaction of powerless minorities—racial, rural, aged, sick, prisoners, mentally ill
- Youth disenchantment with features associated with "progress" such as materialism, centralization, institutional rigidity, authority

These trends were strong but now seem dated. There appears to be passion on the first point though it has migrated to environmentalism. The largest "public system" is the earth itself. "Powerless minorities" is a dated characterization, but the impulse lives on under reframed concepts of diversity, inclusiveness, tolerance, and so forth. Social injustice has shifted to new forms or descriptions such as globalized genocide, starvation, refugees, disease, failed states, radical fundamentalism, disrespect, etc., but there is no less passion or substance to the issues. The problems may seem to pass, but they re-form and persist.

In order to take turbulence seriously, one must take uncertainty seriously. If one had gone marching off to solve this or that problem as defined in 1973, the problem might have shifted in a way that invalidated your effort. This is not an argument against making such efforts, only to emphasize that turbulence will be disruptive, and that this should qualify how one acts, and in particular how one prepares to keep acting. Our task is to set up a culture of practice by which we can discover and develop effective responses, even as the agenda shifts. Trist, Toffler, and Schon continue to hold interest to those seeking guidance through a turbulent and uncertain environment. In particular, they provide examples of how not to make inappropriate and self-defeating simplifications, assumptions, and commitments.

Trist had less time to develop major extensions, but he did pursue quality of working life and participation in the workplace. This was an effort to facilitate the shift from traditional to postindustrial values, from achievement to self-actualization, self-expression, and interdependence, but this movement dissipated. As one of his colleagues, Russell Ackoff, remarked: "The quality of worklife movement has not died, but it is in a coma."

Toffler continued to chronicle how new values, much as Trist described, have been unfolding. In Toffler's notion of "pro-sumer" (the consumer who produces more for himself) he finds much more interest in work that is personally involving and rewarding rather than merely remunerative. His stories of astonishing change are certainly diverting, but his prescriptions to do something about it have had a mixed response. He helped Newt Gingrich with some momentarily refreshing ways to reframe intractable political conflicts. Toffler explored additional means of engagement by setting up others in a strategy consulting group called Toffler Associates. It developed an unusual array of public and private clients but has not been especially influential in developing new structures.

Donald Schon took a different tack, in exactly the direction of our study. He examined professionals in the new environment.[8] Complex situations are commonly mishandled with "cookbook" solutions. A superior practitioner not only relies more on judgment honed through experience in complex situations (a feature of traditional craft work) but in addition is "reflective." Such a practitioner is sensitive to his own role and limitations, and to the changing environment, and can learn at a great rate through interaction with each situation. Being open and reflective is something that one can aspire to and achieve, and it will often be the key to effective practice in complex situations, although results are never guaranteed. Schon's work on practice has driven a new way of thinking and acting that is appropriate for the times. Though the audience has been limited, several academics have been following up with further research and courses.

## Lag in Professional Culture

Trist, Schon, and Toffler were employing cultural lag theory, which was first articulated by Ogburn in the 1930s.[9] According to Ogburn, economics had two-way linkages with many other aspects of society and culture, and he maintained that these different aspects of social reality would tend to shape each other over the long run. In the short run, a change in one aspect of society might require changes in response that align society with the initial innovation, but that response may be difficult and may be delayed. Typically, cultural patterns are slow to respond, hence there is cultural lag. This formulation asserts that where there is a mismatch between different forces in society, there is unrest, plus a tendency to resolve the mismatch through accommodation to the reality of the initial change.

Ogburn had critics, mainly among the newly ascendant positivists who found the notion of cultural lag too vague and untestable. On the other hand, the formulation was sensible on its face to anyone who had a feel for the conservatism of most institutions. Many interests were in conflict with the social conditions that arose due to technological innovations such as the car, radio, electricity, and so forth. Modernity brought with it significant change, and indeed may even be defined by it. Ogburn generalized the process, however, and did not attribute all the initiative to technology. Any change of condition can potentially initiate a tension with some other component of society, and the accommodation of the two may be painful and delayed. While Ogburn worked with more tractable cases, his framing device, consciously or not, is often invoked for larger contemporary problems.

The lag in response to pervasive turbulence is of a different order. One can at least conceive of a way to accommodate a specific change while maintaining overall "stability" and "control." The condition of turbulence is different. It is a perpetual wild card, demanding a perpetual capability to accommodate unknown challenges. With turbulence, we don't know what a solution would be, for we cannot formulate the conditions as a problem that would be solvable. Trist and the others are suggesting to us that we have something else that we are facing, perhaps a challenge rather than a problem. Anything that we produce that is stable may be an appropriate patch for a time, or it may not. In an unstable environment, the whole drive to find stability is nonsensical. But that doesn't mean that all is hopeless and chaotic, and that a cultural response is not necessary. There is a better response to the challenge that doesn't assume away the difficulty. Professionals need to think differently. They have to overcome the assumptions baked into their training and culture. They have to set sail for the unknown, in the unknown.

The cultural lag that Trist described is for the culture as a whole. It is tempting to think of this lag as characteristic of the unenlightened masses, and that the people who recognize this lag (such as the readers and writers of this book) have broken free of this lag and are well on their way toward a different culture. They may even believe they have achieved a new ethos and are fully adapted. While the unenlightened population is unable to escape the pull of habit and tradition, the educated and insightful professionals are (a) privileged observers who can perceive the difference and (b) cultural creatives who are able to make a transition and live in a different way. Enlightened professionals, in this view, are not full participants in or otherwise locked into mass culture. Institutional inertia may force them to go along with the crowd, but many of them are able to understand what is needed and are taking the initiative to change their own culture, and that will influence others to follow. That is a reassuring view, but that is not how culture works, nor is it even how professions work. Professionals may enjoy special roles and capabilities that allow them to vary their thinking and behavior in certain respects, and they are able to establish professional subcultures, but they are not separate from the common culture. Consider Karl Mannheim's classic argument that intellectuals don't have a place in society on their own, but take on and speak for groups that have interests, and in that sense they lack independence.[10] While intellectuals have certainly grown in number and can be said to now form something of a class on their own, this is a recent development and their common interests are not clear. Their interests are regularly trumped by those they serve. But to the extent they have an interest, it will favor guild habits, for which there is a favorable return in a current economic sense. Of even greater importance, professionals are not separate from the habits and traditions of their own subcultures, no more than mass culture. All we can do is get a glimmer of how to operate differently, and to initiate movement toward something that works better.

We will be calling these professional subcultures "practices" shortly, but we are emphasizing at the moment that the patterns we are referring to belong within the more encompassing category of culture. We do this to emphasize that these professional patterns have all the characteristics of culture that make them extremely difficult to change. A look at individual cultural change will make the difficulties clear. Sally is an American who wants to speak Japanese. After long training, Sally has enough vocabulary and grammar to get along, but she has a nagging accent which throws off native speakers that she encounters. Much worse, however, is Sally's inability to use indirection and politeness as a native would. Japanese find her brusque and do not include her in normal activities. If she hopes to be included, not only does she have to pay attention to new ways to think about everyday situations, but she needs to stop thinking about them in ways that have been successful for her in the past, that she has spent a lifetime perfecting in America. Most experts say that it takes about four years to become fluent in a foreign speech community, assuming that one is consistently seeking to make this change, and that one is spending most of one's day fully engaged with those who have mastered the new culture.

Playing back those considerations from language learning to the task of acquiring a "foreign" professional subculture, there are many similarities. One can pick up the vocabulary and grammar, even the accent. But what makes this transition unusually difficult is that you tend to remain in an environment where prior cultures (the ones you are fully acculturated to) are active, even dominant. You are constantly expected to "speak correctly" using your old language, as you always have in the past with your colleagues. It is easier to speak the old language because you have so much practice, and on top of that you are rewarded socially for maintaining cohesion with those who are not striving to change. There isn't a thriving new culture to become immersed in.

The difficulties of individual cultural change, Trist observed, add up to a lag in cultural adaptation. People take their cues from the culture around them. These cues may be at odds with what is actually adaptive in the long run, and even with what the individual wants, but the cues are nevertheless salient and effective. There are cases where a resistant culture persists in the face of environmental conditions that drive its members to extinction. The eventual total loss of the culture, and the inability or unwillingness of its members to acquire a new culture, can be psychologically devastating. (Certain Plains Indians, such as the Crow under Chief Plenty-Coups, suffered from this hopeless situation.) Western societies have been pushed along through the last few hundred years and, for the most part, however painfully, the population has been able to continue to adapt to dynamic economic structures. This is not to say that adaptation is good in any absolute sense, and individuals will often reckon adaptation as a net loss. Nevertheless, adaptation is required to achieve some measure of peace, safety, and success in the new environment.

## The Crisis

Turbulence creates challenges to adapt, but the amplitude of today's turbulence is what catches our attention and requires that we find ways to deal with it. We will refer to the crisis and not qualify it as being of a particular kind, only that it is very large and highly connected. Wherever one begins in one kind of crisis, one is led to another kind of crisis, and there is really no root crisis or cause. One of the best indicators of the crisis is the loss of species. This evidence communicates well to our feeble senses. It gives us something to see, name, and count, and affords us a point of comparison on a geological scale. Biologists can say, based on simple observation, that we are living through the moment of the sixth extinction.[11] There were five cataclysms that wiped out most life forms. These periods are fascinating to contemplate. The earth went into an extreme state not seen for eons, and in a short period, most life forms perished. Many of us may muse, how strange it must have been to live through such a rare event. But we are in fact right in the middle of one. With just a little imagination we may perceive this epochal event for what it is. I underscore "event" because it is occurring more quickly than most of the other extinctions. (The exception is the fifth event, when an asteroid impact set fire to the earth and wiped out the dinosaurs.) While humans have put pressure on habitats since civilization began, it is really only in the last hundred years that we have applied the coup de grâce. It would not be implausible for the human species to be among those that perish.

It is difficult to select an image that prevents one from misinterpreting the crisis as a set of isolated, solvable problems. Friedman succeeds with his image of three bombs.[12] He explains that the first bomb, the nuclear one, has now become worse due to weapons of mass destruction and proliferation. The second bomb is climate, and the third is debt. These bombs in the political, physical, and economic spheres can each tip into a runaway condition that sets off the others.

It is not certain how to fix any of this, both because we don't understand any of the issues singly, and because they connect in ways we cannot fathom. Not that we could control our response, even if we had one. This does not mean that we should not have a program. We most definitely should, but it should be an adaptive one in sum, a program that recognizes our ignorance and acts sensibly within the situation we actually face, not in a system we may imagine that allows our calculations to work out. It is not a problem to be solved. We have to stop thinking and start adapting, and professionals are in a position to lead.

We have been emphasizing the stubborn nature of culture. Yet cultures do change. More specifically, as Trist points out, a new ethos is emerging that is adaptive to turbulent conditions. In professional subcultures there is an emerging ethos as well. Although the general culture and the professional subcultures are not identical, they have a family resemblance and they move together. Let's now look at that subculture.

## The Professional's Predicament

The professional practitioner is relied upon for reasoned judgment developed through professional education and experience.

Professionals conduct projects and contribute expertise in support of the goals of major institutions that order our social and physical world. We exclude from this group those who are not expected to exercise judgment and political skill in uncertain settings, though they may have deep technical skill. The number of professional practitioners in the United States would be within the range of the 38 million "creative class" or the 50 million "cultural creatives."[13] We will de-emphasize the executive decision makers who are receiving the services and advice of professional practitioners. Many of these executives were once themselves operating in the role of expert practitioner and may still do so from time to time, but we are not focusing on the decision-making role and are instead concerned with the people who prepare information and advice for decisions.

Managers and implementers work alongside the professional. They are highly skilled experts in their own right and will often know more of what is relevant than does the professional. The professional will sometimes appear to be ridiculous and superfluous. Nevertheless, modern society has carved out a function for professionals, and most institutions expect them to be present and to do their part. Their proportion among the working population, over the long term, is growing as well, especially as laborers continue to be replaced by machines. But there are gut-wrenching reversals in such trends. In the post office a few years ago, a new executive came in ready to sweep the place clean. He said, "If you don't touch the mail, your job is in jeopardy." He thinned the ranks of managers, but he was most severe with professionals, such as those studying human factors engineering, logistics, pricing, promotion, competition, and so forth.

The professional's *practice* is what he does and thinks on a habitual basis, what is most characteristic of his role. Some care is needed to recognize that while practice includes explicit procedure, there are additional layers of cognition and action that conventional formal descriptions of procedure do not account for. There is nothing surprising or mysterious about these additional concerns, for example, how one employs teams or networks with peers. These other factors aren't secondary to procedure and can be crucial to success.

Practices are usually spoken of as "the practice of something" in a rich context of a particular field. To speak of practices as an abstract concept leaves little to hang on to and seems to violate the nature of the concept, which is to be situated and embedded. Also, the frame of mind that is necessary to practice well is to be fully involved in action, which presents a dilemma. By talking about practice abstractly we are failing to act in a concrete situation and are, therefore, not practicing. This dilemma occurs when talking about any skill. To swing a baseball bat well, it is best not to think about how one does it, but to engage the mind in the performance, which often translates into relying on habituated action, where one is sensitive to the particulars of the setting and in a state of keen awareness and flow.

While reflection on practice is disengaged from practice, it is not entirely disengaged. That will disappoint those who expect fully abstract formal analysis and believe that is a requisite for making any sense. To see how partial disengagement works, consider how Tiger Woods remade his swing. To accomplish this he didn't merely continue to practice and concentrate on more predictability and control. Instead, during a period of analytic disengagement, he decided to use his musculature differently. He reconfigured his swing rather than simply continuing to polish performance within his existing configuration. For a time, when he was setting himself differently, his attention was on establishing a new channel, to canalize differently within the surface of possibilities afforded by his mind-body. His new motion was not habituated, and his scores were initially poor but ended up better once he habituated to the new configuration. Most duffers never really habituate to the level of a professional. For Woods to have done it once, then to intentionally deviate and to reestablish a new swing, is evidence of a deep level of plasticity and control of the integrated body and mind. To have the intention to change one's stroke and to experiment to find a new configuration and then canalize, requires some level of reflection on and disengagement from practice. But doing so is itself a kind of practice—reflective practice. After one disengages, one may be tempted to remain there or continue in the same direction and take up a different set of concerns, such as coaching, or to recede further to science, theory, and finally philosophy. We will attempt to stay moored to action, but like Woods, we also want to take a detour to find that new swing and to incorporate it back into practice. (We will not detour further into Wood's personal life!) While our work will be *like* setting up a new swing, there are differences that make this effort even harder (and, we must acknowledge, a huge challenge for all of us duffers).

First, there is the difficulty of even knowing whether you are performing well in a professional practice. You can know if you are making a living at it and you probably know whether you have the respect of your peers (though that respect is rarely more than grudging). You may even claim responsibility for some good outcomes. But it is useful to apply here Carse's distinction between finite and infinite games.[14] In a finite game, there is an agreed upon resolution, a score. We can act as if we are playing such a game, and we can aspire to "join the leader board," but in actuality we are playing an infinite game, one that does not resolve, and one in which our understanding of the situation, our role, the payoffs, and the problems to solve, may shift. There is evolution and not resolution. It is hard to know whether you are doing well in such a game, and it is not proved by your score every day. You may be in a cul-de-sac, unable to continue or to generate new paths.

This uncertain situation is still not turbulence, merely the vicissitudes of any life, in which you have a dim possibility of insight and are tempted by illusions. What is doubly confounding about a turbulent environment is that you may very well have achieved a kind of wisdom and a capacity for adaptation that helps you play an infinite game. You are able to recanalize and to know when that is necessary. But now we are faced with situations that are less familiar and less easily read on a regular basis. We can continue to play "our game" and others might expect us to to do so and reward us for it, but we may nevertheless be misreading the situation, reducing it to what we can cope with and not treating it as it is. This book is an examination of whether it is possible to expand our capacity for practice, to play without the fixed playing field or the stable environment that always seemed to be a necessary condition for the development of any practice.

Few people want to become a better practitioner "in general." Whenever one practices, effectiveness has a lot to do with what one knows about the situation and one's specific field. However, this does not mean that we can't speak of practices in general, nor gain significant benefits by doing so. Assuming that we gain from such an excursion, the remaining trick will be to reinject what we learn from the general case back into the topical fields of practice.

Despite the high hurdles to achieving any provable excellence, professional practices are surprisingly stable and surprisingly influential. When a professional is wrong, he can easily jam things up anywhere along the path of action, from policy formulation and approval through project execution. There is no lack of awareness of this power, nor of the lag in developing effective practice for the times, but we just put up with it. As Trist points out, there is a cultural lock-in, an arrested development, an obvious mismatch between our actions and the conditions we find ourselves in. Yet it is not just a simple refinement that is needed, but a letting go to a thorough realization that turbulence undercuts central habits. This initial diagnosis seems to also question, if not invalidate, not just the professional's skill, role, and perquisites. We won't go so far as to recommend a cut in pay, but in order to save the role of the professional, we really do need some seismic adjustments. Nodding assent to the fact of turbulence is not enough. In particular, residues of inappropriate practice confound and disrupt the transformation to new practices that work.

This lag in professional change, we assert, is one of several constraints on broader cultural emergence. Traditional social analysis would suggest that other constraints are stronger, such as the status quo interests of the wealthy. Yet even this interest responds to incentives, such as investment returns or innovations that break up established markets. In our professionalized culture we now have a much larger population of professionals with significant power to mediate the action of others. Yet, surprisingly, professionals are not adept at changing their own standards and culture, capabilities, and biases. There are few levers, and it is a hard problem.

In this study we examine regular flaws in the professional's thinking and action. Some of the cognitive habits that he achieved, after great struggle, now place him in the way of general civilizational adaptation and, potentially, survival. Put aside for a moment what professionals say and watch how they they actually practice. They continue to assume, implicitly, that the environment will stay put and that their solutions will hold. They are astonished when events don't work out according to plan. This is chalked up to bad luck (or to any number of other excuses). The professional can only repeat himself, as if he were one of those poor souls who cannot form new memories. This "brain damaged" routine is based on an outdated, uncorrected understanding of the situation we face. Our professional cultures enforce this condition, inhibiting an effective response to global turbulence. A change in practice is required, beyond a change in opinions and attitudes. Making such a change depends on individual and social learning of unprecedented magnitude.

## Professional Cognition

We will employ a generic framework similar to Boyd's OODA cycle: orient, observe, decide, act.[15] OODA is a staple in the military, used for tracking the cognition of the actor in a stressful situation. Boyd developed this model because he felt that decision making was not being described in terms of how it is actually experienced, and without that,

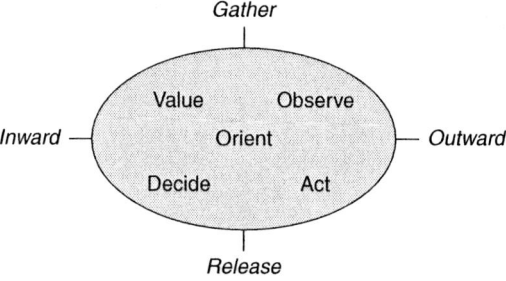

**Figure 1.1** Generic model of practitioner cognition.

training at every level in the military was bound to be off the mark. The model is appropriate for organizing professional practice for the same reason. Although we did not begin with this model at the outset of our study, we recognized, after generating five variant models, that a generic model was lurking underneath, and that it resembled Boyd's. But there are some differences from Boyd in how we depict our general model, shown in Figure 1.1:

- Boyd's "orient" is divided into a less variable portion (value) that constrains reframing and a more variable portion (orient) that generates concepts or frames grounded in the situation.
- Linkage to underlying experience of world: We locate the model on a landscape describing more fundamental features of experience. Observe, for instance, is more about gathering than releasing, and is more outward than inward.
- More emphasis on a fractal quality or mesh of relations: There is no "main" set of relations between the terms, no beginning and end that form a specific cycle. While a person may want to think before he acts, often he doesn't, and often it is more advantageous to think after or while acting.

We don't need to analyze the model further, just put it out as an organizing device for describing specific, contrasting, professional configurations, to which we now turn.

# 2

# Reflexive Practice for the Times We Live In

Becoming a reflexive practitioner can hurt your head. Normally, you fit a concept into what you already know, but that operation subtly reinforces what you already know. It is also an easy operation, what you are good at, and what you try first. But if the new concept is supposed to modify or replace the structure of what you already know, that's when it hurts.

Yet our aims here are modest, to simply instill an awareness that reflexive practitioners see the world differently, and that they may be on to something. It is not a complete account: the new cultural pattern itself is unclear, and our survey is selective. The account will also seem strange because we present it as a reflexive practitioner might. That is an additional way by which we hope to communicate the difference.

Reflexivity refers to a technical distinction concerning social systems, one that is especially relevant for success in the turbulent environment. That is just one feature, however, of a pattern of thought that emphasizes several other distinctions:

- Social systems are **reflexive**. The perceptions of the actors often lead to a change of state that leads to subsequent perceptions. There can be mutual, positive feedback between objective conditions and perceptions. The two can diverge and do not necessarily settle into equilibrium or predictable trends. The practitioner will have facility in reading and acting within reflexive social situations.
- The practitioner is **part of the system**. The practitioner is sensitive to his own perceptions and continuing impact within the systems of which he is part. The practitioner, as a reflexive element, tests his own thinking and actions in relation to others and to changing situations for continuous learning.

- Social systems are **complex**. Interactions are unpredictable and connected. The practitioner avoids simplifying assumptions and artificial bounding of problems.
- Practical **judgment and action is uncertain**. Models and research may aid sensemaking, but all representations of reality are incomplete and unreliable. Interventions have unanticipated effects and upshots. Interventions take account of impermanence and the need for continued development and intervention.
- Systems have **developmental potentials** that can be elicited or suppressed as they interact with environments and agents.

These features of thought help the reflexive practitioner act adaptively in turbulent conditions. By adaptive, we mean open to favorable evolution that avoids systemic risk. Some examples:

- The reflexive practitioner has an awareness of and capacity to make sense of phenomena at the periphery of any focal concern. "Outside" issues are sensed and accommodated in the response. There are fewer overlooked risks and surprises.
- Because the practitioner does not require or assume certainty, he can proceed to act with less anxiety or delay, and is keen to continue learning from the response and to modify prior assumptions and plans.
- He applies indeterministic methods to obtain available and relevant information (such as heuristics, multiple perspectives, action testing). He does not presume that right answers, right methods, or right data are available or reliable.
- He is prone to move, act, and change thinking as a way to turn up opportunities, even when this is uncomfortable personally or for the client institution. He is open to the discomforts of personal, professional, and institutional change.
- He is reflective concerning himself as part of the situation and as one prone to illusion and ignorance. He examines himself and the possibility of his own continuing deficiencies with respect to adapting to the environment and facilitating institutional adaptation.
- He examines his ethics, avoids exploitative relationships, and seeks the common good.

Although we have no instrumentation that allows us to measure, our estimate is that 5 percent of the population would qualify as thinking in a manner generally consistent with Trist's postindustrial ethos, meaning generally nonideological, seeking potential, and tolerant of large amounts of confusing information. A guess would be that the same percentage of professionals would share the general ethos and would likely have made it a part of their professional practice, and hence exhibit reflexive practice. (See chapter 8 for psychological tests that might be used as measures, and see the Appendix for some sample data on C-SPAN guests.)

A person is not born to reflexive practice; it is a cultural pattern for interpreting the world that one has to learn. (An argument can be made that reflexive practice is attuned to self-organization, and that self-organization is a natural process often suppressed. But even if the underlying pattern is "natural," it needs to be developed as a cultural and cognitive pattern in order for the person to function as a professional.) One may learn it later in life; in fact, that may be typical in our society. Reflexive practice does not appear to be an elite attribute. A few elite professionals have it, but many of the most famous professionals don't. The reflexive mindset will sometimes be associated with the weak because it does not always win or insist on winning, and also because it has many detractors among the strong. It is certainly possible to have this posture and also be disagreeable, dull, or have many other objectionable characteristics.

Table 2.1 lists terms that describe how the reflexive practitioner thinks, overlaid on the terms taken from the generic cognitive model presented in chapter 1. One may read a cell this way: The reflexive practitioner, like all practitioners, needs to "value" in some way. The particular way he does this, which distinguishes him from other practitioners, is to "potentiate" (described later). We have selected terms that will draw into high relief how this configuration differs from the other four at-risk practice configurations that we review in the next chapter.

We will now address each term of the model separately, but keep in mind that it is a unitary posture, an integrated way to play. This is the recommended posture for the professional who is playing an infinite

Table 2.1 Cognitive configuration for reflexive practice

| Potentiate | | Scan |
|---|---|---|
| (value) | | (observe) |
| | Reframe | |
| | (orient) | |
| Prune | | Elaborate |
| (decide) | | (act) |

game on the turbulent playing field. Stylistic variations are certainly possible. But on this field of turbulence, in this infinite game, we hope to show that reflexive practice is the posture of the true champion.

## Reframe

We begin at the center where the other elements are synthesized. One normally expects to build up a "foundation" of parts and then add a "crowning" synthesis. The reflexive practitioner doesn't think that way! The machinery of synthesis is always on and ready. It is not a stage, not an afterthought.

The reflexive practitioner (XP) is aware that when we perceive the world it is already framed, often to our disadvantage. Other professionals, even those who are aware of this, are often satisfied to leave the world framed conventionally, obviously, in a default manner, thereby inviting unexamined assumptions and losing opportunities to learn, gain insight, and communicate options. Alternative ways to pose a problem are often just as legitimate as the way that is expected or that requires least effort.

Gary Klein has created a more extensive set of operations for working with frames in relation to data:[1]

- Frame: Define, connect, filter data in relation to event flow, goals, mental models.
- Elaborating the frame: Seek data, extend frame, fill slots.
- Questioning the frame: Detect inconsistent data, violations of expectations.
- Reframing: Find new anchors, recover discarded data, reinterpret data.
- Preserving the frame: Explain away or distort data.
- Seeking a frame: Search for alternative information anchors.
- Comparing frames: Sharpen distinctions, test against alternatives.

These operations don't merely juggle your analysis; if taken seriously, they are a useful way to perform diagnosis and pose creative actions that would not readily occur otherwise.

George Lakoff has taken framing into the realm of rhetoric, politics, and morality. He has shown that political speech interacts with deep-seated psychological frames (e.g., strict father versus nurturant parent), and that knowledge and use of these frames can have a dramatic impact on getting anything done in politics, but also in organizations and families.[2] His work has been quite influential in partisan politics. While his intention is to not hide anything and to simply make the best argument for policies that enlist moral feelings, his framing of political messages tends to devolve into a manipulation. It is a clever way to "push someone's buttons." But Lakoff often goes further, to consider reshaping the buttons themselves to facilitate social adaptation.

Schon proceeded along these lines in his last book.[3] He showed that the toughest, intractable conflicts can yield to reframing. Indeed, there is no other way to make progress. He describes how parties can be persuaded to find different frames that allow for mutually acceptable solutions, even if not always ideal. On a finer scale, Roger Fisher makes similar arguments based on his research on negotiation strategies. It is interesting to see how Fisher has lately added a great deal on the reflexive and emotional aspects of negotiations, beyond the rational calculation of interests.[4] This points to additional layers of the situation for reframing—framing of ourselves, and of ourselves as part of the situation. The last step is the hardest, because it is rarely under control.

Clearly, a facility with framing is an important part of making sense of what is going on. But there is more to sensemaking, which we also locate here at the synthesizing center of complex practice. Weick[5] and Klein[6] elaborate sensemaking as a kind of judgment process that is not well accounted for in much of the literature on decision making. Uncertainty does not allow for the smooth application of an evaluation function. In a situation of true uncertainty, in an infinite game, we cannot engage in formal decision-making analysis with any reliability. Weick and Klein are able to describe better ways to make judgments in these situations we actually find ourselves in. One finding of Klein's is that the best deciders decide early and don't wait for all the data, nor do they delay decisions until the last moment before a response is required. But there is an important condition: the best deciders remain alert to what might not fit their conclusion, and they are able to change their conclusions rapidly. Making a decision and taking an action gives them something specific to deviate from and to refer to for continuous testing, comparison, and (of course) reframing.

Nonaka adds something else that has not been connected to the sensemaking literature, and that is phronesis.[7] Phronesis is a richer concept for describing this integrating function, one coming from an entirely different tradition that was nearly eradicated by positivism.

Phronesis is practical judgment in political matters. It isn't just getting matters settled among interests, but perceiving and acting on the common good within specific situations. Aristotle contrasts it with *episteme*, scientific knowledge, and *techne*, an artisan's skill that isn't social or moral. Nonaka adds some phrasing around the term: "distributed strategic phronesis." This is also helpful in emphasizing that judgment is not the job of a few elites, nor is it strictly a local matter. It is interpretation of the whole situation by all with respect to the good that is always being sought.

## Potentiate

What is the good under turbulence? One thing that is advantageous about this goal—and is not the detriment that is often supposed—is that it isn't specific. It therefore won't lock onto specific goods that may become maladaptive. It encompasses both greater good and achievable good. The elasticity will cause some difficulty through frequent reinterpretation and disagreement, but that is a fair price to pay for necessary flexibility, and an upshot is that there are more opportunities to have many players learn again what they think, learn what the group thinks, influence the group, and maintain cohesion. Being a common good, equity is an explicit concern. This obviously breaks the rule that goals must be clear, or at least seem to be clear. What is clear is that there is a process and an explicit result that is subject to reinterpretation. When one has a "clear" goal, it may actually not be clear how it is being interpreted or applied or how it can change. It may simply be an aspiration without consequences, and the real goals are opaque or hiding. The only effect of last year's "vision" poster hanging in the lunch room is to engender cynicism about the undisclosed real goals. But even if the explicit goals are sincere, their application may be clumsy and commit the organization to efforts that are not working well but must be maintained in order to show compliance with a dated, independently derived, top-down strategy. The uncertainty of the turbulent environment argues for less certainty in goals, and continuous reexamination in the context of cases, plus reexamination of the assumptions that underlie the goals.

It is difficult for us moderns to admit "good" into the picture. Science, allied with rational practice, would prefer to separate valuation and come up with a best technical solution in relation to a criterion given from outside. But the very notion of what is best is in motion and in play. It is artificial to leave the good out, and also debilitating to not develop the skill to interpret the good within the situation (phronesis), and to instead accept abstract and arbitrary criteria that typically devalue solutions that participants know to be good and would support, in favor of mindless score-keeping against abstract criteria that discourage further striving toward the good.

When there is uncertainty, one especially wants to preserve the resources and capabilities to change. This can be inefficient, but it is commonly done and not always recognized as such, in matters such as the continuing education of personnel. Personnel are often hired on the basis of matching extremely specific needs on a project today, yet sometimes those needs change even before the project starts. Needs certainly change at the end of projects, when the organization is left with a specialist who may have no further contribution, unless of course the person happens to have a general education and a strong ability to learn, plus the organization has the capacity to reintegrate such personnel. As often as not, the person is fired, others are hired, causing untold expense and heartache, and making for a dispirited workforce even among those retained. One wonders why this sequence, which is so common in a turbulent environment, does not become more of a factor in the initial hire. The drive to hire the "perfect match" is an optimization strategy that makes little sense.

Building and maintaining potential can be done in more ways than through hiring, of course. Contrary to the imperative to focus, an organization can choose to use such concepts as general, flexible platforms or capabilities, or keep some variety in product lines, even if some are not highly profitable today. On the other hand, one must guard against simply retaining the old and comfortable, but also take opportunities to open new areas where one might learn and acquire new skills in preparation for possible growth or rapid shift in the market. When times are tough and there is uncertainty about where the new opportunities are, an investment in general infrastructure is not a bad bet. It keeps you in the (infinite) game, and increases readiness.

Those who demand clarity, specificity, and fixedness will shirk in horror. It seems to them as if we are arguing that anything goes—there is no state, goal, or interest to guide you. But you do grab on to development capacity, along with a more protean sense of the common good, to be expressed through situations as you find them or as they develop. We don't sacrifice for a specific future that we are betting on, but we do sacrifice for a high-potential process that keeps moving, keeps open, and points toward the common good. It is important not to get hemmed in, to lose capacity and readiness and willingness to adapt.

Some writers on adaptation stress movement toward a goal, the more specific the better. We reject that, because the good isn't something to be reached or calculated. It is a good that encompasses, contingently, many needs and wants without creating an image of an optimum solution, which inevitably won't be achieved, leaves some out of the calculation, may be oppressive, and may limit options and potential needlessly. Evaluation doesn't occur that way in an ecosystem. The members simply keep balancing as excellences are found. We don't want a low variety ecosystem, nor an arms race, but we also accept strife, pain, and loss as a normal part of it, as a goad to forbearance as well as excellence. What we don't want to do is set the game off in a direction where it is relentlessly brutal, or goes into a cul-de-sac and limits the infinite game. This can seem like spineless compromise or inconstant leadership. But it is open to aspiration and multiple paths, not one solution for all. It is neither nostalgic nor contemptuous of tradition. The reflexive practitioner will not always arrive at the best solution compared to other practice styles, or even arrive at a solution. He will, however, tend to do less damage to the commons, or even improve the common resources and his own resources for the next round.

This is the criterion that many writers on resilience or robustness generally describe. We prefer to use the term "potential" because, unlike the others, it does not emphasize either strength (as does robustness) or perseverance under adversity (as does resilience) but combines both. The practitioner will also have learned more that will be useful in the next round (about the situation and not just a repetition of a "perfecting" procedure). Thus capacity is increased at every move at low cost, resulting in a distinct advantage in a turbulent environment.

In discussions of strategy much exhortation is focused on the result and the action but does not question the motivation or path. One is always trying to finish. For an image of how endings give a sense of satisfaction but aren't necessarily the best objective, consider the *renga* form of Japanese poetry. Several members join in this game. After somebody closes the poem, the next person is challenged to add another verse that both reopens the poem and closes it again. The most fiendish competitor will make the closure so tight that it is impossible for the next person to add to the poem. The result is a poem full of explosive shifts with little continuity, not unlike other forms of Japanese fighting and competitive games. We seem to do this to ourselves without even realizing it. We close off the possibility of successors, always producing a "once and for all" solution, then jump in later, claiming that the old solution is wrong, and that we will need to (heroically) make another, much finer solution. The new leader attempts to bury the old. This may also be behind the drive to create remarkable success, which is often purchased at the expense of any safety, and ending with unsustainable financial structures (a topic taken up in chapter 5, on economics).

We can be more precise about staying in the game for the long and short term. Paul Light's account of strategy is interesting in this regard. Light claims to have developed strategic principles empirically, as a pattern from cases. One can doubt the strictness of his procedure, but his results do reflect the unusual set of cases that he worked from.[8] He worked exclusively with the records at RAND over many years. RAND advises many government, military, and nonprofit organizations, as well as profit-making organizations. One could argue that this is a biased set, and that whatever conclusion are built from that set are going to be inappropriate for profit institutions. On the other hand, one could easily argue the contrary, that taking only profit-making institutions is highly biased and a poor basis for learning anything in general about the management of human institutions. The recent collapse of profit-making institutions gives weight to the latter opinion. Major financial institutions, the ones that were too big to fail, were surprised to learn that they had responsibilities for protecting society against unusual losses, and that their approach to risk and risk management was tragically narrow-minded.

Organizations in the public sector, and especially in the military, are of course much more aware of large and systemic risks and their responsibilities to insure against failure. They are, as Light says, robust. But we are led to modify his work in the following ways, in that we think he shrunk back from a general formulation and added some language that, while it might have attracted more readers by accommodating their expectations, muddied the message.

It is evident from the text and from the author's course notes that his working title was "Robust Organization," not his final title, "High-Performance Organization." His publisher must have thought that people would not buy a book with that title, that they will only buy a book that promises, like all the others, "high performance" as a direct and immediate result of reading the book. Light's actual message is that, in a turbulent environment, you have to build in a capability to achieve performance in multiple, different ways. This is not efficient, nor is it a direct path to high performance. But if you do it the right way, it is extremely efficient insurance, and an insurance that many organizations don't have or throw away needlessly. It is an important line of argument, especially for organizations of last resort, such as any federal or military agency or, we may now add, the largest profit-making institutions.

Light wants a "robust" organization that performs well over time because it is able to perform differently as turbulent environments dictate or as opportunities arise.

In a stable environment, an organization may not need to perform differently and hence doesn't need the capacity to do so. Stripping that capacity may save money, making the organization "optimal" within a stable environment. But place that same organization within a turbulent environment, and it would be more accurate to call that organization "brittle."[9]

It would be preferable to use a model that admits the possibility of high performance due to optimality, but at the same time shows why it is risky to aspire to optimality when the environment is turbulent. This can be done by introducing a variable that is independent from performance. I name it simply "potential," meaning available and uncommitted capability. Once this capability is separated, it is possible to create a unified model in which all of Light's distinctions can be located, plus identify other distinctions that are implied but not stated. The new model is in Figure 2.1.

The robust organization is now redefined as one having both high potential as well as high performance. If the organization happens to have high performance yet its potential can be criticized, we would call it brittle. But this creates two additional cells that we can name.

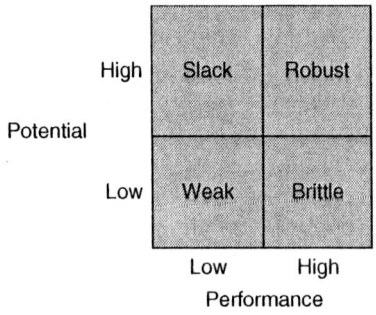

Figure 2.1  Two factors of robustness.

It is possible to have high potential but low performance—the slack organization. Finally, the low performer with low potential is simply weak, doing poorly today and unprepared to do better under changed circumstances.

But what is potential, exactly? Light says that there are four "pillars" to performance under turbulence: alignment, alertness, agility, and adaptiveness. After having separated performance from potential, we now see that these pillars are really close correlates of, and hence factors of, potential. They are not, in fact, closely correlated with performance! Performance can vary independently from them, but potential cannot. An organization simply has to have these attributes in order to have potential, and in turn, in a turbulent environment, potential will often and over time provide the opportunity for achieving higher performance than it might otherwise obtain. Slackers become interesting under turbulence. They will be able to turn themselves around if conditions change, and may even break out to perform well. Optimized organizations, on the other hand, are unlikely over time to do well in a turbulent environment—they do not have a deep well of capability.

Many indicators can be generated to get a fuller measure of potential. These should vary depending on the situation, and one can learn something by generating indicators. A tool that is helpful is Katsenelinboigen's generic list of "parameters of potential."[10] His list was developed by contemplating all the advantageous relationships that one can have on a chess board. From this list, one can interpret how a chess advantage translates into another context. I used this list to generate a comprehensive set of indicators for security in minerals markets. In a different study for the Navy I consulted the list again to develop measures for interorganizational alignment, a portion of potential. An interesting aspect of this project concerned a previous assessment of alignment. That study operated on the bland assumption that if everything was in agreement among several internal factors, this was good. That study found that the client organization was humming along, but when I reached the client, they were in turmoil. They were now responsible for getting several large organizations to work together as an "enterprise." Each organization hummed internally, but almost all the relationships between the separate units were troubled. Clearly, they were not aligned where it really mattered, and the enterprise was failing to adapt to what was now expected. Given turbulence, a maximum alignment score either internally or externally would not necessarily mean that alignment was ideally contributing to potential or to performance. Scores became a diagnostic tool, as a way to organize information on differences, changes, and explanations. In turbulence, there are simply going to be tensions between nodes in the system at any level. The challenge for interpretation, in this project, was to distinguish between appropriate tension attending adaptation, from excessive and destructive tension due to cultural lag.

A final example was a project for an Air Force organization that was growing rapidly to cover new responsibilities that were not well understood and that military personnel were not well prepared for. The commander could have collected a lot of conventional data, or just had his section managers report on whatever they were doing, but he was highly concerned with the ways that people were rushing off to do things that surprised others and made things difficult in the relationships between offices. He had no way to organize and communicate about all these matters. He was intrigued by the alignment diagnostic schema and adopted it (during his rapid growth period) for continuous monitoring of the health and integration of his organization. The model was a great success in framing management meetings around "misalignments." This reduced guesswork and recriminations and helped communicate to everyone that they were encouraged to succeed, but only as a team.

## Scan

Strategic environmental scanning makes sense and is often recommended. It is hard to deny the need to look outside the organization, to track changes that have large impact and will require significant adaptation. As Peter Drucker remarked in 1998, it is something of a scandal that massive investments were being made to manage internal information with little strategic significance, such as backward-looking accounting, while outside information that does matter to survival is barely noticed, let alone used for decision making.[11] He foresaw a rebalance of attention. That may have occurred, but not in the way he expected. A few organizations churn through awareness publications, and some decision makers consider the results, but there are breakdowns at every step, even where this style of scanning is attempted. Various kinds of intelligence services have grown, many of which use specialists and semantic tools to scan the web or to gather information from broad sets of experts. This doesn't guarantee that anyone pays attention to the results, however. The connection to decision making is loose, and is sometimes focused only on a limited set of risks, such as defense against disgruntled employees and whistleblowers. (The reasons why the organization generates disgruntled employees is not part of the research.)

There has been more promising development in cross boundary personal networks, where enough professionals maintain collegial links, and everyone acts as everyone's scout, and where colleagues listen to each other. The social networking software services have real consequences in maintaining voluminous peripheral links among professionals. There are positive effects of online professional networking, tempered by the negative effects of the overall decline in professional conferences.

What one hears from colleagues often comes in the form of narrative, which is another skill of the reflexive practitioner. You want to listen to and interpret with some care what people are saying about their experiences. It is good for gaining clues and shreds of evidence of what will shape co-evolution. It is a job done poorly by those who are impatient to "get the facts" or "apply the model" or "adhere to rules" or "take what's yours."

However it is done, scanning for significant and fast-moving change in the outside environment is an important component of reflexive practice. The maintenance of relationships with well-informed people on the outside, such as bloggers, writers, headhunters, and the like, seems to have become the sweet spot for reflexive practitioners.

## Elaborate

Here we draw on the imagery of biological growth and evolution. Many projects should be launched and run quickly at low cost. It is inevitable that some fail. They should be run to the point of a fair test to see whether they give evidence of being effective. If results are positive, they can be scaled up. If not, the projects can be pruned at low cost. Minimal effort should be spent on evaluating start-up projects because evaluators, regardless of their level of expertise, simply don't know what will work. Knowing a lot does not necessarily make you a good judge of what is new and what (or who) will succeed. This fact of ignorance is well known but is not always controlled in the peer review processes in various technical, research, and investment fields. Good ideas are cut off because they don't appear to be "building on" research programs that the reviewers cherish but which may have become obsolete. Those who propose projects may know better what they can accomplish, and it would be wasteful to not let them run with what they know and are committed to.

3M enshrined an elaboration and pruning process. Google and others have following with something similar, where professionals are required to spend 20 percent of their time on personal investigations. Professionals in 3M were required to work on their own projects in secret. When they were ready to present a project for scaling up to the next stage, testing was brutal and many project were pruned at that point. This worked for many years, and 3M was able to continue to be profitable based on revenue from new products. This is a case of rapid learning, but note that in a turbulent environment, little that you learn is of permanent or cumulative value. The permanent part is the learning process itself, and the courage to actually apply it. The harder part, more than starting projects, is pruning them. Even where an activity has little or diminishing benefit, it may continue because it can be done efficiently, it is somebody's domain, and it is expected by some customers. A reflective practitioner is ready to prune it, but not because it is an utter failure, but because it frees up resources to continue to invest in a portfolio of rapid, high potential explorations toward development and performance.

"Secondary" effects are often ignored when both starting and stopping projects. The explorations will build new skills that can be reused, regardless of whether the projects succeed, and the very fact of acting to investigate and intervene positively creates new potential and opportunities. Consider the placebo effect and the Hawthorne effect. One often gets good outcomes with a placebo, equal to or better than the "real" medicine. In the Hawthorne organizational experiments a wide variety of interventions had good effects, as long as they were monitored and the participants were aware of the monitoring; it turns out that the monitoring, not the interventions, were causing the positive outcomes. These are not anomalies, just cases where certain pretenses of control were dropped and the unforced adaptive responses of participants (including investigators) were elicited. Many practitioners aren't themselves learning from what they have seen. If they were, they might consider initiating more no-cost placebo-like relationships, and not depend entirely on the expensive control "medicine."

One could describe Appreciative Inquiry in these terms. Ask what has worked for participants that truly pleased them or that represents the best of the organization, and a way might be found to do more of it. This only seems like mystification to those who must document a process that is held apart from themselves and is imposed on the subjects, focused on a chosen influence, all other influences being suppressed or discounted as noise. This emphasis on neatness can be costly by reducing opportunity and by suppressing adaptive, self-organizing behavior. It can also simply be doing the wrong thing that, in addition, reduces the chances of finding out that it is the wrong thing. Elaborations don't need to be free, they only need to be lightly resourced in order that there be many. What can be done is to use not just other people's money but other people's dynamic. If somebody has a problem, it is often the case that somebody sees how they can benefit themselves by helping. It takes some creativity to find such resources and to match them up. The practitioner who does this will not be given permission. As a reflexive practitioner, your way of acting is connecting, then letting the rest happen if it is going to.

To whom do you connect? In many organizations, those with long tenure allow both grudges and deep linkages to constrain their network and what they can accomplish with it. Mancur Olson argued that the German and Japanese economies succeeded after the war precisely because long-standing economic networks broke down.[12] He argued that the old relationships prevented innovation because of elaborate sets of agreements, loyalties, and threats. After the war, the relative freedom to make new relationships drove the economy forward.

## Prune

In one's life work, rapid change with no payoff can be unappealing. As Tom Peters became more fervent about speed, change, and project work, it became less and less clear what happened to the "excellence" he once trumpeted. There may be an unresolvable difficulty here, of leading a meaningful, coherent life within turbulence.

Anyone protean enough to keep up with the pace of change, even if outwardly successful and aimed at something meaningful, may still suffer from disorientation and alienation from a world that does not offer the satisfactions of enduring experiences and relationships. On the other hand, this may be a problem that can be solved through reframing. Csikszentmihalyi tells us that many professionals at the leading edge of their fields are highly engaged and in a highly rewarding flow state most of the day. They face hardship and turmoil, but are highly motivated to exert themselves to the level of their expertise and skill. At any level of expertise it is possible to achieve flow states. It is like playing a game, he says, "It usually has clear goals and rules of practice. It provides feedback... in the form of knowing that one has finished a job well done, in terms of measurable sales, or though an evaluation by one's supervisor. A job usually encourages concentration...it also allows a variable amount of control at least ideally—its difficulties match the worker's skills."[13]

It is apparent that the infinite game we have been referring to needs to be dialed down in some cases to create conditions conducive to flow. The large fact of uncertainty may be tolerable if elaborations are structured as a series of brief, well-bounded finite games that support flow states. That could provide for satisfaction and growth without misconstruing the environment or insisting that situations be over-ordered. The XP could accommodate this need for a moderate pace and for frequent feedback through a pruning process. Some of the practitioner's creativity comes, not from starting more elaborations whose ends are not known, but from drawing opportunities to a close. Give them a time limit or performance limit, and shut them down with the understanding that every conclusion, as long as one learns from it, is an accomplishment.

Another approach is to make much smaller interventions and let the system adjust itself. The task is to insert a strategic "nudge" and see what happens. In Thaler and Sunstein's telling, a nudge is a "choice architecture" that one sets before an operating process.[14] It includes incentives but there are many more ways to channel decisions in favorable directions, such as through setting defaults or providing high impact information at the right time. The idea is to not remove variety that comes from different choices being made, not to remove the freedom that people want to pursue different paths, but to simply boost a pattern that would be more adaptive and generally beneficial. A simple item is to set a default for new employees to automatically join the savings plan. Giving employees the choice to opt out rather than to opt in is good social policy. The input is often small, and one can then learn from well-prepared feedback. Negative trends within the system can be pruned in this manner.

## Evidence of Reflexive Practice

Over time, the growth of reflexive practice will shift professional culture. It will become expected and easier to perform out in the open, with less cutting criticism from those who practice differently and whose authority is waning. We have not developed the evidence but will just mention where instances of reflexive practice are often found. The practice is frequently displayed by those who appear on PBS news programming and on C-SPAN interviews. There is remarkably little evidence of it on network broadcasts. One indicator of the audience for this style of though was PBS's 3 percent audience share during the presidential debates. The video feeds on the other networks were identical, and the only basis for choosing one channel over another was the different commentary that the viewers were anticipating.

Reflexive practice is the focus of several new awards (though always with different labels). The judges are able to identify those who exhibit these inclinations consistently. The thrust of these awards is to praise those who are not otherwise well known and who have been passed over for awards by the traditional guilds that usually reward at-risk practitioners. These awardees have combined ideas and addressed complex social threats in fresh, arresting, and nonideological ways. The following are examples:

- Right livelihood awards: http://www.rightlivelihood.org/
- Nobel Peace Prize
- Wired Magazine's The Smart List: 15 People the Next President Should Listen To[15]

## The Generality and Necessity of Reflexive Practice

Systems thinking is a first approximation of reflexive practice. As Trist was writing about turbulence, his colleague Russell Ackoff was separating himself from operations research. Ackoff wrote that there were larger problems that concerned managers and that the mathematical models were no help. They could not represent the changing and uncertain situation and offered no reliable solutions. He and many others set off developing an approach with many of the features we have been discussing. Systems practitioners of many varieties were participatory, crossed boundaries, used multiple methods, and evolved. But Ackoff and others, to a greater or lesser extent, retained the rationalistic frame of goals and plans.

In 2004, Ackoff lamented that the systems program that he so energetically pursued since the 1970s had not achieved what it should have.[16] There were still crushing problems in all institutions, and systems thinking could no longer plausibly claim that its program offered the most hope. Confidence and manpower had drained out of the movement. In Ackoff's memo he included some broad suggestions which we interpret as supporting reflexive practice. He observed that systems thinkers were talking to themselves rather than to policy makers, and they had also been captured by the academy. His recommendation was that practitioners shift toward communicating to their clients. Find out what could be presented at meetings that clients would find compelling. He briefly mentioned the need to pursue development projects in which participants were allowed to make mistakes and come up with bad results, which suggests a break with rational practice. Like Moses, Ackoff prepared us but could not transform with us. His parting words: "I believe we have an obligation to the global society of which we are part to make every possible effort to bring about a radical transformation of that society."

Ralph Stacey argues that systems thinking is entirely discredited and eclipsed by his complexity thinking, but we find that claim unconvincing and unnecessarily shrill.[17] Both complexity thinking and systems thinking are good sources. We find it helpful to view organizations as complex adaptive systems that self-organize. Of immediate interest, Stacey discusses three cognitive orientations: rational, political, and judgmental. These match fairly well with our rational, interested, and principled practice types. Stacey gives each type a domain of legitimacy, defined by the level of certainty and level of agreement, and he reserves complex decision making for when both of these levels are low. We would add that in turbulent conditions these situations are more common, therefore complex decision making should be more common. Yet we are wary of reserving reflexive practice for special cases, to be available just in case there is a situation of unusual uncertainty. Doing so assumes that we can reliably determine this and that we have prearranged agreements that allow us to shift to a different decision-making process. It is just those uncertain situations that are routinely "reduced" or simplified or treated for the most obvious, popular, and short-term remedy and not seen for what they are. We would argue instead that in a turbulent environment every situation needs to be looked at from a complex or reflexive perspective first. Also, many people should have these practices and support each other in their application. It is not just for high-level gurus or special case problems. If reflexivity is not a daily and "practiced" practice, it is not going to be effective. From the viewpoint of one of Stacey's alternative cognitive types, the landscape does not look the same, but is biased to make its own perspective dominant, and that is what we cannot afford.

Another similar schema is Snowden's Cynefin framework.[18] Snowden insists that a determination of the level of complexity of a system not be imposed, but that it emerges through interaction with the data. This is good advice but maddeningly difficult to get across to professionals who have never before refrained from or even questioned rapid stereotyping. In this framework, problem solving styles are again associated with levels of complexity, but the styles and levels are somewhat different. The unordered domain is chaotic, and there is little that one can do except act in novel ways and see what happens. From the other end, in a known region, it makes sense to apply best practices. In a knowable region, professionals need to examine and adapt best practices before applying them. But more and more situations fit within a disordered regime he calls complex (which we would identify with turbulence and uncertainty). It is there that "emergent practice" is applied (which we identify as reflexive practice). Snowden has perhaps done the most thinking on what to actually do as a professional in this regime of order, and he is articulate on why the common error of mistyping a complex situation as a knowable situation can lead to trouble. He warns practitioners to stay alert and not collapse all situations into more orderly regions simply because they prefer the solutions and tools that are available there.

Gareth Morgan has a similar argument, favoring the skill of reframing and the rest of complexity thinking only secondarily. Morgan argues that it is necessary to frame a situation in a particular way in order to learn anything about it, but that all frames are based on a dominant metaphor, and that every time you use a metaphor you reveal something and at the same time conceal other perspectives that might just as readily have been used. His argument is that any practitioner in complex systems will have to read situations, and that no single frame will be reliable or sufficient, and in particular that the most common frames that many people lock onto will be anachronistic. To think mechanistically about organizations will often not give you the understanding you need to be successful. A sophisticated practitioner will need to be able to use more frames. He does not claim that the set he describes is necessarily the best, and he invites the reader to use other metaphors.

Where we differ with Morgan is that, given a turbulent environment, we think that some framing metaphors are more useful than others, though we would always want a variety. While the metaphors that he presents do not clearly match the practice types we describe, there is obvious similarity: his mechanistic frame is similar to the rational practitioner, his interests metaphor would be favored by our interested practitioner, and the flux metaphor is where the reflexive practitioner would tend to begin and then proceed to use others, particularly the cultures and the learning and self-organization metaphors.

Phronesis recently returned to topical importance through Flyvbjerg's argument in favor of "phronetic social science."[19] Nonaka extended this work to a practitioner's version he calls "distributed phronetic strategy." Flyvbjerg's work engendered some very heated disputes in the academy over his idea for fusing practice and social science, not as a mere concession to relevance, but as a different concept of what science is within the social realm. Into social science he sweeps narrative, aesthetic judgment, and a more frank accommodation to interests and politics. This is a congenial "scientific" grounding for reflexive practice.

Stacey, Snowden, and Morgan tend to give professionals a pass from the rigors of turbulence and reflexivity, offering that there are plenty of situations where reflexive practice is not necessary. While we would prefer to agree with them, it may not be wise to do so from the perspective of pedagogy and out of concern for the global sustainability challenge. The practice types are not mere eyeglasses that one can take on and off to suit the situation. They are starting points that one never deviates from, because to do so would require a sort of biculturalism. There are defaults that, once set as an option rather than merely a comparative dimension, crowd out the others and are very difficult to dislodge. The situation is like learning languages. If you reserve a new language for special occasions, such as in a classroom or only at home, you will never master it. While it is possible to be fluent in multiple languages, each has to be learned in an immersive manner and ready for use for all occasions.[20] You will not become fluent in a new language if you don't think in it directly but translate from your native language. Reasoning can't dislodge this sort of foundational thought pattern. Professionals need to have a practitioner's cognition as an ingrained, habituated manner of thinking and acting, in order to have it be effective. And once that happens, it becomes the starting point, and the alternatives become, at most, second languages.

## Vulnerabilities of Reflexive Practice

Turbulence can disable any practitioner, including the reflexive practitioner, despite the comparative advantage that he can claim. But there are additional ways that a complex practitioner is prone to perform poorly. They are unavoidable consequence of his strengths. We will mention a few areas where the practice is most likely to break down.

The reflexive practitioner (XP) can lose to competitors who retain influence. The at-risk practices remain a prominent part of the turbulent environment and often cannot be bypassed. Clients will often know the at-risk approaches and will simply not understand or tolerate deviation. The XP should resist capitulation. Time must be spent educating the client, and it is best to simple demonstrate the alternative, even if not asked. Quick results might matter.

By avoiding thoughtless closure, the XP loses the advantages gained from forcing rapid closure. The program leaves itself open to disruption, and participants can contribute negative disruption. If the XP extends his period of appreciation, he may be perceived as floating without sure results, unable to show that his early accomplishments logically or obviously link to conclusions. The XP can seem aimless, but he is open to aspirations and wider solutions, not final results and not on one track.

XP will not always arrive at the best solution compared to other styles, or even arrive at a solution under many definitions. The XP thinks in terms of perseverance and evolution. He will tend to do less damage or even improve the common resource for the next round, which may not have been asked for or even valued by clients who are focused on the short term.

All practices have their excellence. The XP doesn't always privilege his perspective above the others. Part of the common good is tolerance, to allow deviation and to accept that there are different interpretations of the good. Yet we are justified in criticizing interpretations if they are not authentic responses to the good but are intolerant and limit the common good. The XP is political in the manner of phronesis. Wise judgment isn't a new invention for our time, of course, but the need for it has become greater because of the high velocity of change that introduces huge vulnerabilities, and because the default approaches are poorly matched. When we see failure all around us, do we not see that it can spread? Do we think we are not implicated personally, that we have no responsibilities? Amid all the extinctions that occur today, do we not see our civilization as a potential casualty? These are not the signs of an ecosystem with high potential for excellence, which we associate with the common good. We want the creativity of nature and civilization to continue, but both nature and civilization can collapse if our practices are not attuned to this vulnerability and grow beyond it. Reflexive practice is difficult because, unlike any other cultural pattern, it is less fixed and less calculable and involves both restraint and rule-breaking. It isn't a new way toward plenty; it dwells in the circumspect world of wisdom and good. We have made ourselves unable to speak of what we need, or can only speak of it in a roundabout, rule-encased way. And then we argue for the rule instead of the good, which shouldn't do our judging for us. We should also question the results from the clash of forces, from one set of hard principles, from scientific economizing, or from tradition, when the ground is shifting below all. We won't remember any judges, unfortunately, because we must keep moving and can't afford to learn too much from any case that threatens to become a distraction. There will be many paths to take, not consistent with any of the methods of inquiry that our training draws our attention to. We need to reeducate our attention, and reduce the siren call of surety.

It is hard to arrive at an image of what life is like when you play this different game, of evolution at speed. Everything that we think about change refers to perfectibility. Getting sea legs is a nice image, but that too is something you learn and perfect. In what sort of funhouse are we in, where we need to keep learning as we influence the house and what we need to learn? A cherished image for engineers is building an airplane while flying it. This image is often invoked when claiming the impossibility of doing what is asked. But it is also an excuse to proceed just the way one wants, to stop changing, or to stop flying. This particular engineering mindset both literally and figuratively doesn't go with the flow. Science was offered as a relief from commitment to unchanging tradition, and it is ironic now that it keeps us not merely rigorous, but in rigor. Let's examine these at-risk practices in more detail.

# 3
# At-Risk Practices That No Longer Work

A primary characteristic of reflexive practice is facility in reframing—the ability to deal with multiple, inconsistent frames simultaneously, creatively, and contingently. Some of these frames are in the shadows; they may be potential or emergent, driven by either external forces or intentional change. The fluidity and uncertainty of reflexive practice makes it difficult, confusing, and maddeningly irresolute at times, but that is the price of facing turbulence squarely, to not assume that conditions are less turbulent and therefore favorable to a different stance that is cognitively or culturally more attractive, convenient, or familiar. To assume otherwise—that there is some other underlying, constant, and knowable reality in our times—is less and less plausible. Nor does society appear to be headed toward any particular regime of stability, based on what we have seen in the past several decades.

Though reflexive practice works, it does not promise to work according to any necessary logic, nor does it give the satisfaction of holding to an anchor of well-defined truth, rule, or procedure, whose understanding and use one may perfect and depend on, allowing one to face any situation fully prepared and fully armed. To argue that reflexive practice cannot be right because it shifts with the winds of what people are thinking and saying is not persuasive. Social reality depends in part on what people are thinking and saying, and that reality is uncertain and shifting.

Even so, the temptation to any number of false or second realities is strong, and such fictions are protected from questioning that would expose these realities as fictitious. Such fictions are a kind of social reality also, of course. They are a self-sustaining cultural fact that must be dealt with. Our task in this chapter is to dispel their charm. This is difficult on many counts, but initially because we ourselves find these at-risk practices attractive. We are not immune to our training and to the rewards for using them. Leaders of these practices are vibrant, successful, and famous. It is a way to get ahead. But these practices are also a way for all social adaptation toward the common good to be thwarted.

One could say that there is little we can do, that if culture and professional subculture are to evolve it will happen on its own, that we cannot either understand or affect it, and can only follow it as we are carried along with the tide. Perhaps so. A handful of reflexive scholars and practitioners are unlikely to be seen as the cause of any change. But striving and participation form the ingredient that will allow the unforced cultural change to emerge. As Prigogine emphasized, self-organizing "dissipative structures" emerge only where there is a great deal of energy flow. That is the kind of new understanding that we are after, one that rides atop turbulence and uses its energy rather than attempting to quell it, either imaginatively or actively. Some directed energy from us may help, though we may be unable to trace the exact path of influence. We are not hapless, but are rather carriers of cultural change.

All can benefit from an understanding of how the at-risk practices are an impediment to cultural change, and how their grip could be released. While the at-risk practices are very different from each other in many respects, they share three characteristics that distinguish them from reflexive practice:

- Fixed frames and assumptions, backed by a self-sealing ideology
- A self-sustaining in-group, a professional subculture
- Advantages in the market that effectively suppress alternatives

If a practice were correct, these characteristics might be accepted as a legitimate means to resist error. The at-risk subcultures certainly think they are right. But if a practice were not correct—or what would be even more difficult to accept, if the practice were *no longer* correct—these characteristics become stumbling blocks for society, preventing the emergence of practices that work better and deal more sensibly with the massive risks and relentless change that society faces.

There are many rival practice orientations that vie with reflexive practice to fill the cultural void in turbulent, postindustrial society. Some of these orientations simply do not reach far enough into the complex of factors, relations, and fields sufficient to the requirements for adaptation. These do not have "requisite complexity," an analogue to Ashby's original "requisite variety" (whereby the variety within the control system needs to match the variety of the target system). Other practices may impose a consistently limiting filter or distortion that prevents institutions from perceiving the turbulent situation with its perils and opportunities. Even when conventional practices are recognized by both practitioners and clients as failing, they have the force of habit and set the standard.

We label these practices "at-risk" because their deviation from what is actually required is not merely a nuisance and a cost but is dangerous. (The allusion to "at-risk youth" is intentional; they have a propensity to get themselves and everybody else in trouble.) These at-risk practices are insufficiently sensitive to, prepared for, and active in dealing with the special challenges and risks posed by the (turbulent) environment. The practitioners themselves believe they are avoiding risk by sticking to what is tried and true. But that is like rejecting the "risky" lifeboats in favor of the Titanic.

At-risk practice orientations will in some cases be driven by ideologies or psychologies that are more easily recognized directly rather than through their secondary manifestation in professional practice. While these connections exist, we prefer not to pursue them here and focus only on what we see in professional practice. (Criswell's chapter 8 does explore these psychological aspects.) It is unlikely, in any case, that any ideology can be successfully opposed head on. One has a better chance by appealing to professional responsibilities and to evidence of outcomes which may, in turn, loosen the grip of nonadaptive approaches. Certainly society expects more of professionals who have been given privileges, who are well compensated, and who are entrusted with the levers to guide major institutions that have serious consequences when they fail. In the case of AIG, if it takes payments for insurance, then business, investors, and the public should expect them to know something about systemic risk in a turbulent environment, not merely about speculation. That fine sounding word, "fiduciary," should mean something.

We will describe four common types of at-risk practice. They are easily recognized and have often been described by others, though not always in terms of how they fail to account for turbulence. We concede that these orientations have been effective in the past, can be effective and appropriate in limited situations currently, and that they arise from legitimate needs within a diverse society. In addition, we have made an attempt to describe them initially in their most favorable light. Understanding their appeal is important for recognizing just how well established these approaches are, and how difficult it is to imagine that they may not be correct for all times in all situations. Even though we proceed to point out their failings in a turbulent environment, they are not entirely wrong. We are simply saying that they are not highly adaptive in the face of postindustrial turbulence, a special case that happens to be chronic. Of course, other criticisms of these practices go further and claim that they are injurious and wrong for other reasons, regardless of the environment in which they are applied. We are not pursuing those arguments. They may be true, but even if they are not, it is still risky to rely on these alternative practices given the environment, and still advantageous to shift to reflexive practice that is a better match to the environment.

## Rational Practice

Conventional training in management and social science insists that there be a method, and that it be applied rigorously. This assures "objectivity," or at least that one's inquiry will be organized, taking cues from an explicit process that is fully separable from the situation. The general cognitive orientation is depicted in Table 3.1.

A succession of plans and adjustments will approach truth and greater power as the system is understood. The practice assumes both that the background is persistent or at least predictable, and that the focal system persists in the state that is intended or represented. Rational practice assumes that the measures and characterizations that are available are sufficiently indicative of how the system operates. The rational practitioner admits that some facts will not be known, some activities not disclosed, and differences of perception and intent not identified. Also, the rational practitioner will admits that the environmental conditions may not last. Yet they will hold out that good solutions may still be determined and can be adjusted to conditions whose drift can be predicted. The disagreement with

Table 3.1 Cognitive configuration for rational practice

| Idealize | | Formulate |
|---|---|---|
| (value) | | (observe) |
| | Optimize | |
| | (orient) | |
| Adjust | | Plan |
| (decide) | | (act) |

reflexive practice comes to a head on the question of whether there is significant, inherent uncertainty; whether it can be reduced or ignored, and whether the model of the system can be resolved (i.e., optimized) to agree with what is known or can safely be assumed.

The reflexive practitioner prefers to have the system itself learn or come to know itself in a collective way as it incorporates adaptations. The observer cannot know it or drive it according to an orderly, formalized model. Such a representation is inaccurate, or quickly becomes inaccurate, such that it is an unreliable basis for understanding the system's behavior. Rational practice assumes that a level of certainty and understanding can be found and represented independently from the system. There is temporary and defined uncertainty regarding hypotheses, but these questions are clearly stated and treated as "not yet" confirmed but knowable by tests. One operates on that basis. But it would be more reasonable to keep the question open and arrive at resolutions through different means, rather than resting on (or ignoring) broad assumptions of stability that are untrue. Also, it is in those very times when a system changes that are most important from the viewpoint of safety and survival. These moments would seem to be a greater priority for the attention of professionals.

Rational practice also assumes that good method leads inexorably to good practice, or rather that they are one and the same. The practitioner can appear dogmatic (except to others in the fraternity). The rational practitioner becomes invested in an idea and in improving its results. The effort to repeat and refine might be better spent in exploration of options. Much data is piled up with diminishing increments of insight, with the upshot that, even if the *status quo* isn't supported directly, it isn't challenged either. While this pattern of practice is not overtly hostile to creativity and discovery, it offers little room for it and must confine itself to verification of thin, well formulated questions.

The contemporary upsurge in modeling, with or without a computer, has kept rational practice vibrant. Modeling can become quite "sophisticated" and give one the illusion that the technical representation is a sufficient guide to action. At the extreme, technical-rational practice substitutes the model for reality, and claims that the model is a necessary guide. The image of success is sufficient, and if the world doesn't follow the model, it is just not being rational. Indeed it is not. There are different ways of using modeling, of course. Role playing games, where modeling facilitates exploration and experience with uncertain situations, are quite different. Even in these situations, however, the rational practitioner may attribute accuracy to the model, and seek greater fidelity toward the goal of prediction. Many rational practitioners will explain that they no longer seek to predict or optimize, but the decision maker still perceives the result as "a decision made, not a decision aid." This is merely a loosening of terms with the same basic posture. They still want to determine through objective methodology the "most likely" states and "overall best" options that will be a reliable guide to corrective intervention, and all the while retaining assumptions of stable environments.

## Focused Practice

This practice pattern is suspicious of theory, qualitative reasoning, strategic uncertainty, and vague external factors. It assumes that if one finds the facts about immediate matters under the control of decision makers, understanding will be sufficient so that one is naturally led to right action.

The professional has a necessary role in performing research, understood as the assembly of a fine-grained description of the focal system whose performance is to be improved. This has merit in looking for the uniqueness of every case, but much is missing. The questions tend to be rote, driving a procedure toward description without examining how the situation is being framed. The function of the system and its interaction with the environment are underappreciated. There is also a tendency to simplify, to come to rest on single, clear, or favored causes.

The approach allows the practitioner to develop great confidence over a narrow range of what he deems to be relevant, and when turbulent reality crashes through to ruin the picture, that is unforeseeable and not within the purview of his services. One can, for example, attribute results to bad or good components—persons, actions, rules, and so forth—that are said to be key parts of the process, singled out for praise or blame. Most modifications replace parts that will elevate the system to standards that assure effectiveness. There is either a denial or willful ignorance of many other potential influences, and a reluctance to pursue alternative or sketchy explanations. Above all, it is sensitive to efficiencies and asserts that a complete job will be a detailed job within boundaries. It is not concerned with change except within its chosen purview. It wishes that influences outside that purview weren't important and proceeds as if they weren't.

Who could ever argue for such a position? Remember that it is not espoused theory that we are discussing here, but actual practice.

Table 3.2  Cognitive configuration for focused practice

| Bound (value) | | Collect data (observe) |
|---|---|---|
| | Describe (orient) | |
| Make accurate (decide) | | Fix (act) |

A focused practitioner may argue that there is an awareness of more and a plan to do more, but the center of the effort is on description, parts, and efficient corrections. Their project typically collects "the basics" and then runs out of time before being able to do anything more. They will also attack others who appear to them to be engaging in "hand-waving" without enough "hard" information. Our diagram in Table 3.2 shows how all this fits into a pattern of practice.

One must bound the system. Other criteria may vary—one may improve it in some way or redesign the system—but the emphasis on bounding the system influences the practitioner to look inward. The main action is to fix the system to make it consistent with how it has been bound. The practitioner gains knowledge through description of the bound case. What else is there? The description will be data-rich and accurate, and this will reveal what to fix and solutions will fall out from the analysis.

One may doubt the prevalence of this practice type or the level of damage that it could inflict. It seems like a somewhat benign fact-finding activity that perhaps is needed as an auxiliary effort, one that can be delegated to less senior professionals due to its limited demand for judgment. We would argue, on the contrary, that this style of practice can easily get out of hand just because it is so mindless. There are always more facts to find and polish. It gives in to the urge to collect, one that humans share with pack rats. But sticking to our theme, we are simply examining the practice and not its sources and motivations. We agree that it is a useful activity to pursue, especially where the environment is stable, and when one has the opportunity to perfect a certain configuration before shifts in the environment require a reconfiguration. But of course the turbulent environment breaks with that assumption and reduces the legitimate scope for this practice.

One of the great waves of management reform—business process reengineering—fits this practice type. The projects that pursue reengineering are often expensive, describing new processes with many details that analysts, not workers, arrive at through laborious procedures and documentation. Six Sigma is the later version of this tradition, tarted up with the heroics of GE, with the total quality movement locked in the back closet.

For almost any movement there will be denizens who can answer any criticism and who will attribute every failing to practitioners who did not understand the program or who were unskilled or unlucky, and that these failings should not be attributed to the source method and to the method's most faithful practitioners. Surprisingly, reengineering leaders have not taken this stance. They have been refreshingly candid in recognizing failings and taking some responsibility, either for weaknesses in their initial efforts, or for letting things get out of hand as the movement snowballed. Davenport offers an interesting *mea culpa*, explaining that the focus on process improvement combined with information technology (IT) and radical redesign became too mechanical and strident (partly his fault) and that it became associated with mass layoffs (not what he ever recommended, but how it got out of hand).[1] In all, it became a movement that left out the human element and caused destruction without producing the (oversold) benefits.

Hammer sounds similar notes though he does not let go of his commitment. Well after the peak of his fame and after widespread criticism and rejection had sunk in, he published *The Agenda: What Every Business Must Do to Dominate the Decade*.[2] Putting aside the overblown title, he continues to find the efficiency of the business process all-important, and that's what makes him fall within focused practice. He explicitly dismisses talk of the "business model," an abstraction that is more congenial to rational practice, where alignment of many factors optimizes performance within an assumed or predicted environment. Hammer instead looks to the internal details: What are the direct measures of customer satisfaction and of cost? How can you rearrange the use of IT and processes to speed everything up and reduce cost and give customers exactly and only what they want, without error? The mantra is "discipline, structure, repeatability." Some analysts from a marketing perspective observe that fixing a problem for a complaining customer is often a golden opportunity to create a positive relationship and loyalty that would never occur with fault-free service. For Hammer, the need to fix is evidence only of a process failure to be stamped out. Hammer's "no nonsense view" is that he can "tame the beast of chaos with the power of process." However, in his last chapter he admits there is this little troublesome issue of environmental change. He exhorts companies to do the following:

- Prepare for an uncertain future
- Develop early warning
- Become proficient in responding to change
- Add supportive structure for accomplishing the above

He offers no explanation of how to do this, nor does he acknowledge that his program may add to the difficulty of doing so. A reviewer on Amazon asks himself who this book appeals to. He speculates that it is meant to reassure engineers that their cultural prejudices for tidy structures are all that the world needs, that the uncertainties that other people struggle with can be dispelled with an engineered system.

Large process projects are rare in corporations these days but persist in the federal government. In these, the largest proportion of time is spent on "as-is" description, supposedly because it is absolutely required that there be detailed documentation of the failing system before anything of importance can be done with any confidence. Why must one assume that the people who run the process every day of their lives don't know enough about it already? Or is the point that the consultants have to learn first from the workers, in order to tell the workers what they already know? Few process-based management reforms are ever actually implemented in government, but even fewer are directly informed by the as-is description. At the beginning of the wave of reengineering in the Department of Defense (DoD) during the 1990s, in a program called Corporate Information Management, the primary success story was a new system for delivering medical supplies. Impressive results were achieved when managers risked making some obvious changes that were well understood by the drivers and dispatchers. This change occurred before the DoD-wide program began, however, and no as-is process study had been done. All that they did was agree to the following:

- Everyone would collect and report relevant, minimal performance data
- The old rules about how to pack a truck and when to deliver were suspended

The $1 billion program that followed was never able to produce another success of the same magnitude, and certainly none at the same speed.

Let's examine a more recent project that highlights the mismatch of focal practice to turbulence. A DoD program from the Bush years, renamed and redirected several times, was generally aimed at fixing financial management. The "stretch goal" was to have auditable books for the first time. Hundreds of experts were sent out to study hundreds of information systems and business processes. As-is process description was always a major element. The intent was to load it all into a modeling tool that is compliant with arcane government standards for enterprise architecture. In one such study Myers spent several days describing a small office in the Navy that reimbursed salaries from one agency to another when Navy personnel were temporarily assigned to a different agency, usually for educational purposes or to foster integration. This record-keeping challenge had spawned a mini-bureaucracy. Most of the reassigned individuals had unique situations requiring elaborate formal agreements, forms, schedules, set of signatures, special accounting codes, and so forth. One intelligence agency refused to reimburse according to their agreement, and the Navy administrator could never raise anyone on the phone or get a response to a series of dunning notices.

What was the conclusion to this piece of analysis? One adviser on the project, an old-timer, said that the Navy should simply stop bothering with this record-keeping and leave the Navy personnel on the Navy books, regardless of where they are assigned in the federal government. First of all, the dollar amounts were small. Second, it was not even certain that the Navy was giving up value since it gained education, corporate relationships, and other benefits. Third, temporarily taking personnel off the Navy books created havoc in the accounting for the home military units, an effect that the focused study did not take into account. There are those who want to know how many people have been temporarily reassigned, but that information can be added directly as an accounting footnote, a simple headcount of people out on loan. This would be more useful information than the obscure fund exchange reports that were currently prepared. Not running these transactions through the accounting system would actually improve transparency as well as save cost. The adviser's clinching argument was that his solution had been settled practice only a few years previously! A hyperactive political appointee had instituted the new practice, and that appointee was now gone and no current manager was defending the change. The analytic team was congratulated for identifying a clear improvement that was well within the power of the administration to implement immediately. As one might guess, nothing was changed.

The point we are making is not the difficulty of making changes in government, but the irrelevance of the detailed analysis in the face of a complex situation. Other factors mattered more. It was possible to take quick, decisive action based on a simple reframing. One could have started with examining the necessity or value of this whole category of accounting information, conclude quickly that it wasn't necessary and that a better, proven reporting technique was readily available. The current way was clearly frustrating, expensive, and error-prone, both for DoD and for the other agencies. The exact steps of the current process were irrelevant, not worth improving, and couldn't ever become smooth and repeatable because of the uniqueness and annual change in each relationship. Yet the mindlessness of this focused practice required the generation of information that was not relevant either to a decision or to meaningful accounting. It was only relevant to an image of complete and perfect accounting that was not achievable in the situation, given the incompatibilities and constant churn of processes and new leaders and direction, combined with staff and procedures that could not possibly change fast enough to keep up. Focused practice mired the client in failure. Reflexive practice, as demonstrated by the adviser, offered a way out, one that on the surface appeared to violate proper accounting but that appealed to the greater good of what accounting should accomplish, and it also offered a real and feasible solution in the form of a bypass. However, that solution was buried within a larger package of as-is description and the presumption that the solution would need to be in the form of a fix within current assumptions of "full accounting" that many had come to expect but never question. The notion that one could simply stop keeping records, rather than "improve" their production, didn't fit the frame.

The irony was that the espoused theory of the program was that the leaders would in fact "break some eggs" and turn off some systems that were costly and widely recognized as irrelevant. The executives could speak this way about major systems in the far future, but actually turning off anything specific proved too difficult. This small matter in the Navy was perhaps too difficult, not because of any detail, but because of the difficulty of getting anybody (of the focused practice persuasion) to move from what they wanted to believe was feasible stability in their record-keeping. Even though the consultants clearly had a better answer and pressed for it, the consultants didn't escape being implicated in the failure because they reinforced the at-risk practice to begin with and failed to educate the client on a different way to think.

Corporate reengineering projects have taken bold actions that are rare in government, but even so, corporate projects are generally a colossal expense that may have any of the following results:

- Doesn't achieve much
- Highly disruptive (even without layoffs)
- Fixes have little lasting value
- The project is overtaken by "external" forces, such as mergers or changes in leadership

Davenport says that reengineering can be seen as the final push of industrial engineering. All work was conceived of as IT-mediated procedure, to become standardized and highly controlled. Big money was spent on software that promised efficiency. This widespread adoption of IT-based procedure has settled in, but it now appears to have become normal infrastructure, no different in principle from efficient telephones. Further investment in IT-based procedures and records will no longer achieve a marketplace advantage. Therefore a continued high rate of spending on business IT would be unwise. This argument was highly controversial, mainly because so many reputations and businesses were dedicated to extending this wave.[3] A lobbyist for IT argues that investments in IT will continue to have returns, though even he admits that returns are not endless.[4] He may be right, but diminishing returns are certainly setting in, and better investment opportunities pop up (and down) with the vagaries of the economy.

We won't deny that having effective internal procedures are important, but high attention to perfecting them and low attention to environmental turbulence and to many other opportunities and dimensions of adaptation is an at-risk practice. Focused practice should not set the pattern for professionals if they are to serve their institutions beyond the level of conventional expectations, to the level of their need to adapt to complex challenges that are larger and less clear than the challenges they would prefer to work on.

## Principled Practice

Principled practice centers on applying an abstract causal framework to specific settings. The framework stresses internal coherence and yields distinct recommendations and promises of success. The practitioner has a plausible claim that the theory has been proved and there is no need to modify the frame, though a great deal of work is required to assure that the principles are properly interpreted and applied. This orientation may take the form of applying "best practices," or it may point toward the purchase of "off the shelf" software that is presumed to work everywhere and is being improved for all users through constant revision. This orientation is associated with ideologies such as libertarianism that promise excellent results if only it is truly and fully applied. To modify one's principles is to risk losing their benefit. One merely has to turn the crank on their application. When there is a failure, it is always possible to develop an argument as to why a violation of principle was the cause of failure, never a failure of the principles themselves. This strategy can only work if the assumptions of the theory are constant in relation to a constant environment, and the two are synchronized to yield benefit, but no part of this stays put in a turbulent environment.

This style of thinking, as depicted in Table 3.3, is particularly adept at masking any evidence that would put the universal applicability of its frame in doubt. There are often troublesome situations in which the principles have been applied and have *appeared* not to work, and this level of evidence can be admitted, but it is then dismissed in either of two ways: explain that the solution was incompletely applied and requires rededication, or claim that the solution wasn't fully understood and is subject to further principled clarification. The solution, in other words, is always to redouble application of the principle.

If a corporate transformation doesn't work, a common explanation of failure is that the CEO wasn't "really" behind the change. This charge always sticks, no matter how many hours the CEO has spent pleading for the program, no matter how much he has funded it. Next time there must be even more management sincerity and "change management" to cram down the correct solution.

Every once in a while extraordinary events expose the irrational, mechanical nature of principled practice. During the initial financial

Table 3.3  Cognitive configuration for principled practice

| Polish template | | Find discrepancy |
|---|---|---|
| (value) | | (observe) |
| | Align to template | |
| | (orient) | |
| Rationalize | | Instantiate |
| (decide) | | (act) |

bailout discussion, several dissenting Republican Congressmen were aghast at the size of the interventions being proposed. Rather than simply seeking ways to counter it, they proposed drastic, correct intervention of their own. Faulty regulation was to blame. So far, so good. But their remedy was not to improve regulation, but to eliminate it entirely. Unfettered markets would somehow restore prosperity. They had apparently learned their lessons too well. No responsible economist backed them up, and even some convinced libertarians found the argument a bit over the top, and perhaps not in their interest to pursue at a sensitive moment for the nation and the world. For some, it seems, it hardly matters what the principle is, as long as there is one that generates the preferred answer.

The more normal move is to take principles for which evidence can be marshaled, such as "market solutions," but then to still just push the application. In a turbulent environment, the conditions that would be most supportive of a principled solution may not obtain, or may not obtain for long. To hold to that frame no matter what is simply misreading the situation and wishing it were otherwise. At best, some principle may be useful or moral in the long run, but they are often too rigid and blind to the opportunities in a turbulent environment. To decide by principle alone is to never allow evidence to draw the principle under question. Evidence, to the extent it is used, is used to either confirm the principle or to suggest that rivals fail because they lack the right principles. It is a dance around a prior and controlling commitment.

This practice is not limited to economic principles. There are those who promote inflexible readings of many canonical texts, be it the constitution, Bible, or the writings of a cult founder. These interpretations do not allow that there is need for interpretation (beyond the interpretation that is offered), and that this interpretation itself has never changed, or would never need to change or even deviate temporarily. Again, there are some embarrassing cases where one is asked to look the other way, to not notice the opportunistic violation of principles, such as with the Supreme Court ruling on the 2000 election. Regardless of one's opinion of this ruling, it is a demonstration to all that situations arise for which there is no principled resolution. Such situations are frequent in a turbulent environment, if one is open to recognizing them.

To a principled practitioner, any issue can be solved based on a reference to an authoritative text or practice. It matters less whether the resolution works. Rather, it must be correct, and the practitioner's job is done. The principled practitioner may be extremely influential because he can engender confidence through bold promises, clear linkages between principles and action, quick and precise answers, and skillful demonstrations honed through many repetitions. Such practitioners can be lionized as "brilliant" in fields where their technical bent can be showcased, such as in computer programming or in stock manipulation. The "quants" from the Long-Term Capital Management hedge fund, for example, received the Nobel Prize in economics mere months before their trading algorithm nearly destroyed the financial system and required a bailout. At the time, the bailout was considered huge. If the size of the disaster that one can create is a measure of brilliance, then perhaps the inventors of credit default swaps deserve the Nobel also.

We are not saying that principled practitioners are not skilled or that they haven't achieved. We do argue, however, that they do not hold the answers for managing through turbulence over an extended period, or for facing uncertainty and learning in the direction of the common good and sustainability. They are very capable, in fact, of leading people off a cliff, and not being aware that they are doing it, or even allowing that it is possible.

## Interested Practice

At the center of interested practice is a "position." This may seem like a very free sort of framing, in that one could arrive at a position through any means, be it a process of inquiry or of imagination. But the position we are speaking of is the expression of an interest, and that is actually quite confining. The detached professional might not immediately realize this, in that he senses in himself no compelling interest until he has studied a matter, but in many jobs he might find himself in, he will be taking on an interest. We mention again Karl Mannheim who spoke of the intellectual having no interest of his own, and that the only way he can be socially effective is to associated with one who does. Today, owing to the large population and high income of professionals, they have come to have the appearance of a class with interests—the "creative class" as some have called it—but these interest remain diffuse. In the pre-WWII German milieu that Mannheim referred to, it was clearer what side one was taking. Today, an American professional in many institutions will be much less aware of whose interests he is advocating. He may think that the market or democracy neutralizes interests or bends particular interests toward common interests.

Nevertheless, interests remain embedded in most institutions, whether recognized or not, and professionals often become their advocates, wittingly or not. Of course large groups of professionals are quite aware of this role as mouthpiece and pursue interests vigorously, sometimes nakedly, sometimes cloaked in an apparent dispassionate analysis that happens to turn out right for one's client. Interests are being played out, for example, in scientific drug efficacy studies funded by drug companies. We will include as interested practitioners those whose work is consumed by exposing and countering the interests of others, which would include "attack" journalists. Their positions may seem to change depending on who they are attacking, but their discourse is always structured by the position frame.

A position seeks a particular good, not the common good. There are many theories that contend that everyone needs an advocate, and that the clash of positions is a process that gives rise to as fair a solution as any, assuming that some rules of process and fair play are adhered to. This is certainly enshrined in our legal and political systems. However, it is also well recognized that it is a costly and bruising arrangement that tends to structure disputes as zero-sum games and will often drive toward deadlock as incompatible positions are set against each other.

Here again we may revisit Donald Schon[5] who worried over the large number of intractable disputes that have arisen in the postindustrial environment. These fights are either never resolved or are resolved badly. He argued that it is precisely reframing that can unlock such disputes and allow for movement, or at least back people away from deadlocks and allows them to explore peripheral concerns where compromise and accommodation are possible.

The most obvious example of policy deadlock is over abortion. It is also an issue where a reframing strategy is relatively obvious, though only recently brought forward. The United States has a greater rate

Table 3.4  Cognitive configuration for interested practice

| | | |
|---|---|---|
| Read constituency | | Read opposition |
| (value) | | (observe) |
| | Find position | |
| | (orient) | |
| Revise and extend | | Advocate |
| (decide) | | (act) |

of abortions than any other advanced society and all agree that fewer abortions would be better. This is common ground where effective steps could be taken, while steering clear of prohibitions. That's what President Obama has suggested as a place to restart, and many have found favor in it.

But interested practitioners are wary of solutions that, regardless of how beneficial to themselves, also benefit the interest of opponents. Promoting one's position to the maximum and above others is the point. Deborah Tannen has chronicled how strident we have become, even to the point of seeking out conflict and being aggressive without provocation, just because we think of it as our job as an interested practitioner.[6] She shows how this has developed as a self-reinforcing culture, cut loose in many cases from any sensible notion of how to manage our institutions or society. Concepts such as accommodation, compromise, comity, bipartisanship all used to be cultivated and valued. Compromise was not a weakness but a sign that one was doing his job as a leader and politician and creating broad benefits. One could be interested but also practice phronesis.

Interested practice, to the extent it elevates its interests and advocates to the utmost, tends to exert power negatively, against opponents. This can be very effective in rounding up adherents, churning them with constant reminders, and providing daily talking points that they dutifully repeat among themselves. Rage can be wicked up in a moment. Of course there are many other positions that are promoted more quietly, and with more apparent rationality.

The U.S. population certainly accepts the interests of business as legitimate, and the Chamber of Commerce attempts to explain what these interests are. But the issue comes over what is the common good, and whether any interest can any more afford to work against it. Several members of the Chamber of Commerce recently defected because the position the Chamber had take on climate was contrary to the public interest. It is very uncertain that a free-for-all of interested practitioners, many of whom cancel each other out, will in the end arrive at a good solution for all.

We are not saying that interested politics as we know it could or should go away. But professionals don't need to lock in on it, especially since it is often at odds with the solutions that are available in a turbulent environment. There are opportunities to co-evolve. In a stable environment, it is perhaps more important to keep the pressure up through interested practice, in order to keep one's place in a web of stable competitions for advantage. In a turbulent environment, the interested practitioner may find himself in a futile fight where the stakes have fallen off the table and the opportunities are unfamiliar, undetected, or undeveloped due to an inability to reframe one's perception to recognize the opportunities.

The classic case of pursuing interests is advocating for a labor union against management. In the case of General Motors and other major manufacturing operations that are on the ropes, to press to retain advantages can easily break the company, and then the union and its members follow. However painful and humiliating it may feel, the advocates for labor may need to think creatively about how to succeed when times are turbulent. Slicing a few dollars off existing benefits may fall short of the creative solution that is necessary for transformation leading to success. Smaller companies have made more breathtaking changes in the area of employee ownership that have worked out well, at least for a time. (We will examine this more closely in chapter 5, which discusses economics.) The union could, for example, accept all the salary and benefit concessions that are requested, but also take significant ownership of stock, just as the bond holders and management are forced to do, plus take additional representation on the board.[7] Then the workers can participate differently in the success of the company, and more particularly in the upside of the stock price, if it occurs, and will be increasing their chances of this happening by making the wage concessions. Of course they could go down with everyone else, but they would at least have a chance and a stake in a success that they could have some influence over. An interested practitioner would find this solution anathema. The practitioner would prefer to imagine that the world is as it was, or seemed to be.

A committed partisan also finds that his supposed rock-solid, constant interests are sent into gyrations in a turbulent environment. There are some issues on which partisans are regularly forced to flip flop, which causes consternation for those who purport to demonstrate constancy. For example, many conservatives promote open trade and free markets, which produces interdependence, though they preach independence. Many liberals promote trade and market restrictions, where the implicit value is independence, though they preach interdependence. Dick Cheney informed us that "deficits don't matter" and attempted to prove it. Now suddenly deficits do matter for Republicans. Some choose not to explain. Each of these values can shift depending on the restriction one places on one's horizon or what other issues are added, such as legal and illegal immigration, outsourcing, and which party promoted which trade agreement in the past. What we can learn from so many reversals and paradoxes is, simply, that the postindustrial environment is one in which one must navigate interdependence, dependence, and other values without being overly quick to capture a short-term, one-sided advantage, but to consider the potential of the whole and how many of us might work together, including opponents, for success in an infinite game. One may very well seek interdependence yet with looser coupling, with the understanding that linkages remain and change, and that they require constant awareness and reframing.

An interesting case is Michael Gerson, a Washington Post columnist and former Bush speech writer. He shows sensitivity to reflexive practice while plying his trade as an interested practitioner. He finds reflexive practice appealing yet he pulls back from it, asserting that what is really needed for today's trouble, after all, is straightforward partisan domination (i.e., interested practice). He writes about Obama:

> His entire manner douses inflammatory charges of extremism. So conservatives are left with what might be called the Niebuhrian hope. One of Obama's favorite philosophers is Reinhold Niebuhr... Niebuhr's thought is complex, but he is properly known as the theologian of conflicted humility—for his belief that human nature is flawed and fallible even, or especially, in the pursuit of good causes. ... In Obama's case, this humility might translate into an administration focused on achievable goals, run by seasoned, reasonable professionals,... reaching out to Republicans in the new Cabinet and avoiding culture war battles when possible. But there is a reason we don't generally praise Niebuhrian soldiers, Niebuhrian policemen—or Niebuhrian presidents. Sometimes events call for courage and clarity, not a sense of irony.[8]

It will be interesting to see whether Gerson's contemplative side grows with age, and whether he can accept that a politician could be anything other than an interested advocate.

## Roundup of Practice Types

From the foregoing review, one may conclude that proponents of at-risk practices are a hard-headed group. They are committed to a constrained way of framing situations, are not open to evidence that would draw their frames into question, and are holding on to practices that have made no fundamental accommodation to the turbulent environment. On the other hand, to deviate from their strictures invites even worse criticism. If one simply negates the at-risk practices, the result is:

- Irrationality
- Lack of focus
- No guiding principles
- No value to anybody in particular

That is not what we recommend as either the transition to, or the end point of, reflexive practice. We instead recommend a circumspect position that can apply each of these frames and additional frames and actions bur remain open to adjusting them all, while promoting opportunistic adaptations, and building capacity to continue on co-evolutionary paths for the common good.

None of these styles of practice is either simple or easily defined, but more can be learned about them by comparing them against several additional dimensions beyond those shown in the basic cognitive model. The following table shows several contrastive sets of characteristics. Not all practitioners within a type will exhibit all the characteristics shown, but they would be unlikely to be diametrically opposed to any of them. For some dimensions, a practice type may have no strong tendency, but we have filled these cells with a plausible preference.

## Comparison of Practices

Table 3.5 contrasts the characteristics of various practice types.

Table 3.5 Contrastive characteristics of practice types

| Dimension | Reflexive Practice (XP) | Rational Practice (RP) | Focused Practice (FP) | Principled Practice (PP) | Interested Practice (IP) |
|---|---|---|---|---|---|
| Goal | capture opportunity and maintain potential | achieve objectives | make an accurate account | illuminate the pattern | gain against opposing forces |
| Unit of analysis | influence network | abstract system/ business model | autonomous institution | rule-based structure | a conflict |

Continued

Table 3.5 Continued

| Dimension | Reflexive Practice (XP) | Rational Practice (RP) | Focused Practice (FP) | Principled Practice (PP) | Interested Practice (IP) |
|---|---|---|---|---|---|
| Method of inquiry | interpretive reframing | convergent demonstration | detailed description | match reference model to situation | biased reframing |
| Evaluation criterion | common good | optimization of factors | efficiency | correctness | advantage |
| Favored type of knowledge | phronesis | episteme | facts in focus | authority | opinion |
| Recurrent cognitive posture | questioning | converging | finding | explaining | arguing |
| Persuasive offering | hope | reason | accuracy | deduction from premises | winning |
| Recurrent frame of reference | common good | theory | delimited system | principles | interests |
| Intervention | shape co-evolutionary paths | implement strategic plan | adjust to standard | apply correct ideas | persuade and expose |
| Write-up style | appreciative aesthetic | tight analysis | complete account | didactic | rhetorical |
| Conversational quality | dialogical | logical | descriptive | evaluative | debate |
| Direction of seeking | to horizon | top-down | inside | to mirror | to motives |
| That which reveals | viewpoints and context | best path | details | repetition | power |
| Place and time orientation | situational and emergent | enterprise and planning period | address and dates | tag from timeless to instance | stakeholder envelope |
| Quality of abstraction | conceptual | categorical | grounded | ideological | social type |
| Coherence sought | multi-perspective | non-contradiction | exhaustiveness | logical derivation | clinched argument |

## The Transition to Reflexive Practice

While reflexive practice may not satisfy many when considered in isolation from the environment, we have argued that when one keeps turbulence clearly in mind, this spoils the ambitions of the at-risk practices and allows reflexive practice to emerge as the prudent choice. The conditions that allowed the at-risk practices to be effective no longer hold. Yet as a culture, we have not actually come to terms with turbulence. Despite the near unanimous recognition of turbulence and the clichéd statements about its importance and how it changes everything, the condition continues to be strange for us, and the practices that work under those conditions will necessarily be strange to us also.

An analogy—a disturbing one—can be made with combat. Under the harsh conditions of combat, it has often been observed that a new set of leaders emerge. Fear can induce a group to take cues from members who are better at fighting and survival, whose calculations are reliable in the new situation. These new leaders may have been shunned as uncouth or unintelligent at the country club or at the company planning retreat where there is an orderly culture and a longstanding web of connections that dictates who and what will be heard. The complex practitioner may be like these emergent combat leaders—perhaps not someone you would choose to be seen with at the professional conferences, but nevertheless a person for the times who will get the job done for your imperiled institution.

The conditions are right for the development of reflexive practice, and there are increasing opportunities to learn this pattern, yet this is not enough to guarantee that the practice will flourish. Practitioners also need to be weaned away from at-risk options. These options won't go away soon, but they can be moderated, especially in turbulent situations where the advantages of reflexive practice can be recognized and employed at least as a supplement. Rather than launching a frontal assault, one may instead point out that the reflexive practitioner can add something that addresses a visible risk that isn't "core" territory for at-risk practitioners who are in charge. Table 3.6 presents

Table 3.6  Strategies for avoiding confrontation

| If This At-Risk Practice Is in Charge: | This Aspect of Reflexive Practice Is Least Offensive: |
|---|---|
| Rational | Cultural change |
| Focused | Developmental potentials |
| Principled practice | Wider scanning for threats |
| Interested practice | Relations with those who are not a party to the conflict |

some ideas on what kind of help, if offered, might be accepted and provide a point of entry for reflexive practice. Another approach, which may be interpreted as a frontal assault, is to appeal to the at-risk practitioner's responsibilities and ideals. One may simply ask, if professional practitioners are here to "solve problems," then why have so few been solved, or stay solved? Also, since we are reasonably certain that things won't stay the same, could we take the opportunity to innovate rather than to perfect the current approach? Where assumptions are unlikely to hold, responsible practitioners should not proceed mindlessly as if they will, or just take somebody's word for it that they should continue. If one stops thinking and simply takes instruction, then that practitioner is no longer a professional (able to advise) but has become a functionary (doing what either the procedure or the boss dictates).

To be able to advise under these conditions means changing practices that allow one to deal with broader, uncertain environments in more prudent ways. Not everyone needs to become a strategist, but one should accept responsibility, and expect others to be responsible, to be honest about dubious projects, and to keep generating a rapid succession of projects that make more sense, even though they break the old rules. We should expect to see portfolios of inconsistent projects, honest assessments of their usefulness and effectiveness as time goes on, continuing identification and testing of assumptions, and decisions that take this information into account.

We are just opening up the question here about how to transition, how to establish complex practice as a cultural norm and to allow at-risk cultural practices to fade from their aggressive position of priority. How we go about making this transition to postindustrial culture and to the professional's portion of that culture is a topic that will be further elaborated in the context of several domains that we now turn to, as we pass from the kernel section to the facets section of this book.

But a little more on the game first, which is a significant factor driving the need for new professional thinking. The reader will often have read the quotation from Keynes, "In the long run, we are all dead." This is usually brought out to make the point that it does no good to look too far ahead, that it is important to get today's problem solved, and especially to reap the benefits for oneself. The phrasing also connotes that this is a manly approach. Yet this quotation is out of keeping with the rest of Keynes, who certainly had vision and a great capacity for contemplation. As with the Einstein quotation discussed in the preface, one gets a very different impression by reading the Keynes quotation in context:

> *In the long run* we are all dead. Economists set themselves too easy, too useless a task if in tempestuous seasons they can only tell us that when the storm is long past the ocean is flat again.[9]

Keynes' point was that when technical analysts are content in showing that equilibrium returns, they ignore the pain of getting there and the need for social action to patch the damage of an economic crisis. He didn't deny the long view at all, only the type of analysis that overlooks the role of practice in dealing with important challenges along the way. He was speaking ironically and critically about those who overlook institutional reality. Practitioners cannot, or at least should not, sit back and wait for their models to come true. There are flesh and blood issues, people die, and scientists, or at least the useful ones, need to deal with policy along the way. Thus, Keynes was playing an infinite game in segments, as a practitioner and not as a theorist. He was criticizing those who played it poorly due to principled disengagement. He was not arguing for a finite game, which would lead to a different posture than the one we are describing here.

II

Facets

# 4

# Intelligence for Security

A National Academy of Sciences (NAS) panel in 2009 took on the question of how to change the thinking of U.S. intelligence community (IC) analysts who had, in the opinion of many, been performing poorly in the turbulent terrorism environment. Brent Scowcroft began the panel session by asking what had changed for IC practitioners.[1] Porter Goss, George Tenet, and many IC directors before them described their work as "stealing secrets." Scowcroft remarked that, while stealing secrets is indeed a unique responsibility, it has been oversold and leads to the denigration of openly available information. Scowcroft asserted that the purpose of intelligence is to reduce the uncertainty of the policy maker. Open source information is not only necessary for this purpose but is often superior to stolen secrets. This sounded a theme often repeated by critics of the IC, that more and more effort is spent on traditional collection activities, while less and less of that effort actually helps decision makers make sense in today's unpredictable and ambiguous situations. While it was not clear to Scowcroft what would work, he was sure that intelligence practices that ignore or misconstrue the ambiguities of decision will not work.

Scowcroft then turned to take a shot at the behavioral scientists on the panel. Scowcroft said that intelligence is a practice that has something to gain from behavioral science, but one should not presume that a major infusion of behavioral science is necessary or always helpful. Many panelists acknowledged his point but were unable to prescribe anything other than the science that qualified them for panel membership.

Scowcroft then began painting the challenge and implicitly criticizing current practices. Situations are "usually very unknown," and what the intelligence analyst can offer will be "comforting" if it meets the following guidelines:

- Communicate. Analysts often seem to be talking to each other more than to the client—the decision maker or policy maker. What does the information mean to the client?
- Distinguish what you know from what you don't know and explain each. Don't hedge concerning what you don't know.
- Avoid code words to denote levels of confidence and probability. These are not really quantitative and don't communicate well. It is better to add context, different judgments, or reasons why you are confident or skeptical. Let the decision maker balance among competing judgments and sources. Save the language of precision for things that you can be precise about.
- Describe the information source and your confidence in that source. The Iraqi informant named "Curveball" had rich details on chemical weapons, but he was known to be a fabulist and this fact was obfuscated.
- Find and state your assumptions. The President's Daily Briefing (PDB) that was issued just as the Yom Kippur War started in 1973 read, "The Egyptian and Syrian military exercises are unusually realistic this year." Since exercises occurred every year, the assumption was that they were continuing, despite strong warnings from Israelis that many conditions had changed, and that President Sadat had an interest in creating a threat to Israel and then negotiating. Intelligence analysts could not make sense of this new information because they were locked in on an assumption. Surfacing the assumption might have allowed for the possibility of concluding that it was wrong.
- Provide analyzed intelligence, not raw data that can be wrong or misleading. Analysts have an important role in selecting and interpreting, not for the purpose of controlling the message but to make the information useful and focused. From raw intelligence, a client could latch onto anything and make the favored case.

Scowcroft went on to describe unavoidable tensions in the advisory relationship, where reflexivity is on full display. Should the Director of National Intelligence (DNI) sit in on National Security Council (NSC) policy deliberations? Some say he needs to understand what people are thinking to tailor intelligence to what decision makers need. Others argue that the job of intelligence is to provide an objective picture, like a journalist, not tainted by interests.

When a President has made a dubious decision, intelligence is in a tough spot. Do you continue to provide information that undermines the decision to invade Iraq, or do you stop questioning and offer only support and help? Some decision makers prefer to use red teams that provide alternative findings based on different sets of assumptions, but the interpreter who synthesizes contradictory inputs needs to be careful. How do you handle dissent against your analysis constructively? The solution has typically been to present a compromise and suppress sharp differences within the analytic community. The notorious 2002 National Intelligence Estimate (NIE) on Iraq's weapons of mass destruction (WMD) was not agreed to by everyone, but the reasons for disagreement were not shown. Information on yellowcake uranium ore and on aluminum tubes was used to suggest that Iraq was intent on developing nuclear weapons. Dissenting views were not completely scrubbed out, but they were obscured and demoted from the main text.

Outside critics fault the IC for failing to detect the impending collapse of regimes. While this failure has occurred, it is neither that surprising nor significant, Scowcroft argued. Contrary to general opinion, in 1989, evidence was presented to President George H.W. Bush of an impending Soviet breakup. He wisely didn't use the information. He didn't know how a collapse would play out, and if he had intervened it would have tainted the events and made it difficult for the eventual winner to work with the United States. In the case of 9/11, generalized warnings and predictions were briefed to President George Bush, but what was he going to do about it? If the government had suddenly started major security checks at airports (as we have today) people would not have accepted it. When leaders fail to act on a warning, though, this induces the production of more warnings, leading to "an excess of prudence." Decision makers don't really want prediction. What is more useful are alternate courses of action and responses.

Intelligence analysts can often be dragged into a policy failure and then catch the blame. Secretary of State Colin Powell needed to make the strongest case for invasion in his United Nations speech in 2002. An analyst ends up giving him what he needs, even though the analyst has become implicated in a "partial deception." Such a person might agonize over those situations, which bend one's role. The role the analyst wants, and usually has, is to present balanced information accompanied by doubt. George H.W. Bush did not include his intelligence adviser in meetings, in order that the adviser would avoid taint and pressure to take a position.

I asked Scowcroft whether he supported the recent expansion in the range of intelligence subject matter, with a new officer for economics, and the production of a national intelligence estimate on climate change. He said that it is perfectly legitimate to use whatever information is available and answer security questions, to include economic information and open sources. The process of intelligence is powerful and can be used for a wide variety of issues. Yet the community, despite its massive capability to collect information, has surprisingly small capacity for analysis and interpretation. You can't study everything and must make some choices. George H.W. Bush was familiar with the CIA and understood uncertainty and limited resources. He didn't expect more than was possible.

An officer on the National Warning Staff asked, since everything changes so rapidly and everything is decided at a high tempo, is there value in strategic or long-range warning? There is value, said Scowcroft, but it really depends on how the information is presented. There is pressure to please other analysts with thorough products that might run to 60 pages. But look at your audience. Decision makers won't read more than a few pages. You also need to connect long-range thinking to the decision maker's current concerns.

Scowcroft gave us a taste of the reflexive dilemmas of the analyst. While it was encouraging to see serious questions raised at this panel session about practice, the main response to the challenge of international terrorism and weapons proliferation has been to simply throw more money at it. DNI Blair estimates that intelligence programs cost $75 billion and employ over 200,000 "core" intelligence personnel, not including about the same number of contractors.[2] One would think that this amount of money would be enough to cover the comings and goings of bad actors, plus surveillance of trouble around the world, yet many topics are not covered, and many decision makers who could use help receive no support.

Terrorist attacks on America may not rate quite so highly when one considers all national security risks, such as cyber attack, climate change, and financial collapse. Even the terrorist threats are changing. Various biological scenarios can result in more damage than a nuclear bomb, and the WMD Commission now feels that we have an even chance of seeing a biological attack before 2013. Taking responsibility for such nontraditional threats puts the IC in competition with outside expertise. But why not join them? If the IC operates as if none of that outside expertise exists, there is no reason to wonder why nobody listens to them.

## At-Risk Practices

We will sample a few instances where at-risk practices in government intelligence appear to be a significant drag on adaptation. Let's begin with focused practice. Only a few years ago the word "petabyte" ($10^{15}$ bytes of data) was spoken of in hushed tones. All text ever written by humans amounts to 50 petabytes. To intelligence collectors, that amount of data has now become a mere file folder. The latest estimate is that, by 2015, stored sensor data will reach "yottabytes" ($10^{24}$).[3] To many in the community, there is something mysterious and compelling in these numbers. Data volume is framed as a great test of technological leadership. The National Security Agency (NSA) had warned that vital programs were in peril because the East coast grid could no longer accommodate their computers. NSA is now building colossal computing centers in Texas and one in Utah with its own generators (which protects against intrusion via the power grid.) It is ironic that NSA's former chief, William Odom, pointed to the National Reconnaissance Office (NRO) as being truly awash in expensive data with no compelling benefit. NRO has at times dumped data that it could not process. That seems reasonable–who has not erased a bad photo?—but NRO could not admit to this practice because it has always argued that all data were precious, and still more were needed. Yet the resource that limits NRO is not power or even money but its own competence in designing satellites. Several launched sensors would not light up. One of these duds had to be shot down in 2008. The volume of imagery actually fell by a third during this period. As Senator Bond put it, "The IC has spent nearly $10 billion on advanced imagery satellites that have never produced a single picture."[4] Minions at National Geospatial Agency (NGA), Defense Intelligence Agency (DIA) and lesser of the 16 agencies in the community are indexing all sorts of data to maps, the preferred medium for the military which conceives of targets as something fixed in a location. Unfortunately, the entities associated with terrorism and proliferation tend to move, or may not relate in any useful way to a map.

The assumption among technical collectors is that a total record of everything is the foundation for conclusions. Yet data that actually matter are usually sought as a result of an hypothesis, then are collected as needed from cheaper sources. The anomaly in this enterprise is State Department intelligence, which has a mere 300 analysts. When Hayden, the deputy DNI, was told that a man from State Department intelligence had been selected as the initial head of analysis, he was pleased, saying, "The State Department is the only group batting over .300."

Robert Jervis, a systems thinker with intelligence expertise, looked into the errors over Iraq WMD and concluded that, while nobody could be expected to get it right given the confusing information, the application of "sound" analytic standards make analysts more confident than they should have been.[5] They simply didn't consider the full variety of perspectives that fit the data, nor were they skilled in using different kinds of data to corroborate hypotheses. There was a pervasive blindness to deception, both regarding Saddam's effort to fool his enemies, and the effort by members of his regime to fool each other. (It has been suggested that we need to recruit those with street smarts and criminal experience to be analysts. Young analysts will have done well in school but typically have no experience with thugs and deception.) This is a cognitive problem, which both Jervis and the 9/11 Commission called a lack of imagination. What stops the imagination is a premature imposition of order within an uncertain and changing state, an instance of rational practice.

Many practitioners cling to outmoded bureaucratic control procedures. This is a kind of principled practice, common throughout government, but particularly corrosive in intelligence. An emphasis on written policies can lead to the most absurd bureaucratic thinking. The official National Security Strategy was placed on the reading list for a course for new executives. The instructor, quite reasonably, pointed out that this document was obsolete and that other documents might be used to learn about current strategy. The education director replied that, while the content was of course wrong, the point of the course was to instruct people in "how the system operates" and that it was essential to use this obsolete document and no others. This "advanced" course was not only training new executives on irrelevant formalities but also preventing them from discussing current national strategy.

New IC-wide policies have been helpful for changing direction, even though much energy is spent over fine wording. The chief of policy points out that his policies are where a bureaucrat can make a lasting mark, and if one has the opportunity to do this well, one should take it. But in the end, a finely crafted, long-lasting policy may be no better as a guide during turbulent times than a mindless formality.

Intelligence professionals aspire to "speak truth to power" and are careful to avoid taking the side of the administration or to exhibit partisanship. This is a commendable ethic and, despite temptations and failures, it prevails in the long run. An interest that is often indulged in, however, is a rather simple-minded construction of the national interest: the United States should gain advantage over others at every opportunity. Since most of the "targets" that the IC studies are clearly hostile, and many military clients only want to know how to defeat them, this assumption works well enough. But national intelligence should serve peacemaking and diplomatic approaches as well, and if all foreign entities are framed as the enemy, the consideration of options is highly constrained.

## Reflexive Intelligence

Transformation efforts in the IC have created opportunities for reflexive practice, though they are often not articulated and are underappreciated as aspects of the cultural change that leaders have sought. Some visible changes in professional IC culture that we associate with reflective practice include the following:

- Attention to adaptation (of both adversaries and self)
- Attention to networks rather than hierarchies (in adversaries and self)
- Attention to the advisory relationship with decision makers
- Openness and collaboration
- Use of multiple perspectives

These trends may sound ho-hum, but their more specific application can be very disorienting. For example, William Nolte, an educator and retired IC reformer, writes: "The better integration of open source information and expertise,...information sharing, and a fundamental review of security practices represent an iron triangle of intelligence reform and re-conceptualization. Success in any demands success in all three."[6] But each of these elements has been very hard to change, and as Nolte says, each reinforces the other. Yet in a turbulent environment, there will be some "out of control" situations where intelligence just has to get the job done, and adaptive practices can emerge quickly. In the field in Iraq and Afghanistan, and in "lift and shift" operations (including Lebanon, Darfur, and Somalia) efforts have often integrated successfully. The pace is high, the work important, and the feedback swift. There is flow, quite different from how things work back in Washington. There are exceptions, such as the National Counterterrorism Center (NCTC) where agencies began to cooperate under conditions of forced contact and full disclosure within a single room. The CIA and DHS teams were at opposite ends and acted as if the other didn't exist but eventually learned to trust each other. Work with partner countries is also better because of the NCTC.

An interesting experiment was conducted for a major estimate on Nigeria. The project leader wanted a "swarming" approach, set up pages in the Intellipedia wiki, and asked everyone to post their contributions there over a short period.[7] This was clearly a faster and better way to put together a draft product, and it was also a positive experience for participants to become acquainted with previously unknown colleagues who had different information and perspectives. This swarming approach is now often repeated on a small scale, and there are new interagency workspaces that some can reach, but the results often have to be regenerated through a formal process that adds delay and little else.

What perhaps matters the most, according to a former CIA executive, is simply allowing individuals to contact peers in other agencies when they sense a need. One still needs to have permission in some agencies. A few can't even send a classified email outside the boundaries of their agency.

## Reframing the Adversary

The presentation of alternative perspectives can be helpful in uncovering more adaptive choices and their consequences. Even something as simple as using graphics in the President's Daily Briefing was hailed as a breakthrough allowing the presentation of different kinds of information in different ways. More ominously, policy makers and intelligence advisers often have a weak understanding of adversary motivations, or at least choose not to dwell on them. It may make sense for President George Bush to tell the public on the eve of the invasion of Iraq that the enemy is one undifferentiated mass of terrorists who "hate freedom," but invasion forces soon need to make friends among the vanquished, a process requiring some empathy and negotiation. As disaster loomed in Iraq in 2006, senior advisors in the Iraq Study Group strongly recommended that the United States attempt to understand Iraqi insurgents and the role of militias. It really hadn't been done. As soon as the question was asked, an alliance with the Sunni Awakening made sense. This alliance was perhaps more important than the surge of troops, just as rethinking how the United States deals with partners in Afghanistan may ultimately turn out to be more important than any change in troop level.

One initiative that illustrates the difficulty of stepping up to the challenge of cultural knowledge is the Army's Human Terrain System. Civilian anthropologists were embedded in units and collected and applied information about how social relations were affecting behavior of the population and adversaries in Iraq and Afghanistan. This program was first deployed between July 2005 and August 2006, before General David Petraeus's broader shift to counterinsurgency. The program generated valuable information that commanders appreciated. It was curtailed, however, due to casualties among the researchers, but also because the Army felt that it was not in a position to support this specialty. They thought intelligence should take over this sort of project, yet no intelligence group stepped up to continue it.[8] This innovation, widely recognized as worthwhile, became an orphan, and its demise can be taken as evidence of the IC's inability to adapt. Useful parts of this work continue in various locations, but a real-time, in-depth cultural approach in support of current operations is missing.

## Scanning for Threats

The National Intelligence Council's global trends program addresses risks that have been out of bounds for most of the community, even though clearly important to the nation's security.[9] The program also gathers many participants from outside and offers a rare forum where large issues can be discussed freely. Focused practitioners ridicule the work because it explores broad interactions qualitatively and without proof, even though this is how turbulent reality presents itself and how some decision makers need to face it.

A simple inspection of prior global trends reports shows that conditions and perceptions have changed in significant ways that were not anticipated. Typically, the response would be to try to improve anticipations, which of course is not possible on general philosophical grounds, but certainly not possible in a turbulent environment. The program leaders, thankfully, did not take that course. They understood that the task was neither to predict nor to recommend a policy. Rather, it was to change the thinking of decision makers, to sensitize them to aspects of reality which are crucial for sensemaking in national security, and at the same time loosen unhelpful assumptions and biases. One way this has been pursued is by deriving brief scenarios from the main study. Even so, it will be difficult for decision makers to apply what they read unaided. The decision maker will not immediately see how the trends affect their decisions. This is work that analysts need to do in partnership with the decision maker. That step of interpretation, if done without the intelligence advisor in the room, may cut loose both from the specially prepared information and from reflexive thinking that is needed to use it properly.

Of course, it is also essential that this step be anticipated from the beginning, that the intelligence information be grounded in and address available decisions. The intelligence analyst should be afforded status as an interlocutor with decision makers, even though his judgment will not be controlling, only flexible and varied. An intelligence team could, for example, iteratively arrive at the strategic decisions that are available to the NSC or to other forums. This will provide focus for research on just those factors that impinge on available decisions. This follows recent top-level IC policy, to provide "decision advantage."[10]

Scowcroft points out that many intelligence clients don't read, and that this reality shouldn't be ignored. What they like to do is talk, and informed dialogue might be the target communication medium and that documentation should be designed accordingly. The United Kingdom's futures intelligence product is twice the volume of the U.S. *Global Trends 2025* and includes a comprehensive section on technology issues. At 180 pages, it demands a great deal of dedicated reading to profit from the scholarship. Ways should be found to give more rapid treatments to a whole network of issues, while also making it easy for the reader to delve into details according to interest and need as the occasion arises. Information format, navigation affordances, and other cognitive human factors are a significant concern.[11]

The global trends products are expedited through the publishing process. Even so, some statements are out of date before the ink is dry. Readers these days tend to look at a publication when it is issued, but interest tails off quickly, even where the materials remain relevant. Users want a sense that recent events are fully accounted for and integrated into any intelligence product. The cost of meeting these requirements for futures intelligence would appear to be prohibitive. But the answer lies not in applying more resources to the existing method, but in changing the method to one of continuous reporting. It is interesting that the IC's newest creation, *Intelligence Today*, is a continuously edited website. *Intelligence Today* is directed at several top government executives who are not currently allowed to see the PDB but presumably are in need of something similar. The website was chosen as the only feasible way to distribute the information, but it may in fact prove to be superior in many ways to the PDB.

Perspective needs to be developed over time, ready for when one is thrown into the heat of current events. For the decision maker, the question properly becomes, "What are we up against in terms of broader evolution?" not "What was today's take?" without any frame of reference except what one cobbles together from personal prejudice. For any surprising event that pops up, what is needed is a more reliable, shared context of consequences for deciding what is important in the light of what can be done. Uncertain conditions and expectations can be reported in a matter of fact way without going into contortions over likelihood estimates of events that are inherently unpredictable. Of course, it isn't a snap to do this work or to present it. (A structuring tool that might help, Spire, is described in chapter 11.)

Global futures is an important intelligence genre (different from "normal" products about current regional concerns) that struggles to work properly under conditions of secrecy, traditional analytic craft, and discontinuous publishing. It can do quite a lot if given the proper infrastructure and relationship with decision makers, but the ultimate aim would be to help structure deliberations in the new interagency process, discussed next.

### Project on National Security Reform (PNSR)

In 2005 Jim Locher, the brains behind the Goldwater-Nichols reform of DoD, was asked to bring in a new set of thinkers to redesign the national security decision-making process. The products from this project were strangely compelling, but I only understood why when James Orton, the project's resident organizational theorist, explained how they were constructed.[12] Many prominent individuals on their "guiding coalition" could only conceive of reforms that met their own criteria, which were often highly conventional. Christopher Lamb (the chief writer) and Orton devised a "Trojan Horse" technique that would allow them to inject a reflexive approach without requiring approval from the coalition. They stated that, since the coalition could not agree on any conclusions, multiple arguments would be presented. The way in which they did this was the clever part. They first presented a conventional argument, then exposed weak assumptions, and followed up with a reflexive alternative. Often an intermediate, more sophisticated conventional argument was required as well.

Orton constructed a table that tracks the locations of all the alternative arguments. Rows in the table correspond to 12 subjects in organizational change, beginning with broad strategy and ending with fine-grained sensemaking. In each row there are three columns. The first column has recommendations based on simple, nineteenth century concepts that, in his words, appeal to White House staff, undergraduates, and novices. The second column indexes what professional practitioners and graduate students tend to prefer. The third column locates the reflexive concepts that some national security scholars recognize as having a good match with current conditions, though these concepts often do not have broad currency. In the passage below, one can see how a conventionally "right" answer is deftly turned into an alternative from the third column.

> Many Conference participants, as well as scholars and practitioners, attest to *the overriding influence of individual leaders in managing the current national security system*. Many conclude that finding good leadership is therefore the solution to poor performance. The Project, however, accepts the growing body of analysis that supports a different interpretation. Since only the president can compel different agencies and departments to collaborate, subordinate leaders must attempt to capture his attention and assistance, or work around the system to make integration possible. From this fact some conclude that only individual leaders can make integration possible. The larger picture suggests that if we remove the impediments that constrain collaboration in the first place so that it is much more the norm, *leaders could be both more successful in their integration efforts and more accountable for doing so*. Even if good leadership can on occasion make a bad system work, it is not a prescription for an organization's efficiency and effectiveness over the long term.[13]

Orton points to some self-inflicted turbulence in the interagency decision process. Institutional memory is wiped out every four years because the National Security Council literally begins with empty safes at the change in administrations. The papers are carted away for the presidential archive.

In this fast-moving atmosphere, national security professionals rarely reflect on how they are part of making their reality. The National Security Strategy begins, "The US is at war," and Orton argues that we are making it that way. He was in the middle of teaching a seminar for special operations personnel on 9/11, and the next day he asked how we create our environment. The students told him that they could not discuss that question since it would interfere with their warrior mindset. Given that opportunities to self-correct are limited in such an environment, he suggests that an evolutionary micro-strategy (or "small wins"[14]) offers more promise than a large-scale, lengthy, or radical plan.

Orton also observes that "sensemaking chains" are broken. Whenever there is a problem, control tends to be pulled up toward the White House and out of the hands of those with situational awareness. Proposed Interagency Regional Centers might be a better "whole government" integrators than the combatant commands that exist today and are dominated by military concerns. This change would be consistent with the smart power strategy, by which *all* governmental influences are used in concert.[15] That is also consistent with the military's own intention, that what they are really after is positive effects. If those effects can be generated by less costly and risky means than war, then the U.S. government should rearrange its capabilities to achieve it in that way. Even so, DoD has most of the funding, yet it is missing some of the skills and capabilities that are needed for smart power. Secretary of Defense Robert Gates has said that he wants a better balance between the Defense Department and the State Department and USAID, but funds cannot be shifted because of Congress. Orton likes to point out that Eisenhower's original phrase in his 1961 speech was "military-industrial-congressional complex." The congressional element was considered too provocative and was removed at the last minute.

Orton's technique of backtracking to what people want to hear, then adding what they need to hear from his "third column," is an excruciatingly polite way to write a report, but a good, convincing way, and perhaps the only way to make the needed points. Admiral John Poindexter, several years ago, had sponsored a project called Genoa that redesigned the very same national security decision-making process, but the work was thrown out when Poindexter's other, deliberately provocative surveillance projects made news. Dave Snowden, the complexity practitioner introduced in chapter 2, had a hand in injecting sensemaking and complexity concepts to the Genoa project. Snowden has since found another client for his work in the Singapore government, which is making drastic and creative changes in intelligence. Several other countries have shown an appetite for new ideas that the United States has funded, then spurned. Eighty countries signed up to attend a PSNR conference in Montreal in August 2010, but Congress terminated the project.

## Reflexive Intelligence Practitioners

There are many reflexive practitioners in the national defense and intelligence field, though many of them end up cast aside. That result is not in itself a recommendation for their work, but it is an indication of how this system is particularly resistant to alternative thinking. We profile three of these practitioners.

### Edward Luttwak and Grand Strategy

Luttwak writes history books, but he also conducts intelligence operations. These two pursuits converged when I arranged to have him visit the Office of the Director of National Intelligence to give a talk on reform. He had been listed at the Center for Strategic and International Studies as an adviser to their smart power project, but he moved in a quite different direction in his talk.

Luttwak was finishing his book on Byzantium's strategy. He used this history to offer a different perspective on how an empire conducts intelligence for long-term survival.[16] He argued that Byzantium, rather than Rome, is a better model for the United States to follow. Byzantium saw that any attempt to conquer one opponent would leave it vulnerable to other opponents. It instead contained and redirected opponents against each other. Enemy councils had to be infiltrated or at least understood. An extensive infrastructure supported this effort, including manuals and training, an expert staff who worked alongside the emperor, and comprehensive language skills. Whenever a clever foreigner from unknown lands showed up, he was called to the palace for an interview (often with the emperor himself), and offered a job as a cultural expert. (When Kublai Khan sent his first message to Constantinople, someone was on hand to translate from the Chinese.) Military commanders who were posted to outlying districts were required to learn local languages. Luttwak compared this policy to the case of Michael Sheuer, the former head of the Bin Laden unit at CIA. Sheuer did not know Arabic and did not attempt to learn it, even though much of Bin Laden's appeal stems from his poetical use of Arabic. Scheuer's understanding was systematically limited.

Luttwak argues that satellite images, telephone intercepts, and much else in the technical intelligence arsenal are expensive leftovers from a different era and don't match up well against terrorist adversaries. He points to examples in Latin America. The Peruvian government took back their country from the Sendero Luminoso. The government, unable to afford helicopters, trained a committed group of infantrymen who walked endlessly and took full advantage of intelligence on the ground. Luttwak compared this to the approach taken by Colombia. Colombia used many helicopters supplied by the United States, but the FARC insurgents could never be found, except when they chose to surround and capture unprepared helicopter crews. Nobody considered learning from what had been successful next door in Peru. The Americans knew better, and they had the technology.

Luttwak emphasizes that the Byzantine intelligence staff was small and was housed in one building with the emperor. All the knowledge was held in common, without any compartments. He compares this organization to British Scientific Intelligence in World War II headed by R.V. Jones. Jones was inept as a bureaucrat, unable to grow his staff at a pace with other sections. Yet he had remarkable success in producing intelligence. Looking back, Jones concluded that the small size of his unit was key, even though he didn't realize it at the time. Luttwak says that the benefits of understaffing are well known in the financial community. The brokers who do well have little support and work long hours. When support is added, the same brokers typically lose intensity and perform poorly.

Luttwak accepts that the new approaches to collective knowledge, such as Wikipedia and more specifically the classified Intellipedia using the same process, could allow dispersed and larger groups to be effective. But this would be an advantage only if knowledge were not compartmentalized, and instead was put out for all to see, even publicly open with only the smallest exceptions to protect cover and sensitive sources.

Luttwak thinks that Bin Laden should have been captured long ago, not because it is necessarily the most important thing to do, but because this failure is evidence of the lack of capability. The way to capture him is relatively straightforward, though not easy, and that is to infiltrate Al Qaeda. Recruit young intelligence officers who want the challenge. Have them convert to Islam in Detroit, go off to study at Leeds, then train in Pakistan. These young agents would need patience, endurance, and courage when the moment comes. This is not impossible, and can be compared to the courage of regular military troops who are taking casualties today.

Setting the Iraqis against each other is a way the Byzantines might have kept them occupied and no longer menacing. He offers that President George Bush's greatest accomplishment may have been to reignite the quarrel between Shia and Sunni. Luttwak argues that the U.S. government needs to get used to dealing with unsavory characters and stop making excuses for failures. It is in the nature of the job. The "high tech," stand-off approach doesn't work and is wasteful. His advice to the DNI: centralize and focus on what we need. If you claim that Congress ties your hands, then go beg them to cut your budget! They will be interested in such a message. The National Reconnaissance Office (NRO) is a prime example of gigantism and lack of discipline. Smallness will create urgency and coherence, and skilled professionals keep their edge when they are harassed and reacting to threats. The Italian intelligence operation, which Luttwak joined for a time after 9/11, was hapless, but because it was small, it quickly became serious and then competent. The DNI should stop pressing for interorganizational coordination, which he calls a fantasy. A committed group of analysts needs to be able to ignore others and not be hemmed in or slowed down with constant merging and checking.

But don't we need to have a large reserve of analysts, for when the targets shift to some other threat? Luttwak says that we have such a reserve at hand—civil society! Walter J. Levy was an oil man who had encyclopedic knowledge of the German oil industry. He offered his knowledge to the Office of Strategic Services and they took it. Terrorism threats come and go quickly, so the IC does need to pick up quickly, but it should also drop targets. (He noted that Jihadists had a foothold on the Indonesian island of Sumbawa, but the natives decided that they preferred beer and popular music instead, and they drove out the fanatics by themselves.)

IC analysts could lobby Congress for permission to radically declassify, put everything in a wiki, and then join the journalists. Today, all analysis is in-house, and an analyst is forbidden from calling up journalists to ask for details. However, it is not outlandish to cultivate such partners. Britain in World War II decided to publish widely what they knew about radar, minus some technical details. The result was that the Belgian underground learned what radar was and what it looked like, and they were able to find and destroy the German radar stations.

Byzantium eventually failed—after 1,000 years! They were never outmaneuvered intellectually, and they were able to resist an implacable Islam for centuries. After a brief hiatus of European colonialism, we are back to the same situation with Islam.

The audience was impressed with Luttwak, though nothing much could be done to implement his ideas. I blogged my notes, and there was an outpouring of commentary, but nigglers on Byzantine history (focused practitioners?) took over the discussion, and the event was soon forgotten.

## Robert Steele in the Open

Alvin Toffler once profiled Robert Steele in a chapter on the future of the spy.[17] Steele had succeeded as a spy of the past, by recruiting sources and finding secrets, but he soon realized that much of what he collected didn't matter and that gathering secrets put people at risk. The information that mattered could often be collected more easily, reliably, and safely by working with what was in the open (meaning information that could be collected without theft or deception). It is important to note that Steele wasn't simply saying that more information had become available, but that open sources were actually better for the problems faced by decision makers. Several senior military officers, among them General Anthony Zinni, agree with Steele, explaining that they rarely use secrets and often rely on openly available reports, and often from organizations not in the IC. This is not an argument for skipping all secrets, but for radically redefining how to serve the decision maker. Steele built a Marine Corps organization around open sources, and later when working as an independent contractor wrote manuals for NATO and others, and supported several Combatant Commands with news scanning and rapid collection on specific questions. Some of his military clients had stopped asking the Defense Intelligence Agency (DIA) for help because DIA simply could not answer questions swiftly. DIA analysts would actually laugh at the requests from special operations personnel because DIA was completely unable to respond. Through the nongovernmental network that Steele assembled, he could offer world-wide coverage in all languages, using trained local investigators who performed piecework. (Local investigators did not know who was asking the questions or why.) Steele was able to outperform not only the government but also several larger commercial services. He won a timed contest pitting himself and a telephone against a team of CIA experts, and he was even able to supply a better map during that test. While he is just a node, his network is powerful. Several governments have paid attention to his methods and have taken training.

In agreement with the recommendations of the 9/11 and WMD Commissions, Steele pushed to form a strong open source intelligence agency to serve all federal users. The preexisting organization that collected foreign media was renamed to the Open Source Center, but little else was done. Steele's criticism became increasingly strident as President George Bush's radical agenda developed. When it became clear that Steele was no longer welcome in government, he reconceived his program as a more comprehensive system for serving the common good, which he called Public Intelligence. He borrowed a United Nations list of global threats to use as intelligence priorities, which differs greatly from U.S. government priorities. He writes: "... In the context of poverty, disease, genocide, and all the other effects of our corrupt mis-management of Earth, terrorism is a traffic accident." He doesn't recommend retreat from terrorism. He instead recommends addressing the crisis of missed intelligence across the IC in terms of developmental dynamics. He continues to promote a shared human network and to attract participants, and in many ways the nodes are already coming together on their own, though having an institutional home would certainly help. He had piloted a Public Daily Briefing, parallel to the President's Daily Briefing, only better. There are problems, of course. Public Intelligence can look a lot like the news or think tank papers that we have today. What differs is the insistent questioning and testing for whether the work is for the common good. The result is a floating, unstable synthesis of a variety of informed (and sometimes fringe) perspectives. What the system would be able to do is detect unnecessary assumptions, such as those used by the at-risk practices. And there would be optional actions to pursue at all levels, with notes on what can be learned from further monitoring and experiments. It is a platform for inquiry as well as reliable information about the global crisis situation and its players—all of us.

Steele will sometimes assert that there is a right answer and will rail against others who disagree. At times, he seems to share with Buckminster Fuller a nonreflexive faith that a technical design can be found that works for all and that can be imposed. Yet rather than shy away from such a battle, he invites people to take him at his word and contend over what is right to do now, it all its complexity. Just don't use an ideological starting point, but argue anew from the situation and the common good. The plan of inquiry does not need to settle into a reassuring set of answers, and would be dangerous if it did. Steele has been more than vigorous in attacking cognitive weaknesses of at-risk practitioners. He is also reshaping himself and giving a running account of how his thinking is changing through extensive reading and interaction with vital practitioners. Recent reading, he writes in his blog, "moved me further down the road toward Evolutionary Activism (focus on connecting all humans to all information, not on arriving at specific answers)."[18] That is a perfect way to marry his combative energy with a reflexive stance.

The ideal client for a public intelligence function would be a governance function in pursuit of the common good. The two functions, intelligence and governance, would tend to draw each other forth. Partisanship, however, is a structural feature of U.S. politics that creates distortions, and it has rarely yielded to direct challenges. The public intelligence function may at least reduce these and other distortions. In a simple case, personal financial corruption on the part of a public official might be reduced by an intelligence function that improved surveillance of potential conflicts of interest. In another simple case, a public official might be ignorant because of poor staff work and might have nothing better to rely on. In a more difficult case, there may be a systemic bias toward "low cost" alternatives where costly externalities have been left out of the accounting. Creating better intelligence on holistic cost could remove distortions and make the common good alternatives more plain both to the public official and to the citizens. Once plain, the public good would be more difficult to avoid.

We don't need to have the ideal governance function in order for the public intelligence function to be effective. The knowledge that it generates will be avoided or denigrated by officials committed to distortions, but the knowledge will nevertheless expose distortions for more to see, which, through citizen pressure, will help drive the governance function toward the common good. In those instances where the common good is genuinely sought by decision makers (such things are known to happen), the work will have been done and available through the intelligence function that has been waiting for such clients.

While professional intelligence analysts may be free of many of the pressures placed on public officials, they can also be guilty of distorted thinking due to poor understanding, ignorance, or illusion. A proven way to reduce this distortion is to generate intelligence from a crowd whose members are biased toward the common good and to relevant truth. The members of the crowd are selected to engage in a process of inquiry and correction. Participants must develop and maintain a reputation among their peers as pursuers of the common good and relevant truth, or else they are dropped from participation. Judgment requires interpretations. The intelligence crowd would serve the governance function by elaborating alternative interpretations that would be a plausible basis for wise judgment.[19]

Nevertheless, in Steele's opinion, there is a pervasive deficit of integrity that thwarts good governance. Steele toyed with the idea of running for Congress as a libertarian, giving him license to attack partisans and demonstrate the kind of governance function that he would want to serve. He also considered taking an offer of a tour in Iraq where his speed and honesty is appreciated and his rough manner tolerated. He recently took a task with the United Nations where some have appreciated his vision. Wherever he goes, he has decided to be a zealous advocate of the public intelligence process and will subject himself to its rules, not lock into a bias or assumptions other than a bias to consider the alternatives openly, and to continued learning with others who are similarly committed. Here is a sample of his political platform, which is continuous with his intelligence platform:

> The central problem of our time is the failure of human organization-its failure to scale, to adapt, to assimilate. We believe the failure stems directly from a rejection of diversity and a falsification of feedback loops-the absence of integrity. We've come to the conclusion that the discord between politics and intelligence is contrived-there is no inherent opposition between politics (choice of best path for all) and intelligence (presentation of best achievable truth for all) provided one condition is met: integrity among the majority of individuals engaged in each. If intelligence loses its integrity and allows itself to be politicized or worse, ignored, then intelligence fails. Similarly, if politics loses its integrity and overplays the secrecy card while also shutting out the diversity of views that are essential to achieving a sustainable consensus, then politics fails.[20]

## John Bodnar on the Inside

Beginning in 2001, John Bodnar, then a senior analyst at Defense Intelligence Agency (DIA), took advantage of the new atmosphere of reform and tried a new approach for researching the secret weapons labs of adversaries. He patiently identified and built relationships with analysts at other agencies, made full use of open sources, and shared notes in a simple hypertext collection. (Contrary to what many people imagine, few intelligence analysts have advanced tools. Microsoft applications are one or two versions behind what the outside world uses.) This work became a strong foundation for defining gaps, testing hypotheses, and linking new data. Without official approval, this small cross-agency group of analysts met weekly. Each person was asked to share the week's "take" of data. A language expert from one group had known little about the technical subject of weapon labs, but after listening to the others was able to produce a photo showing lab leaders. The location of the photo was not known, but the overhead imagery analyst was able to match the building shown in the background of the photo. The linguist continued to collect innocuous notices from newspapers and journals that were then used to infer organizational relationships and research interests. Findings began to pile up until there were extensive profiles of two previously unknown labs. Each analyst reported the group's findings through their own organizations but never mentioned the cross-agency team as a source. This group and another similar one eventually revealed themselves and received awards for providing exceptionally good intelligence. Bodnar published a book on his sensemaking methodology and conducted popular workshops on it. He also advised a major government research program that developed unique prototype IT tools that would support such collaboration.

It became very clear to Bodnar that there is a foraging analyst who is quite different from a sensemaking analyst. They often work separately and hence both fail, but Bodar saw that, if they join as different aspects of a shared intelligence process, and if they think and act reflexively, they can contribute to a much superior team effort. He finds that Intellipedia, though an extremely helpful resource, is insufficient. "Finished" intelligence is still required, but by different means, including interaction with multiple analysts, or ways to propose inclusions, and ways to discuss issues in the context of what is known and established. There needs to be many more ways of indexing information to make it easier to share. Authors rarely index well; librarianship plays an important part, but there is little support for this part of the information problem within the IC, unlike in medical research where findings are indexed extensively and are much more accessible and readily built upon.

Bodnar's information-sharing practices, bridging disciplines and agencies, fell apart when Bodnar became a contractor and began working for a different intelligence agency. DIA erased his files—standard procedure for departing employees—and it took a full year before his clearances and access were restored. He had mothballed his work and was able to have it restored at his new agency, but under the unremitting pressure for current reporting, there was little support for continued basic research, though his new colleagues did appreciate the answers he could give based on prior work. His separate collaborative software research project ended in April 2006 without any of the technology being picked up for use.[21]

Bodnar's experience shows that individuals can indeed make huge strides through collaboration, but such accomplishments are very fragile and do not have consistent institutional support. It was like chestnuts sprouting in the woods—the promise of mighty trees, all doomed by the blight. Bodnar is quite concerned, not for himself or others soon to retire, but for the next generation of young analysts who are not being acculturated to better collaborative practices. "If that cadre is lost, the IC will have to rebuild itself virtually from scratch, and will not have the expertise to do so for at least a decade."[22]

# 5

# Economy for Good

Few people express any doubts about what is right and what is wrong regarding the economy, despite the fact that the majority of people, relying on well-worn opinions, were surprised and made poor decisions recently. One would think that this experience would engender a little humility and curiosity. We will sample from those few who take the turbulent situation seriously and who are led to think differently.

We begin with some stage-setting. Our contribution here is less on the facts, which are everywhere, and more on framing and the professional role, which are often overlooked. A useful first step is to disorient the reader. We will not focus on the immediate past, nor on the sweep of economic history through ages or even the Great Depression, but return to the period when turbulence first became obvious, the 1970s through 1990s. Writers at the time could speak of the condition more clearly, with less layering of subsequent interpretation. Yet this period of commentary is regularly avoided today. Perhaps it is just normal to avoid reference to the recently deceased. Contemporaries are assumed to have incorporated whatever the prior generation had known and have now gone beyond it. Tastemakers are given an opportunity to sort through the old materials and select a few classics, at which point they will be safe to read. Yet, if one recklessly proceeds to read a recently obsolete book, it can be surprisingly compelling on live issues that have since become obscure. It is we who have allowed ourselves to become confused in our up-to-the-minute sophistication.

J.K. Galbraith's, *The Culture of Contentment,* has this surprising quality.[1] His academic contemporaries dismissed him as "not an economist," but he, more than they, grasped the situation. Galbraith observed that every generation reinvents debt. It used to be that people had to forget the tragedy of risky debt before they started a new cycle, but since the 1980s debt bubbles in various forms have been nearly continuous, including junk bonds, S&Ls, dotcoms, collapsed hedge funds, and so forth. A recent *New Yorker* cartoon is hardly an exaggeration. One wealthy person turns to another: "I just don't see a new bubble to invest in." Is that all that business offers? Why do we persist in such a system, and does our professional thinking have something to do with it?

We have been reassured, after every failure, that there have been enormous strides in technical understanding of how the financial system works, coupled with exquisite control and elaborate governing capacity. But to delve into the details of each bust, each instrument, and each fraud distracts from the systemic character of these events, and also distracts from so much else that is also disturbing but doesn't immediately strike us as being connected to these narratives. In fact, one of the useful results of the 2008 crisis was that it became starkly clear that there was such a thing as systemic risk, and that it eluded representation in the most "sophisticated" models used by economists and insurance "experts." Many professionals had no idea of the game they were playing, transfixed as they were by what they saw on the surface in terms of prices, and what they and everyone else around them thought was the limit of their responsibility. But what else strikes us when we defocus and attend to the shadows in our peripheral vision? Here are a few observations:

- After many decades of having familiar names on the Dow Jones industrial list, there is now a high rate of adding and dropping. General Motors was one of the remaining old-timers and is now off the list. Major companies that remain, such as GE, are hardly recognizable compared to what they were doing a few years ago.
- The average number of employers that a professional worker has over a career is high. This doesn't even account for the type of job where one is bid out to perform on short-term assignments, effectively multiplying the number of job changes. This suggests a different concept of career that omits any sort of institutional affiliation as a defining feature.
- "Local independent retailer" is an anachronistic term in several respects. Online sales attack from one side, chain stores from the other. Large scale "platforms" have the upper hand in many businesses, especially where information handling, finance, and elaborate supply chains are an advantage. Even the specialists who once served small markets directly have become appendages to central platforms, selling through Amazon and eBay.
- Bankruptcies in the United States became high and remain so, even after changes in the law that make this wrenching personal "correction" less attractive.

In all, there is pervasive insecurity and a great many useless people, even among those who remain employed! Yet many of us choose not to see it. As Galbraith writes, "The fortunate and the favored, it is more than evident, do not contemplate and respond to their own longer-run well-being. Rather, they respond, and powerfully, to immediate comfort and contentment." They don't see themselves as expendable, hence their surprise when they are downsized. A few people are fully insulated, but they are like lottery winners—things turned out well, not solely because of their own attempts at control, but because they caught a temporary updraft. "The result is government that is accommodated not to reality or common need but to the beliefs of the contented, who are now the majority of those who vote." Finally, "It is the nature of contentment that it resists that which invades it with vigor...." He speaks in an exasperated tone about many problems that were longstanding at the time in 1992 and still haven't budged, such as global warming. But to our point, he elaborates on how the culture tightly insulates the economic realm. He sounds quite contemporary: "Support to failing financial institutions—the great savings and loan rescue and later that of the commercial banks—is a fully defended function of the government, however evident the financial extravagance and extensive and visible larceny that made it necessary."[2] While it is a rich set of reinforcing cultural factors that keeps economic rules in place, some of the problem can be located in the practices of professionals to whom we listen on such matters.

## Practice That Is No Longer Adaptive

The most spectacular recent failure of an economic at-risk practice is that of Federal Reserve chairman Alan Greenspan, a clear purveyor of principled practice. Greenspan was well aware of turbulence, using it as the theme of memoirs.[3] He had a complete response to it, however, and that was to let the market work, though every instance of the application of this simplistic principle required that a mysterious obfuscation be added, to make it seem as if he was thinking about it. As an acolyte of Ayn Rand, he asserts that the ideal ordering of society is for there to be no restraint on the creativity—or apparently depredations—of individuals driven by their appetites. Everything works out for the best. A rank ideologue was thus given control over the nation's wealth and invited to protect us against disasters that, by his reckoning, were impossible.

When he first took the job as Federal Reserve chairman, he realized that the job required him to compromise on his principles.[4] It was, after all, a regulating institution. Even so, he would use every opportunity to reduce regulations or to avoid applying the law as it stands. This would increase wealth, and so it does, until it doesn't. When markets overshot in the dot-com boom, Greenspan went along with Shiller's term "irrational exuberance," except that it wasn't irrational at all for individuals to cash in on the bubble. It was irrational on his part to do nothing about it. Brooksley Born, when she was installed in 1996 as the head of Commodity Futures Trading Commission, wanted to do the job that legislation told her to do-regulate derivatives. Greenspan told her not to, and on top of that told her that she should ignore criminal fraud if she should see it. The market would correct. And so it has, after a fashion.

In 2007 Greenspan registered the fact of market failure, compared it to his knowledge that such a result was impossible, then considered that his thinking may have been in error. In a congressional hearing, Representative Waxman asked him: "Do you feel that your ideology pushed you to make decisions that you wish you had not made?" Greenspan: "Yes, I've found a flaw. I don't know how significant or permanent it is. But I've been very distressed by that fact." Greenspan explained further in his written testimony:

> In recent decades, a vast risk management and pricing system has evolved, combining the best insights of mathematicians and finance experts supported by major advances in computer and communications technology. A Nobel Prize was awarded for the discovery of the pricing model that underpins much of the advance in derivatives markets. This modern risk management paradigm held sway for decades. The whole intellectual edifice, however, collapsed in the summer of last year....[5]

The public seemed to demand reassurance concerning stability. Greenspan obliged, though it was an illusion. Rational practitioners as well as principled practitioners can play to these cultural expectations, and they are often convincing. When Larry Summers, former Treasury Secretary and President of Harvard, was still waiting for the Presidential candidates to sort themselves out, he gave a talk to Harvard alumni working in Washington, many of whom had been his students or coworkers. One of the questioners began with a critique of Summers's rhetoric. He said that, at Harvard, it is well known that Summers will say only that which is absolutely unassailable on the facts and logic, and anyone who doubts what he has said will lose the argument. The questioner added, however, that Summers will necessarily neglect to mention something relevant that belies his argument, and on top of that he will disguise that he is omitting relevant information. Therefore the only hope you have of having an interesting exchange with Summers is to ask about what he has not said. That requires some careful detective work before you open your mouth. Summers didn't object to this characterization. For a rational practitioner at the top of his game, that's just how the game is played.

Steve Denning, a rising thinker on organizational cognition, observed something similar in the rhetoric of Robert McNamara during the period when both were at the World Bank.[6] Denning felt that McNamara used his wit to appear smart and decisive, resolving dilemmas with what the right answer should be, but often as not his thinking was a shallow, self-protective arrogance that prevented him from learning anything or allowing others to develop or change the institution. Denning felt that McNamara's rhetoric fit Frankfurt's definition of bullshit: "Saying things where you don't really care whether they are true or not."[7]

Most rational practitioners care about truth, of course, but only as long it takes the correct form. One of the most durable features of rational practice in business is the clear goal. A plan is composed of interventions that will achieve goals. In the American way of excess, many goals, relentlessly driven, is the standard, and if you don't get the results you want, drive harder and add more goals. An expert in best practices who spent years pushing such rigor on corporate clients encapsulated his argument in a paean to "strategic clarity."[8] He saves his worst taunts for those who give into the temptation to make many changes without a precise structure and control scheme, though he admits that "it increases the likelihood that at least one of the changes you make will actually improve results." He warns darkly of "chaotic strategies" in which "there's no way to tell what went wrong" if goals are missed. In other words, if the organization ends up achieving a goal other than the way the planner prescribed, or if participants learned from mistakes something other than what the planner expected, then this is a problem. It's really only a problem, however, for the planner whose first priority is to validate his models, plans, and goals. Even Harvard professors have noticed that strict goal-setting methodologies have been grossly oversold, and that their pervasive harm has been ignored.[9] We select just three problems with goals, the ones that most visibly suppress reflexive practice:

- Neglect of nongoal areas, especially the management of risk andpotential. In the balanced scorecard approach goals are supposed to at least be distributed into areas that are routinely overlooked, principally the "development quadrant," though this is often filled by something vanilla and automatic, such as the spending rate on schoolhouse training—nothing that will distract from the "real" business.

- Oversimplification. Focus on what is measured and not on the linkages that may be necessary for whole performance. Workers stop asking what is good and what is success. If you take away the question, it promotes a finite game that one can be very clever in winning, while in the meantime losing overall capability and potential.
- Drives unethical behavior. If you reward CEOs for short-term gains in stock price, they will oblige by driving up debt and putting the venture at risk.

Finally, interested practitioners are rife throughout business. Yet along with the trend toward transparency, many institutions have dialed back on the heaviest advocacy. Some have found that, in the long run, it is better to deal honestly and openly and find community solutions that they can live with. Altria, the former Philip Morris Company, comes to mind. An interesting convert from extreme interested practice is Wendell Potter, formerly head of corporate communications (i.e., chief flak) for Cigna.[10] He is now reflecting on the health insurance industry and on what his role had been for decades. He once thought that his role was to serve investors, and that this objective was aligned with "high-quality" operations. But operations in fact aligned against the interests of insured customers. He concluded that the majority of health insurance companies were socially destructive.

Potter was not thinking this way when he took a vacation on the corporate jet back to his hometown near Wise County, Virginia. A health fair was under way and he decided to take a drive and look. He expected to see people handing out toys and brochures, but he quickly realized that this was an outdoor emergency room for very sick, very desperate people, manned by volunteers. The sick were white working people from families who had lived in the region for generations. They were not immigrants, homeless, jobless, or otherwise dislocated. Then he drew the connection. His company was effectively making medicine unavailable to a large percentage of the population of this region. This experience made him examine his responsibilities. He figured that his job was to serve society in some way, with some sort of rough justice. This led him to retire from Cigna and use his insider knowledge to explain how Wall Street interests had overwhelmed the political system and the health system. With no rancor, he simply stopped using the false arguments that were his daily product at Cigna. He described how the companies, under pressure from investors, were drawing huge profits out of the system. He says that the medical loss ratio at Cigna, the percentage of insurance payments that are paid back in claims, went from 95 percent to 80 percent in a short period. If there is the slightest blip in the medical loss ratio, the company's stock is punished severely, and the hugely compensated executives do all they can to guard against that. The only way to keep this game going is to deny claims as ruthlessly as possible, and to explain away the complaints and to pressure politicians to write the rules to allow all this to continue. While each person in the system can claim to be forced to play his role, Potter's example shows that, at a certain point, one needs to consider the common good and start applying a little back pressure. Not everyone needs to or is able to act as dramatically as Potter did. There are many corrupt institutions, and it is a matter of judgment how far they have fallen or whether they need correction, but as a professional in a turbulent and dangerous environment, one must at least ask the question. Potter figured that he wanted to be working for a health system that could stand up to examination as something that most people would find acceptable, even if flawed. He would have been happy to keep selling a service; he just wanted a service that was more worthy. The more he reinforced Cigna's strength, the more suffering he created for the sick, and the more unjust benefits he created for the rich, including himself. He didn't want to end his career in a position he could not take some pride in. All he wanted to do was to speak honestly with a generous attitude in favor of something that works for all. If this is not possible, society is surely in trouble.

## Reflexive Economic Practice

So what to do about it? Common sense remedies are fine, but just saying them often leads nowhere. We will mention some lesser known strategies that exhibit the mindset of reflexive practice, and that we think will become increasingly relevant as other strategies fail. In the economic realm, these reflexive strategies will tend to be viewed as unorthodox, unprincipled, and technically deficient by the at-risk practitioners who tend to be in charge.

### Ownership and Motivation

The technical fact of ownership in a corporation often entails nothing in terms of actions or motivations on the part of the owner. Most owners of stock are passive in the extreme. They may not even know that they own it in their mutual fund, and may even be picketing the company. On the other hand, there are plenty of workers who want to be enthusiastic about the institutions they work for, but they have no opportunity to participate seriously as an owner, or to directly gain from the wages to capital. They are instead wage slaves and know that they are highly expendable. They can easily become cynical during a rough spot when they are asked to sacrifice. Meanwhile, management makes happy talk about how important the workers are and how the company cares. These managers (usually those receiving stock options) are themselves highly motivated and bemoan the fact that the workers are so listless. Russell Ackoff had concluded in late 2009, just before he died, that pervasive lack of worker motivation had become a huge impediment to any adaptation. People are withholding, doing only what they must and no more.

We offer one case that illustrates how ownership, motivation, and the absence of a plan combined to produce high adaptation in turbulence for 35 years. In 1969 Robert Beyster, working as a physicist under contract, was told by his government sponsor that his current company was dropping out but that the program needed to continue. He needed to form a new company to which the contract could be transferred. He gave the company a generic, noncommittal name, Science Applications, which became SAIC. He had no visions of grandeur but simply wanted a company that would support and reward people like himself who had some technical skill and wanted to work on important national problems. He figured that professionals would take care of themselves if they had opportunity to find the work they liked and also could gain an ownership stake in a platform that would continue to support semi-independent entrepreneurs. He set aside most of the stock to distribute to those who could bring in suitably interesting and important professional work. The phrase developed, "You kill it, you eat it." This meant that, if you want a box on the organizational chart and high compensation, don't plan to replace somebody and don't try to drive up your salary that will be passed on to government contracts. Your goal was to create your own position by bringing in work, and accumulate company stock whose price will increase as you and others bring in work. Fairly soon, some clever people figured out how to make this work. SAIC entrepreneurs could regularly read the situation and find new work on new problems where incumbents had little advantage. Divisions within SAIC were constantly reorganizing and changing their names to keep current and relevant. Beyster himself dropped out for a while to run a side company that targeted a field that interested him but that he knew little about. He returned to SAIC full time, however, and tried to learn how to manage a larger company. Some say that he never succeeded, but that's debatable. He had a huge aversion to ethical risk, which led him to refrain from lobbying, a normal practice for competitors. The company also walked away from successful civil development work in Iraq to avoid the corrupt atmosphere. Beyster was famously cheap regarding executive perks, internal investment and acquisitions, corporate staff, and especially advertising. (SAIC was once called "the largest company nobody knows.") His one corporate indulgence was a quarterly company-wide conference featuring technical leaders who discussed new markets and capabilities. He loved to join in the conversation and match wits. His opinion counted, of course, but whether something succeeded was mostly up to the worker's initiative and whether he could find a client to pay for it. A prominent SAIC manager thoroughly internalized this attitude. He knew what the government actually needed and he would encourage people to pursue it, as long as they continued to perform to standard on current contracts. But he had no illusions about what the government was actually going to buy, and everyone was required to work with top efficiency to capture the work that was available. Often enough, the government was buying the wrong thing. SAIC's job was to stay in the game and hope for better days, which often came to those who were prepared and who kept their hopes alive.

There were several occasions when two or more teams wanted to bid for the same government contract. If the teams did not want to join, they were not forced to. Sometimes the government objected when they received two proposals from SAIC. Many thought that this was crazy, that a top manager should be able to choose one best approach and force the teams to conform, split revenue, and thus "save" the wasted expense of bidding twice. But who does the company serve, anyway? And who makes the decisions? The deal that had been made is that people who win work and build programs are not restrained, only supported. After all, the company loses bids all the time, and top managers know much less than either team about what will win. The company decided to let the process play itself out, and that could be viewed as a wise investment in adaptive capability rather than waste. All employees earned stock in their retirement funds, most employees bought or were granted substantially more stock, and few strong players left. Attitudes were remarkably positive for 35 years. It felt like "our company." However, the internal stock system broke down when too many longtime employees wanted to sell back their shares and retire. Also, the company grew so large that the staff was full of younger professionals who did not have the extra cash to buy stock or were suspicious of the vast corps of executives, and the power of motivation through company stock faded. A new CEO could think of nothing else but to go public in 2006, at which point the company was plundered in the conventional manner, rationalized with a conventional functional organization, and brought to heel in pursuit of large contracts more befitting its overall corporate size. It is now a publicly traded company, with a stagnant stock price, shorter average employee tenure, and less authentic enthusiasm amidst all the "we care" programs. It is trying to satisfy shareholders who don't work for the company. SAIC's experience doesn't mean that unusual ownership structures are always doomed, though they may need some of the same incentives that conventional structures enjoy. Alternative ownership structures can be adaptive options that align with positive human motivations and social benefits.[11]

### Measurement

Can one get ahead with reflexive practice? The reflexive practitioner is going to ask what "ahead" means, and will look beyond immediate moves in his own interest. Daly and Cobb[12] record some fascinating inquiries into the meaning of "good" in economic contexts. One theme is simply that an economy needs to be connected to its physical substrate, the earth. In nature, everything that grows tops out, and anything that grows exponentially for very long destroys its environment. So a goal of maximizing growth, both in terms of physical throughput and exponential growth in money—with more money driving more throughput—is clearly inconsistent with what the environment can support. Humans have been able to continue on this path only as long as they had an ability to move to new environments or in other ways separate themselves from spoiled resources. That process has reached its limit and society simply has to find a different conception of the economy, beyond emergency measures, that is integrated with our human home. Daly and Cobb's work is full of nudges that allow freedom while channeling everyone into a lower-risk, infinite game with more true wealth and satisfaction. There are plenty of things better in life than jacking up a hedge fund within a charred wreck of society.

What is interesting is to try to create a quantitative criterion that can be used to assess, at various scales, whether one is approximating a "common good" strategy. Daly and Cobb gained attention by offering a carefully developed index of sustainable economic welfare. Generally speaking, it includes costs that are normally dismissed and benefits that are normally unpriced or mispriced. Similar and perhaps better indexes now exist, such as the Genuine Progress Indicator which shows that Europe and the United States have steadily declined for 30 years. But Daly's is interesting for its philosophical grounding and development through dialogue with critics. Once you have such a tool, you can used it in policy making. A lot of projects don't look as good when their destructive qualities are taken into account.

Measures such as this that give better accounting are a basis for generating pervasive nudges. One can communicate what does not constitute development and can organize communities to avoid it. The futurist Willis Harman, in an interview he gave in 1995, summed up the problem of economic thinking that misreads the present situation:

> It turns out that if you look at the assumptions underlying our economic system—especially the ones regarding the prerogatives of ownership—and then you look at the goals we humans have about how we want to live our lives, there is no compatibility. The assumptions can never lead to the goals. And yet this incompatibility passes unnoticed. I think that's because the assumptions about economic progress seemed to work rather well during the time when you could equate material progress with general benefit. But that equation doesn't work anymore. We now have a system that works to the benefit of the few and penalizes masses of people today and in the future.[13]

## Pick Up the Pieces

Beyond fending off at-risk thinking, the reflexive practitioner needs to be ready to capture some of the odd opportunities that turbulence turns up. Jeffrey Sachs, director of the Earth Institute at Columbia University, argues that the 2008 crash is an opportunity for larger realignment in the auto industry, beyond band-aids that allow manufacturers to resume as before. He recommends investing in infrastructure for electric cars and giving current manufacturers a head start in conversion. This avoids picking a winner—either a particular company or a technology—while accelerating broad adaptation to the inevitable downturn in the use of petroleum.[14]

A surprising trend, induced by the absence of new greenfield sites to develop, is the discovery of the development potential of degraded and abandoned sites and resources. Many ruined sites have no value under conventional assumptions about how to develop, but if alternative developmental dynamics are added—principally the recuperative powers of biological processes plus an alignment with community interests—unnoticed value can be recaptured. Horribly wasted locations have become garden spots where people want to work and live. Every site is different, however, and the practitioners have to be creative. Storm Cunningham, an expert in community revitalization, offers data indicating that there are huge investment opportunities in restoration projects around the world.[15] The State of Wisconsin contact him after they started questioning why they had been using tax dollars to attract depleting industry. Restoration projects offered vastly more return to taxpayers, including more permanent jobs.

## Profiles of Reflexive Economic Practitioners

### George Soros

George Soros, speculator and philanthropist, is very explicit about the concept of reflexivity and says that it is key to how he operates. The recent crash, he says, proves beyond any doubt that the modern edifice of economic theory is wrong, that markets do not always correct themselves and do not seek equilibrium. Alan Greenspan was honest enough to admit that his longstanding belief in this principle, backed up by conventional theory, had been shaken by events. So what is Soros's alternative?[16]

Markets do have quiet periods when they vary randomly and return to equilibrium. Frequently, however, self-reinforcing positive feedback drives the market out of equilibrium. A run-up turns into a bubble. Eventually, speculators are easily convinced that the high prices they have been paying are unreasonable, and there is a rapid drop, again a self-reinforcing trend, except this time it is very quick. During the run-up there are tests of reasonableness. If prices hold after a test, they will then keep rising. These dynamics are quite familiar, but dominant economic theory doesn't account for them. Economists will say blandly that prices reflect knowledge at the time, and that if there is any small misperception of value, the market will correct. The most efficient course is to let participants police themselves. Greenspan said that dot-com stock prices were irrational, but he did nothing about it, confident that they would subside, which of course they eventually did, after causing a great deal of unnecessary havoc.

Soros argues that a pig-headed insistence on market fundamentalism has allowed a superbubble to develop. Tests did occur several times over the last 20 years, and only when governments intervened did markets return to "normal." This supposedly demonstrated that markets do return, but the interventions were conveniently ignored, not recognized as the essential prop that the market could not itself provide. Governments allowed the expansion of debt in many forms to continue. The housing crash, he finds, was just a small bomb by itself, but this time it ignited the larger bomb of layered debt throughout the system, including especially the trillions of dollars of unregistered derivatives for which there was instantly no buyer.

Soros is able to fit the facts to his theory of market dynamics, and that oftenenables him to generate trading profits where others can't. But his other main principle is uncertainty, or more precisely "fallibility," which emphasizes the cognitive state of the practitioner. There is no basis, no possible knowledge, that often enables him to be able to reliably predict the timing or magnitude of these events. Even so, he is better off than the others, who labor under theories that are provably wrong and offer only an illusion of control. He lost plenty in 2007 because he didn't play the volatility swings correctly, but he did much better than others. None of this is predictable but he argues that a knowledge of why you are uncertain and how disequilibrium occurs, combined with a willingness to read the situation and keep learning, can make you a better trader in this turbulent period. Nonequilibrium breaks are quite common, and are also inadvertently driven by the market fundamentalists who dismiss them.

But Soros doesn't just want to make money as a market player; he wants the market to be managed, lightly, to avoid risk and produce social good. It is the government's job to do so, and it has failed miserably. To say that policy makers don't know exactly how to do it, while correct, doesn't excuse them from the responsibility to do their best, which will be good enough if they keep the market within the confines of what is safe. He recommends that central bankers exercise powers that they have today but have avoided using:

- When a sector is overheated, pressure banks to reduce credit in that sector. He says that this was common practice in the 1950s, before the theorists came on board. It is nothing drastic, just a nudge that simultaneously sounds a warning while also reducing the systemic risk that all the players suffer from but that no individual player is motivated to reduce alone. Also, credit comes out in other forms, such as equity leveraging during the Internet boom. The Federal Reserve can reduce the rate of new stock issues. In general, monetary controls are too blunt an instrument and are inappropriate for some situations. Other instruments should be used to counter trends that increase debt in other ways.
- Register and monitor derivatives and disallow their unlimited creation in forms that cannot be explained. To have what was estimated at $27 trillion in unregistered derivatives means that nobody knew the true holdings of the major institutions. The portion of holdings that were reported were thus meaningless, creating uncertainty that made loss of confidence inevitable.
- The institutions that are too big to fail must maintain high reserves relative to credit. The system has to take some responsibility for its own

safety. Speculative trading must move out of these institutions to fully separate hedge funds.

Reflexivity is easier to track in finance, but it exists everywhere else, and Soros would like to manage it better in the rest of the economy and society. After the fall of the Soviet Union, he realized that this created a political and cognitive vacuum, and felt that a small intervention at this fluid moment might make a huge difference later. He generated many small projects through a network of Open Society Institute offices. Some of the projects were successful but came to the end and he stopped them because their time had passed. That is quite a change from most foundations that seek to develop a "reputation" or "brand" through a perpetual program, not considering that their resources might be better spent on a changing portfolio of opportunities. Stopping a program releases human resources, who will then have more opportunities to spread what they have gained. One educator who had conducted seminars for Soros had done his job well but was disappointed when he was cut loose. Yet his subsequent projects in the United States, conducted for another foundation, benefited from the experience. Of course, some of Soros's projects were failures as well, and he doesn't attempt to minimize or hide these results. Soros knew that failures were inevitable, especially in the wild areas of the globe where he has been operating and where no other foundations are investing. His is an excellent example of learning from a rapid process of elaboration and pruning.

Soros's trading behavior probably exacerbates turbulence, such as when his position threatened U.K. currency, but he says he is just doing what the rules allow. He recommends better rules that would reduce his opportunities. His purpose is not simply to exploit the system, but to make enough money so that he can be influential in improving global governance. People have demonized him as a partisan, but a careful reading shows that he is not. He simply identified destructive patterns in the Bush administration and is now finding some issues with the Obama administration. Soros would probably have no quarrel with a reasonably accommodating conservative who governs safely in the interest of all. Certainly he doesn't promote extremes in the Democratic Party, only a responsible program of survival.

In April 2009 Soros opened the Institute for New Economic Thinking. He knows that there is much more work to be done toward a reflexive account of the economy, and he knows that he might be wrong and that others might have useful alternatives. All he does know is that orthodoxy is wrong and that he cannot trust the economic culture to stop on its own, no more than he can expect Marxists to stop until they die, and thus new thinking needs a boost and a protected institution. What is perhaps even more interesting is his funding of the new School of Global Policy at Central European University in Budapest. This is less directed to economic theory and will develop the reflexive practitioner who will gain influence in government and business institutions alike. The school is tightly linked to the Open Society Institute, through which students can find opportunities to gain full experience on live projects under the guidance of practice mentors. The school has no departments and reorganizes itself according to opportunity and need. Research and teaching are focused on practice in a contemporary setting, including the explicit cultivation of phronesis and paths to holistic, social adaptation. Faculty will avoid the common fixation on hierarchies and markets and will explore the importance of networks, especially as an alternative governance mechanism. It will emphasize the role of civil society institutions and supranational organizations. It is a fully international institution, operating as a European, Hungarian, and American university simultaneously.

### Paul Hawken

Paul Hawken, entrepreneur, offers his own account for his success in business, but it is not difficult to restate his story as one of a naturally skilled player in reflexive situations. He never finished school and started his first successful business on Newbury Street in Boston. Newbury Street continues to be an unusual location. Today, one end begins with the most expensive shops imaginable, then trails off to some truly odd lifestyle stores, such as Newbury Comics, where comics are recast into something disturbing, but above all ironic. That's just part of the store. The rest is filled with music, much of which is unknown to most people, plus loads of ironic goods based on traditional children's forms, such as stuffed animals, models, gag gifts, and so forth. The reason I pause to describe the setting is that I think it has a great deal to do with Hawken's success. As a young man he started Erewhon Natural Foods there, which became a major organic food business. The appeal was not just the food, but its cultural meaning. The people who lived there had an active imagination and associated the food with a way of life they admired. They liked the commitment of the owner, and they believed that this was part of becoming a healthier culture. There are some ironies within the organic food business. One of the biggest organic wholesalers told me (in confidence because his customers would not like to hear it) that the business could never have grown without huge advances in refrigeration technology and rapid transport. In other words, the business requires high-energy inputs that customers cover with higher prices. Thus organic food, as practiced within our modern economy, is a kind of a high-tech luxury good. The "crunchy granola" lifestyle that accompanies it is an urban affectation that merely simulates rural life. This is not to disparage the movement, but to simply point out that Hawken got his start in this intense enclave of subjective culture, and he made a good living at it. He said that he sat in on courses at the Harvard Business School and thought that somehow this would improve his business skill, but he was unable to make the connection and came more and more to reflect on what seemed to be working for him. We won't recount his business theories here, but just point out that it has a lot to do with respect for and involvement of the purposes of customers and workers. It is a relationship business. If you can do something delightful together, you can succeed together.

Hawken sold out and eventually ended up in Mill Valley, north of San Francisco. This is where he started the Smith and Hawken company, another rousing success. Marin County is famous for many things, but one of its distinctions is that a high proportion of citizens live off trust funds. Rich people relocate there because of the combination of natural and cultural beauty, and the retail sector works very hard to keep it that way. A lady entrepreneur who had run up several businesses in the area said that her expertise was in "retail theater." It didn't particularly matter what the goods were, only whether the goods were a suitable prop for the show, which was a combination of narratives on how the goods and relationships were going to contribute to the customer's lifestyle. For her, Hawken's original store was something of a shrine, even after he had moved out of it. To the uninitiated it was hardly more than a gas station, but she remembered how the site, the staff working the plants, the beautiful tools, and the charismatic owner were a riveting combination. Mill Valley is a hotbed for expertise on eliciting an enthusiastic response. There are of course all the hangers-on who find ways to amuse the rich people with esoteric massages and so forth. My retail thespian once opined at a dinner party that there needed to be an appreciation book on sushi. She was offered a contract on the spot, and it became the first in a huge series of food appreciation books. Then there is Jay Conrad Levinson in his mountainside retreat, scribbling away on his next Guerilla Marketing™ book, shaping it for maximum response among those readers who are seeking maximum response in their businesses.

Hawken again sold his company. The Scott company invested heavily in its expansion, figuring that the brand was established and that all they needed to do was scale it up. But what was "it"? The catalogue had been successful, but it turns out only as an appendage to a lifestyle, and only for a time when imaginative upper income people were experimenting with gardening and wanted to participate in the entertainment. They were willing to pay for "classic" tools that felt and looked good, and while the customer didn't always articulate this, the setting and story enhanced the look and feel. When you take that away, as one does when you sell Smith and Hawken tools wrapped in plastic clamshells through national chain stores, then it becomes just an overpriced piece of hardware. Where's the delight in that? The Scott company abruptly terminated the Smith and Hawken line and its "superstores" in 2009. On the occasion, fans of the original offered hundreds of explanations of what went wrong, but let's interpret the event through the eyes of a reflexive practitioner. Right from the beginning, customers were paying a premium for a subjective experience. Tool manufacturers had long ago moved on to new materials that worked better, were cheaper to manufacture, and offered better function to those who really needed the tools and needed to buy one. This segment of the market compared the choices according to their function and cost, and Smith and Hawken was a big loser. (Workmen also have their loyalties, aesthetic preferences, and even snobbery. For many mechanics, shiny Snap-On tools from the roving salesman are irresistible, even though Sears tools work just as well.) But Smith and Hawken was a big winner as long as the subjective portion of its value was intact. The company was eliciting a self-reinforcing experience among high-minded people about the beauty and wholesomeness of gardening. But there is an arc to such a movement. First of all, it is rooted, in all senses. When one can no longer associate physical and social places with the goods, as happens when you move the tools to big box stores and lose the flowers, the store, the personality, all of which extended through the catalogue, the goods lose value. Put simply, there is a size and time limit. You can't grow beyond the relationships through which your value is actively being generated. The value is not "in" the package. Another factor appears to be the temporary nature of social learning. A segment of the population had a burst of interest in gardening; they learned and they bought the tools. One shouldn't expect the movement to continue indefinitely. A business can succeed, then move on to something else when the peak of interest passes. The fact that a market concept is temporary doesn't mean that it is a bad concept, especially since such concepts are more and more common. That's where a lot of money is made and what drives a lot of social change. To read the situation and know when to quit is part of reflexive practice. Model-based marketing aimed at endless growth, on the other hand, is bound to hit a wall as tastes change, especially if such an effort has no roots or relationships other than an excess of capital.

Readers of *Business Week* might notice that there is a formula for writing about businesses that perfectly reflects the formula of the businesses they write about. The first article describes a hot new company that is expanding faster than competitors. Obviously, they have the right formula and are poised to make it big. The second article, not many years afterward, is titled, "What Went Wrong at X?" This article talks about all sorts of terrible results and attributes them all to mismanagement. Neither the writers nor the businessmen ever consider that what was described in the first article may have actually been the evidence of mismanagement, whose inevitable result is what is described in the second article. At the time of the second article, the managers may in fact be managing well for the first time, making very heroic and clever adaptations to escape from an impossible mess that bad thinking had created.

Hawken doesn't appear to be in business any more, but with a little defocusing of one's categories, one can see that he is doing exactly what he had done before. His new "venture" is the largest of all—it's just that, this time, there is no product, ownership, or profit in a conventional sense. In his recent book he has asserted that there is a worldwide movement of people who are united in developing a sustainable global culture.[17] At the moment, the members of the movement are not conscious of their membership, are unaware of other members, and have not realized that there is a shared and unified agenda. The way I have stated it makes it sound like this is a lot of Mill Valley hoo-ha. But as we have seen, he is able to sense when the developmental potential is ripe, then fire up the imagination through skillful reframing. The global movement is "realized" in two senses that drive each other reflexively, first as a new awareness that one is acting at this level, and second as a redoubling of action with this newly refined account of its meaning. Many others discuss a global awakening, and they certainly have their contribution to make, but Hawken has a special knack for channeling cognition and energy. His training grounds in Newbury Street and Mill Valley may be early examples of how social nerves become exposed and realigned in a turbulent world. For the same reason that we once thought that fighting and winning in New York made you a master of business elsewhere, now loving and winning in Mill Valley can make you a master of global evolutionary culture.

# 6

# Economy, Environment, Energy: Worlds Apart, or Three Perspectives on the Same World

*David L. Hawk*

How best can we respond to issues that seem ambiguous, unbounded, and increasingly omnipresent to our world? Behind these traits lies change. Change surrounds most of what we decide to do, often so much so that by the time we are ready to do something, the something has become something else. Businesspeople point to the unfairness of suppliers and customers turning into competitors. Students describe their interest shifting from getting accepted to a college, to getting something acceptable from college. Voter attention is moving from how to spread democracy, to why it's not working at home.

Some point to these as characteristic of society undergoing change; others suggest the change has become turbulent. I agree with the second group. Still others, with a fundamental faith in tradition, and a confidence in the leavings of the sands of analysis, see current conditions as simply a cyclical low point. They recommend patience. They suggest we await the forthcoming upturn in the cycle. Of course, while waiting we are welcome to present our methods of analysis and means to measure this thing we call "turbulence." Since those who perceive turbulence see little point in analyzing and no point in measuring turbulence, there is a standoff. The situations in which we participate thus spin further from understanding and the possibility of normative intervention.

More effective ways to reconsider the ambiguity of the present, to appreciate the importance of the systemic, and to respond to the turbulent are needed. People and organizations that are prepared to take risks and experiment with timely and innovative practices are needed, but they should come from the group that is sufficiently ethical to risk their own resources, not those of others. The dilemma for Emery and Trist,[1] as well as the authors of this book, is that a turbulent environment, labeled as "type IV," defies labeling. It is worth remembering that Trist selected this term in 1965 as a construct from fluid dynamics where the normal flow of things (fluids, processes, politics, thoughts, and actions) becomes disrupted, and can be disrupting. The consequences of turbulence can be upsetting and dangerous, especially to those dependent on stability, or who have little insulation from rapid societal and environmental change.

Trist argued for use of systemic thinking to conceptualize and respond to environmental turbulence. This proved to be sage advice, but in recent years we have seen how the systemic is as fluid as the turbulent. To add to the direct instabilities, there are indirect difficulties in failing to manage a generator of turbulence in a timely manner. Quite simply, there has long been a gap between humans sensing that a practice needs to be different, and then taking the necessary actions to beneficially change a practice. During conditions of accelerating change a situation can shift from being a problem to being a problematique very quickly. Humans have long depended on time as insulation against the consequences of unresolved problems. While acting with much deliberation over goals, objectives, plans, and strategies, in response to a problem, it evolves quickly into a problematique with little respect for planning. The challenges from a systemically fluid environment are great.

The difficulties of our situations can be more clearly seen in how MBAs are prepared to lead firms with no desire to be lead, or few opportunities to deviate from what was done in the name of past success. For whatever else MBA training does, it fails to prepare graduates in ambiguity training, or for innovative practicing.[2] Notions gleaned from the surface of industrial age analysis provide structure for case studies but become an encumbrance when surprises call for radical alternatives. The great economic ideas of the 1930s, such as planned obsolescence of manufactured products in order to create a need for ever more manufacturing, continue to provide structure to business school education. Few instructors are equipped to include context and connect these ideas to twenty-first-century economic, energy, and environmental challenges. This idea of managed obsolescence, as promulgated by Alfred Sloan, was a General Motors mission. It now is a symbol of what can go wrong in a company and a society that believes in the company without question.

It is difficult to talk about twenty-first-century systemic phenomena via a nineteenth-century vocabulary of the analytic. It is even more difficult to be able to see the systemic through the eyes of the analytic. Richly connected, dynamic situations require new concepts, vision, and passion. Newtonian metaphors, e.g., leverage to deal with force/counterforce, are not helpful. Our practices need to become as nimble as the environments they will occupy. Organizations and those who occupy them can thus better demonstrate who they are, what they do, and what they ought to become.

Various attempts have been made over the past 50 years to rethink traditional practices in light of systemic phenomena, but the results have not been encouraging. Systems thinking was taken as a term and turned into systems analysis as a practice. Reflective practice became a new dimension of marketing. Something less acceptable to business as usual is needed to shift from what is and to what ought to be. Analytic constructs, such as segmentation, dissection, priority, hierarchy,[3] and rational progression[4] may best be suspended when experimenting with normative action. Alternative patterns of thought can arise from success in action experiments. Open-systems concepts can then be connected to practices that mirror change, movement, negotiated order, and systems of living order. This may need to be done in protected areas of experimentation.

Euclidean geometry can provide a metaphor of how this might work. Euclid's axioms and postulates were suspended within a new form of mathematics now known as non-Euclidean geometry. Development of Einstein's revision of the universe appeared in a similar manner. It arose from those who didn't understand or relate to Newton's world. This may mean that the most radical forms of innovation rely on suspension of what is assumed to be most essential to what is. In the area of environmental concern, current use of concepts like sustainability, recycling, and environmental protection are taken as essential. We might begin to rethink the initial, and strongly justified, environmental concern by avoiding these later concepts in order to see, for the first time, a systemically connected environment. This might provide new constructs for tapping into the human psyche in ways that connect to an enlarged potentiality outside the self-imposed limits of current social regulation schemes established to avoid past errors. Where do we find those who are most willing and capable of experimenting with different practices?

Signs of changing practice can be seen in capabilities being developed by those who survive at the edges of institutions. Their seemingly naïve early responses to challenges of surviving in edge conditions now seem more legitimate than the traditional directives emanating from the core. Even where core management has access to the latest information technology, and information, to efficiently organize what possibly need not exist, they accomplish doubtful ends. New practices emerging from the edges of reality seem somehow better informed than IT at the core, and better prepared to act instead of reflect. From these individuals we can learn. In conclusion, something akin to a new version of open systems thinking is needed, and needs to insure that it can accommodate controversial concepts.

Concepts such as entropy,[5] anarchy, and Faustian bargains will attract new attention, although much of it will undoubtedly be negative. Those involved should come to see how the role of entropy provides a window into the universe of the systemic, and does so in a way that is fundamental to innovation. It had potential to bring fundamental change to the way we apply systems thinking to design, production, and consumption. Entropy is superior to concepts like sustainability in that it provides a less ambiguous means to see meaningful limits on human activities. It also can serve to spark the human imagination to fully engage the power of the design argument.[6] Entropy, combined with design, opens up largely unconsidered practices to improve processes, products, settlement patterns, governance, and relationships.

## Open Systems Practicing

Open systems practice requires open minds, but how can we open what we have for so long managed to close? We have learned to disbelieve our experience while blindly trusting the advice of ill informed, analytically limited experts as well as systemically challenged professionals. This can be seen in fields from medical practice to house building. Illich[7] discussed the problem in his 1977 book. It was an early criticism of the limits imposed on social systems by expert systems. He pointed to the harm from professionals in society, even though society welcomes them, employs them, and embraces their mostly faulty advice. He argued that this begins in an educational disability. It is as new as it is unfortunate, or as Illich said, "When I learned to speak, problems existed only in mathematics or chess; solutions were saline or legal, and need was mainly used as a verb. The expressions, 'I have a problem', or, 'I have a need', both sounded silly. As I grew into my teens, and Hitler worked at solutions, the 'social problem' also spread."[8]

Consistent with this direction of education, students are taught to avoid asking difficult questions. Architecture and management students are trained to act as if they know when they clearly don't know. This aspect of becoming a professional is widely known and little discussed. In education it's quietly known as "learning to wing it." When confronted by a question you don't know the answer to, you simply act like you do and therefore "wing it" through your presentation. Where winging it fails you move to trivialize the question, or then the questioner. Teachers are good at demonstrating how this is accomplished in their responses to especially interesting students. These student's raise tough, interesting questions, but teachers can simply fail them, make fun of them, or simply say "BS" as a student walks away upset.

Instead of facing challenges, architecture students are taught to develop a specialized vocabulary by memorizing unfortunate precedents. Management students are taught in a similar way by memorizing the inaccurate and uninteresting aspects of cases. Both groups deserve better.

Research into how best to instruct executive MBA students in accomplishing biotechnical innovation was carried out in a northern New Jersey company in 2003. Results showed that a major impediment to learning new ways to practice was the need of a student to appear as if they knew what they didn't. Those with the strongest pronouncements of a claim to knowledge were ultimately found to be the least imaginative about alternatives. They were also the most likely to be promoted within traditional management hierarchies.

The systemic works well in network form organizations that are organized non-hierarchically. To thus manage the systemic you no longer rely on a predetermined structure. Remembering that you first expand a problem to include its environment, you can then take advantage of the increased potential for change. Developing an ability to question the traditional, ignore the prescriptive, and expand the limits to the allowable takes effectiveness to new processes and practices. In this way the role of the normative is enhanced.

Open systems practices, guided by ethical challenges, can help manage complexity by allowing suspension of the contradictions that become intrinsic to tightly drawn legalistic prescriptions. Laws are often drawn from and intended for conditions and actions that no longer exist. As laws are more tightly drawn, the contradictions between specifics grow. Standing back from such simplistic rule systems allows practice to evolve and respond in new ways to opportunities not previously noticed, or that were envisioned as unachievable. This was an early intent of continuous, adaptive planning as seen in work from the 1970s. The approach failed in part due to the adaptive being consumed by the rational and the continuous becoming the completed. In this chapter, the emphasis is on practices of the fluid, not the fixed.

Concepts of objective-based plans for solid people carrying out dependable practices in fixed, predictable environments need to be upgraded. Planning without plans for "fluid management of liquid enterprises" requires very different concepts and practices. Demonstrations of this difference were conducted by a Silicon Valley start-up firm,[9] as based on lectures they attended on the importance of redirecting a company via fluid metaphors.

Ideas about fluid management leading to changed practice were also demonstrated in an Energy Star Program in the US Government beginning in 1994. The program was set up as a public response to a societal problem that had emanated from short sighted actions of private citizens and enterprises. Energy Star was established as a non-regulatory experiment to manage a societal problem. It was to encourage the potential in self-management and self-regulation. It assumed a problem-solving approach that would utilize systemic expansion instead of analytic reduction. In it, energy concerns were not reduced to improving US access to world petroleum supplies or to the mobilization of Americans via phrases like "drill, baby, drill." Instead, it came from a reflective reconsideration of ideas about energy gained from examining economic and environmental issues. This was to counteract the training of environmental professionals who had been taught to reduce pieces of "the complex puzzle" into even smaller pieces, prioritize them, and solve them one by one. Responsibility for a "bigger picture" was traditionally left to politicians.

Energy Star was to have been an example of how citizens can confront the dilemmas of a politician's image of the big picture and move directly to engage the body politic. Consumers were invited in to reflect on how energy consumption relates to environmental and economic choices. Some aspects of Energy Star thinking grew out of dissertation research of 1977.[10] Consistent with the 1977 research, Energy Star was to demonstrate how to continuously renegotiate with the changing reality of a surprise-filled, fluid environment.

Energy Star had an exciting launch and was initially deemed successful. It then went through the normal process of feeling a need to become officially accepted, finding a permanent place in the hierarchy, and moving from high-risk to acceptable activities. It became officially welcomed and locked into the Atmospheric Pollution Control branch of EPA. From that point it was never able to again lead or even accommodate change in the water and solid waste pollution activities that were integral to it. Once the program was organized around specific standards the participants could game the program and use it to support the own narrow ends. This was in part done by shifting attention from making products that were to be 30% better than a reference model that represented what could be achieved with a set of tough regulations, to being 30% better than a worst-case scenario of essentially no action. It later became possible to meet air pollution reduction standards by covertly increasing water and solid waste pollution.

Over time, the program turned from fluid management of the ambiguous and the flexible, to picking up one of those Energy Star labels with little to no cost. The program gradually became more like the traditional programs it was originally intended to influence toward innovation. Even vinyl siding, a material known to have no value or justification for use anywhere, was recently awarded Energy Star status because it could be "recycled."

Two years into the project, other significant problems were encountered. They related to differences between industry potential and customer preference for what was. Examples of HVAC equipment and washing machine designs, as discussed later, will illustrate the challenges of any who want to bring improved practice to society. The momentum of the usual, as supported by the power of the analytic, is great. In the Energy Star Homes program there was an explicit reluctance to see problems with energy use in a context of economic and environmental understanding. When these three perspectives are viewed as interdependent, exciting opportunities arise to reconsider and redesign human practices, including those of Energy Star.

## Economy and Environment: Two Perspectives on our Energy Dilemma

Economy, environment, and energy are herein presented as three perspectives on one issue, not three issues to be reduced, analyzed, and solved. Together, the three offer an unusual array of observations on the critical dilemmas facing all three. One of these, perhaps the major one, is how to create the means to get more from using less. Humans seem unhappy with the seeming contradiction in this mission. It may be because they are deeply invested in contemporary practices that keep the three domains as separate. While managing each via business as usual, we see glimpses of systemic hope, as well as the catastrophic in business as usual.

Our perceptions and practices for problem solving seem not to be systemic, yet the problems we face clearly are. Given time to reflect we see early signs of business as usual not being able to continue, but we seem to give up after speculating on what "new" business can mean. It will help to begin with a common framework, even though we are not very good at describing what is common. Such a framework can reduce some of the created complexity[11] in and between each perspective. This may initially seem illogical, because complexity is presumed to lie within each, but as mentioned previously, solutions seem to arise from just this sort of contextual thinking that is excluded by problem analysis.

Economics, energy, and environment are increasingly complicated topics. Each has a set of dangerous consequences if not managed well. The fears in each are great, but we soften them by presuming that society will discover means to manage each in "better ways." On careful inspection we see that gains made in one are achieved at the expense of one or both of the others, or via our misplaced optimism we fall into a Faustian faith in advancing technology that allows the externalities of a former technology to be resolved with a new technology, with its own externalities. We thereby can "solve" an energy problem through increasing an economic or environmental problem, just as Faust "solves" an ethics problem by sending it into the future.

As with all Faustian bargains, it's a "smart" idea to serve your own near term interests by dumping the externalities into your future interests, or better yet, onto the interests of others. Besides illustrating the underlying weakness of the Adam Smith's logic, there are other reasons to reflect on the three as one. Each plays a significant role in our lives, what we do, and what we would do if we could transcend the limits placed by each on us. Each, in isolation, seems to pose greater limits on the human condition with time. Each, operating via a set of its private principles, sets limits on what the science and disciplines of each define as good practice.

### Economics

Economics is often given center stage, but why it is treated with such esteem illustrates an underlying problem. This deeply seated problem can be seen to have been planted in the early part of the industrial revolution via utility theory. This was based on a belief that humans primarily operate to avoid pain and seek pleasure. This, combined with the eagerly accepted beauty of rational expectations, provide humans with a central rule system. In the view of both Smith and Marx, energy and environment are passive resources that await consumption by economic man. From this perspective economic aspirations, and worries, can easily trump the other two.

## Environment

Environment is becoming a more interesting subject for humans, as the consequences of its mismanagement become more dramatic. Early evidence led humans to seek to "protect" the endangered environment from humans. Just now the human attitude seems to be a bit less homocentric.

During the 1960s, environment surfaced in two senses: the social and the natural. Rachel Carson gave importance to the idea that there was a natural environment, and that its existence was essential to all living systems, including humans. She pointed this out in a small way that caught the large attention of society. Fred Emery, Eric Trist, and others, went on to articulate the importance of the social environment as a critical context for the wellbeing of social systems. They illustrated how social systems, when their stability is threatened, react by increasing instabilities.

The idea of an environment becoming more important is similar to having a largely unnoticed stage set as a context for human actions and interactions. In pointing this out, Eric Trist and Fred Emery[12] helped inform a cadre of people in organizations that were trying to conceptualize the changes unfolding around them. The cadre included directors of firms, researchers running projects, and academics seeking to describe the next big thing and to avoid being told that their ideas had already been dealt with. Outside these groups there was little use of the idea of organizational environments in day to day practice. Despite the ambiguity of its use, it seems clear that the conditions of the environment are critical to defining human success, and the importance of it has been growing over the past fifty years.

## Energy

This domain is more mysterious and omnipresent than the other two. Most aspects of economic action rely on cheap energy and most uses of energy have significant environmental consequences. Just now energy signifies high costs, long lines at gas stations, going to war to shorten them, and diverting foodstuffs to make fuel in parts of the world which then leads to famine in other parts. Energy is a mythological aspect of human history, where it begins with Promethean fire. Finding the next Promethean source of energy has haunted human development for thousands of years. Optimists, relying on analysis, generally dream of energy as unlimited and quite free. For example, with the advent of electricity in the nineteenth century there was a belief that energy would eventually become so cheap and plentiful that it wouldn't pay to meter it. Once again, fifty years later, nuclear energy was thought of as a cheap road to industrial progress. Related to this there has also been much human enthusiasm for discovering a perpetual motion machine.[13] In so doing, humans disregard the Second Law of Thermodynamics as well as the consequences to the environment of expanded energy consumption. Humans also disregard the First Law of Thermodynamics, that energy and matter cannot be created or destroyed, by "inventing" a social possibility for the recycling of production mistakes. Consistent with this history, humans can ignore entropy and continue sketching out images of perpetual motion machines.

## Integration of Economic, Environmental, and Energy Thinking

Real advantages are seen in the integration of the three domains into a single field. Together, they encourage creative responses to complete situations. As a teacher of management students it is obvious that most will end up working in badly managed situations while being encouraged to accept the status quo until they retire. What they are educated to practice comes from unhelpful and uninteresting texts, case studies, models, practices, characteristics, and capabilities. Management principles, no matter how "innovative" in their labeling and presentation, presume that there will be no or limited change. Each principle implies that control is the optimum response to problems. Control is seen as more efficient than ambiguous approaches that include the ideas of others.[14] Where control fails we instruct students to grudgingly move on to complexities. As such, there are three essentially choices for managers interacting with others in their environments:

1. *Control*: This is the dominant human desire, and besides, "it's easier and I know what I'm doing."
2. *Manage*: This is a fallback posture, when control mechanisms fail, or can't exist.
3. *Negotiate*: This may be our last best hope, where control is impossible, and management can't manage.

The first is the dream of the engineer, the second of the MBA, and the third introduces the world of living systems. Enough has been said about control. An endless amount could be said about management, but to little end. Negotiation is more interesting. It is used in the historic sense of ancient Greek and Chinese ideals, not the one given by the Harvard Negotiation Project. As such, negotiation needs to be seen as fundamentally different from bargaining. Bargaining is a zero sum game that gets reduced to who takes what portion of a fixed pie. Negotiation is where all participants will be changed in the process, including the size and shape of the pie. There is no static state or controlled stability in negotiation, just as there can be no reliance on statistics or cause-effect thinking. Percentages and probabilities are used in negotiation to frighten, not to enlighten. The process is fluid and the entities are liquid. Negotiators are not controllers or managers. The controller works to divide things into digestible parts and needs no common language; as in the Tower of Babel. The manager, on the other hand, accepts the parts, but works to facilitate by giving them a common interest (usually his), and proposes a common language (also his), and begins the bargaining process. Facilitation is complete when his interests are achieved. For reasons of efficiency, disruptive comments are kept to a minimum.

The negotiator, on the other hand, acts to disrupt arrogance and assured comfort of all involved, including him/herself. Given a choice, most people appear to prefer bargaining over negotiation. It offers short-term certainty of outcome and shifts the costs of bargaining to those occupying the long term, as in a Faustian tragedy. The process and results, even where bad, seem more predictable thus more desired. The pie is fixed, thus attention can be turned to the size of your piece.

Within negotiation, the process is ambiguous. As an open system, even the pie is indeterminate, and ends up smaller, larger, or gone. People tend to shun the ambiguity and uncertainty implied by negotiation. It seems that most prefer the predictable bad to the questionable good. Thus, negotiated order[15] still remains best suited to situations with an air of: "it's too late." The dangers of the negotiation approach to order are considerable, but the seemingly guaranteed disasters awaiting control or management techniques are greater.

Negotiators must be respectful of the systemic, and skeptical of the analytic. Negotiated results tend to take longer to accept, which seems to be a price that must be paid. In each of the three examples that follow there are serious issues but ways to escape the more unfortunate results.

## Environmental Concerns

In the Energy Star example it took a long time to go beyond the assumptions found in the status quo. In October 1977 a box with letter attached arrived at my farm in Iowa. I had recently returned from two and a half years at Sweden's Stockholm School of Economics doing an environmental research project. The project was designed to compare and contrast different regulatory approaches to environmental concerns. The letter, from the then Director of the U.S. Environmental Protection Agency, stated: "Dear Mr. Hawk, enclosed you will find the copies of your report, "Environmental Protection: Analytic Solutions in Search of Synthetic Problems," that were picked up by EPA. We have no further use of them, your research, or you. I will see to it that you secure no government funding for future environmental research. You have done a disservice to your country and the environment."

The essential point of the 1977 research was that the United States wouldn't be able to control its environmental problems because it was using the same approach—a legalistically arrogant, analytically flawed set of fixed guidelines—to control the consequences of what had been initiated by the same attitude. I had argued that this would keep the regulators from appreciating, seeing, or effectively responding to the complexities and ambiguities of the problems, or seeing the potentials of the stakeholders. Meanwhile, the misunderstanding underlying the environmental problems would continue to grow, thus leading those responsible to become angrier. The mental mode, which I called analytic determinism, was behind the industrial processes that resulted in environmental deterioration and then came to be used to "solve" the problem. By failing to experiment with systemic responses to systemic problems the United States was projected to produce an ever more dangerous environment. Other OECD nations quoted from this research in their rejections of presentations made by U.S. representatives preaching that they knew the way forward.

Fifteen years later, in 1993, I received a message from a different EPA director. "Are you interested in a grant to help establish an Energy Star Homes Program? It would be good if you could illustrate some of what you talked about in the 1977 report." Once the limits of the project were established it became clear that EPA had missed the central point of the 1977 work: how to avoid the false security of analytic-based solutions. Regardless, I continued to work with the project for the next two years before giving up.

## Energy Myths

In 1987, an editor for a Harvard Press publication on "North American economies in the 1990s" asked me to write a chapter for a forthcoming book based on a lecture I had given that year in a Texas conference. The title of the lecture was "The U.S. Energy Myth and Its Probable Consequences." The chapter came to be titled "Landing the American Eagle," but it failed to make it into the proposed book. It instead appeared as a last chapter in an obscure book on US-Mexican economic relations. Mexico was never mentioned in my chapter, but I guess it didn't need to be. I later found that my chapter was seen as "interesting" but had a few problems. It was interpreted as a little too "un-American." In it, I suggested that cultures, including the American one, are held together by myths that guide collective behavior. The American myth came from the early days of the European invasion where it was a pioneer nation with unlimited energy and material resources. I argued that the idea of limitlessness in material and energy resources had been an attraction but later led to an unfortunate approach to industrial design, production, and consumption: "use the best, trash the rest."

From this I suggested that the "American eagle," via its guiding myth, was coming in for a necessary landing. It needed to become grounded in a new reality, but would it achieve (a) a graceful landing, seek a better myth, and take off again, or would it (b) come in confusingly and awkwardly and, while bumping along the ground, become damaged, or would it (c) simply crash and blame others for forcing it down with unfair trade and currency control practices? I was told by the editor that my chapter didn't fit with the tone of the other chapters. It wasn't very optimistic. I concluded from this that I should write for books about Mexico, in that they didn't need to be artificially optimistic.

Fifteen years later, in 2002, I was asked to serve on a congressionally sponsored commission via the National Academy of Science. NAS had asked me to give a lecture to program directors on my Mexican "energy chapter." The mandate of the commission was to bring private sector innovations to improving public sector agency management. My role was to secure interviews with executives of ten firms that we could examine in detail. Interviews were held with executives at Honda, Toyota, General Motors, and elsewhere. Only the GM evidence found its way into the final report. This was due to the final review of the report, where "editors" in the 2004 White House felt GM was the best example of where the United States needed to go. I never understood why the final report needed to be approved by the executive branch since the congressional branch had sponsored it. Regardless, my suggestions for bringing private sector experiments into public sector operations were dropped during final editing. While the 1987 interpretation of the American myth was tolerated in 2002, it was again viewed as "unhelpful to America" by 2004. The Committee itself had found Honda, J&J, and Intel as the most exciting places from which to learn about the future. Toyota, on the other hand, was seen as almost as uninteresting as GM. In 2009 GM did prove to be an example of US difficulties in practice, not those envisioned by the White House in 2004. The White House occupants proved to have their own difficulties with practice.

## Economic Understanding

In 1992 a project titled "Conditions of Success" was completed and reported out. Using action research the project centered on executives from 60 firms. They became the action researchers and assumed responsibility for implementing what was being learned. The objective was to improve understanding of internationalization models that had not found their way into textbooks, advisory consultancies, nor the World Economic Forum. Results showed that international success was shifting from quality of decisions to relationship of decision to the conditions within which a decision was made, almost like the Ancient Chinese source book, *I Ching*. The environment was somehow becoming more important than the decision taken within it.

This was the first international study that examined success relative to the conditions within which practice was carried out. Using the Eric Trist contextual approach, the researchers organized the decision models around the three cultures in the study: American, European, and Asian. When questionnaire results were studied and presented in a 1991 Stockholm Symposium, the executives projected that the American model would be further diminished in two decades, and the European model would turn inward in a quest to find new meaning for the European citizens. Only the Asian model was seen to be sufficiently expansive, international, and based in research investments to achieve renewed success in a changed world. The researchers speculated that by 2020 all three, even the Asian, would run into environmental dilemmas that could not be dealt with via current technology and models of business. The researchers then projected that Japanese researchers were best prepared to begin innovative responses to environmental concerns. The Chinese were seen to be too tied to industrial expansion, although they seemed to be aware of its longer term limits.

Except for those participating in the study, the results had little impact on the larger industry or to consultants advising on models of internationalization. The 60 executives were concerned with this and elected to run a symposium on the project results instead of attending the World Economic Forum in 1991. Those running the Davos forum were not impressed with that decision.

The Director of the World Economic Forum visited me in 2007. He was interested in the results from the 1992 report and asked if the Forum could use them to chart development of new industries and to initiate a study of Forum companies. At his request, I attended the annual meeting of the Board in Dalian in 2007, to describe why and how the 1992 research had been done. We jointly concluded that it was too late to use the 1992 model. The World Economic Forum people instead used a scenario forecasting model that only four companies elected to join. It was too late.

## Summary

What does the mismatch between analytic solutions and systemic problems, caught in a fifteen year time lag, mean? It is unlikely that major economic, environmental, and energy problems will be addressed in less than a superficial manner, or without the time lag. In addition to this, or perhaps due to it, there is a lag between individual consciousness and societal unconsciousness, all while the consequences approach the present.

Some have speculated that the time lags are the result of cultural imperatives that do not easily accept change. Others have argued that one of the most effective ways to bridge such cultural gaps is to meet rude experience. A New Orleans hurricane, called Katrina, provides an example, as does an oil spill in the Gulf of Mexico. When experiences become even ruder, as they are expected to become, we will have opportunities for investing in very different practices. During those conditions we can experiment with suspending analytic thinking as it is now used to govern practice and guide political decisions.

This will undoubtedly involve a different conceptualization of communication. This can be seen by reexamining the role of communication in the "Prisoner's Dilemma" game.

## The Practitioner's Dilemma as The Prisoner's Dilemma

Americans consume a great deal of energy supporting life that offers limited comfort and questionable quality. Naturally, many disagree with this, especially those not holding passports, and believing the United States to be a superpower, and thus able to provide the best of the best to its citizens. Concern is directed against anyone proposing that the United States offers anything less than the best in all areas. Nonetheless, the evidence is large and growing that the United States is not the best in all areas, and will have limited success in continuing to attract 25 percent of the world's energy and material resources, and the best and brightest students from other countries, all to serve 4 percent of the world's population.

This thesis is supported by observing the ill-informed practices of the US building industry. There were fundamental errors in the design and installation of the energy consumptive infrastructures that support the American life style. These include home air conditioning design and installation, and washing machine design and manufacturing.

1. Practitioners that design and install U.S. building air conditioning systems rely on a model that was initially designed to overcompensate the need for cooling by about 20 percent. This was due to the poor insulation performance of U.S. buildings. Practitioners, using this model, add another 20%, where the rule of practice is "more is better." This 40% overdesign results in higher capital costs, too high humidity, bad cooling, mechanical equipment breakdowns, and very high home energy consumption. Based on a demonstration project done for the Energy Star Homes Project, this flaw was shown to be prevalent. The industry has yet to change its practices, even though the energy consumed and the problems with the results are large. If we can't get this right, what hope is there for the greater challenges in successfully creating new sources of national energy?

An experiment was conducted to demonstrate there was something seriously wrong with practices in the area. A new air conditioning design was formulated and prototyped. In theory, it would require only half the usual equipment, consume only a quarter as much energy, and bring greater comfort to the occupants. During a two-year period the installers refused to supply the specified equipment on two grounds: they would be open to lawsuits, and they would get a bad reputation with customers. Finally, after pressure from the manufacturers who agreed with the new design, and after signing release forms, the installers delivered the new equipment. The results were more dramatic than we anticipated.[16] In the intervening 14 years installer practice has not been changed to accommodate what was learned from this and similar demonstrations, even though very significant savings in U.S. energy consumption would have resulted, and human comfort world have been enhanced.

2. Savings in a second area of energy use could have been equally as impressive, while water savings could have been even more dramatic. It is not widely known, but the American practice of washing clothes uses an extraordinary quantity of resources to arrive at relatively poor results. American machines for washing clothes, as initiated by GE designers in the 1950s, are different from the rest of the world. They are called vertical axis, or more poetically, top loading. The washing machines used in most other parts of the world are front loading. American washing machines require four times as much energy, three times as much water, and four times as much soap as European machines. They cost about the same to manufacture. When American marketing innovations are applied, the European machines can sold for about three times what they cost in Europe. This results from market segmentation, where "European" machines are advertised and sold as a special environmental item for the more endowed members of U.S. society. Via governmental encouragement U.S. manufacturers now offer some horizontal axis machines but without the major energy saving devices used in Europe. When asked about this oversight, the industry designers argued: "We don't want to confuse the customers." In addition to savings of energy and water in this change in practice, there would be a large reduction in soap additives going into the water supply. The horizontal axis machine also cleans clothes much better.[17]

Large gains can be made via small, humble steps to improve outputs while reducing inputs. Why then is practice not changed? Two kinds of problems seem to impede change. First is the time lag between knowing what to do and being able to do it, and second is a perception that until its "too late" no significant change should be instituted. This may arise as a consequence of our cultural preference to "control" things, as distinct from "managing," or "negotiating," with them. The second kind of problem is that even when we find it acceptable to manage or negotiate toward an improved response, prospects for innovation get sidetracked via a communication deficit.

To deal with this, we can take a lesson from Prisoner's Dilemma.[18] The dilemma part relates to some actors working to insure that communication is defective, thus insuring that practice is defective.

Prisoner's Dilemma deals with what happens when communication is disrupted between two individuals engaged in doing something together. After the prisoner's are arrested, the investigators separate them so they can't communicate. Each is spoken to in isolation to get each to think that their partner is simply not to be trusted. The dilemma is that you are led to believe that if you choose to be disloyal to your partner you will be punished less or perhaps not at all, while much of the burden for a wrongful practice will fall on your colleague. You are thus encouraged to escape responsibility and avoid co-designing a way out from the problem.

In the two examples given above both the customers and manufacturers can be seen to be the prisoners. The practitioners operate as go-betweens to emphasize their own interests while successfully keeping the "prisoners" from communicating with each other about joint interests. The crime in this model is greater than a gas station holdup. It's the large and largely needless consumption of scarce resources to accomplish unworthy ends. The dilemma is kept alive via the misinformation given to each set of prisoners. Each is kept in the dilemma with advertising that implies they can get more than they "deserve" if they don't communicate. Besides, their partner will never find out that they were dishonorable. The situation thereby begins as dysfunctional and continues in a sea of misinformation.

The only way out is for either the consumer or the producer is to improve information quality, so both can collaborate in doing the right thing, thereby forcing change in the world of practice. This model also offers an ideal way to see what it means to get beyond the limits brought on by bargaining and move towards renegotiating the relations between economics, environment, and energy.

# 7

# National Environmental Policy Act as a Reflexive Setting

*Thomas W. Cuddy*

In these days of heightened environmental awareness one could ask, "Was there ever such a thing as environmental stability?" On a beautiful day in May, I put the final touches on a five-page guidance statement for how to deal with greenhouse gases and climate change in the aviation sector, emailed it off for review, and left for a Memorial Day weekend at the beach. Solve climate change, head off on vacation, all in a day's work. If only it were that simple. People must interact with their environment, and for most of humanity's existence on earth a stable environment was an underlying premise. We are only just realizing how wrong we were about the environmental side of it, and in the process finding out how our own cultural complexities further change the balance.

Anthropologist Stephen Lansing provides an intriguing case study of resource management for environmentalists from his study in Bali, Indonesia.[1] Rice is the staple food product in Bali, and is grown in rice paddies, man-made terraces carved into hillsides that form an endless patchwork across the countryside. Rice is best grown in soggy conditions and the terraced walls are part of an ancient technique to trap water in the paddy to nourish plant growth. The terrace walls create a picturesque vista across the landscape, and are linked into an equally important system of water canals that extend continuously across Bali. At each major canal juncture, where the flow of water takes a turn or crosses a property boundary there is a water temple. The Balinese water temples are places for coordinating the complex religious, social, and technical aspects of water control. The water allotment, or "use rights," for each household are based on individual needs, and each rice farmer draws from the canal the amount of water he has been allotted. This integrated system, managed by the water gods as well as the orderly behavior of participants, ensures that water remains in the canal system for those living downstream of the flow. Rice is had by all, and a selfish farmer tempted to take more water than allotted risks his well-being in this world and beyond.

The modern environmental field in the United States is a mixture of some science with a lot of politics and business, and stability is hard to come by. About the only thing not closely bound into it is religion, but that may not be completely absent either. The prevailing U.S. ethos of liberty and individualism has convinced us that the natural environment can be dealt with as an externality, and yet everything environmental is, in the end, not only controlled but politicized. Most people intuitively understand that environmental concerns are complex scientifically, but the untold story is the extent to which environmental concerns are also social, economic, and political concerns. Activities of any size in the United States, and especially federal infrastructure projects, result in the convergence of many influences including governmental policies, public interests, and resource variability and distribution. To modern environmental professionals for whom everything is pushed and pulled by a variety of unpredictable forces, Bali would seem like an unimaginable oasis.

## The National Environmental Policy Act (NEPA)

It is a common misconception that Congress formulates laws and they are simply implemented. The National Environmental Policy Act (NEPA) is the highest tier environmental legislation and the most direct federal environmental mandate that must always be complied with by all U.S. federal government agencies. Passed in 1970, NEPA compels agencies to comply with other existing environmental laws when conducting their business. It is considered "umbrella legislation" because it essentially operates through other laws. Agencies have their own areas of expertise and develop programs for regulating and managing their domains—the Environmental Protection Agency (EPA) setting water and air quality standards, Fish and Wildlife Service (FWS) dealing with living plants and animals, the National Park Service managing national historic landmarks, and so on. But not all federal agencies are natural resource agencies, and those like the Department of Transportation (DOT), the Nuclear Regulatory Commission (NRC), and the National Aeronautics and Space Administration (NASA) still must comply with resource agency regulations when carrying out their own programs. These agencies hire consultants when planning projects to obtain the expertise needed to adequately comply with the diversity of environmental considerations for which they have limited capacity to complete themselves. There are different types of environmental work, but this chapter focuses on NEPA as the best example of the forces involved in professional environmental practice. Since NEPA is carried out for U.S. federal projects, it is the biggest single factor in American environmentalism and is the primary vehicle for considering environmental issues in large-scale programs.

Environmental projects start with patron-client and public-private relationships between agencies and consultants, a working relationship complicated by the fact that many environmental topics do not lend themselves to "command and control" legal regulation. NEPA specifies *what* environmental impacts to consider in project planning, but does not specify *how* to consider them. There are approximately 25 categories of environmental impact, depending on how they are counted, including such different disciplinary fields as water quality, endangered species, public health concerns, and Indian tribal matters. The variables change on a case by case basis, so the amount of interpretive leeway that environmental practitioners have in complying with NEPA is extremely high, almost to a fault. Many federal regulations under the umbrella of "environmental" policies are vaguely crafted in the form of considerations–an agency must consider the effects of its actions on a park, or consider the effects of its project on an archaeological site. These have recently been dubbed the "light green" laws, as they leave much room for professional judgment.[2] Even the dark green laws, the more stringent regulations such as air quality standards or hazardous waste disposal, only differ from the light green laws by bringing more quantifiable data and benchmarks to the interpretations. The agency folks can't just hand the environmental work completely to the consultants, because they will turn around and ask, "So how would you like to work this one?"

If it weren't complex enough that NEPA projects are ad hoc partnerships of public and private professionals interpreting a wide array of different environmental factors on the fly, there is also a requirement within NEPA for public review and comment on the decisions. Agencies send their NEPA documents to other agencies asking for feedback and opinions. They also must hold public hearings to present the information to the public and request comments. A standard project requiring an environmental impact statement will at least have a public meeting early on to scope out the extent of environmental study the project requires, and a public hearing at the end to review the final report. A mega-project expected to last many years will have additional public meetings and may even organize the various stakeholders into technical advisory groups that meet monthly or quarterly throughout the life of the project. This public requirement in NEPA is considered the democratization of the process as it theoretically results in collective decisions.

About 50,000 environmental assessments (EAs) are completed by federal agencies in a year. EAs are the simpler and shorter reports for projects that do not have extensive environmental impacts. An EA can take anywhere from three months to three years to prepare, and might be anywhere from 50 to a few hundred pages long, depending on the environmental issues. The larger studies, prepared for substantial projects, are the environmental impact statements (EISs). An EIS is prepared when an agency knows its project will affect the environment and must offer mitigation actions to reduce those impacts. About 500 EISs are completed by federal agencies per year and they usually comprise two or three volumes, each several hundred pages long. The average EIS takes somewhere between two and four years to complete, depending on the industry, the agencies involved, and the proposed activities. Only rare exceptions come in below this time frame, and if there are complications the time could easily double. A project manager for a highway widening or airport runway extension assumes the EIS will take four years. If the activity is an administrative decision, for example, the Department of Energy wants to establish a new granting program for alternative fuels research, the EIS might be largely a book report and come in under two years. Federal actions with high sensitivities, for example, a site license from the Nuclear Regulatory Commission to construct a new reactor, will face a long environmental process. Adding insult to injury, sometimes the shorter assessments reach the conclusion that the more extensive EIS is called for.

## Complications

The environmental field meets complexity in the structure of policy, the relationships of those involved in the practice, and with the informational content. There are built-in troubles whether you work as a consultant, for the government, or in an environmental engineering firm. The complex characteristics of environmental work are, as the saying goes, not the kind of thing that can be taught in school. Practitioners that get into NEPA work are often motivated by a love of the environment and arrive at the profession from a master's degree program in biology, zoology, or something similar that prepared them to operate within a discipline of scientific inquiry. Many fit a personality that eschews office paperwork and administrative bureaucracy, preferring instead to be outside doing field work or in a lab analyzing data.

The antiestablishment sentiments of idealistic college graduates who enter this line of work can put personal passions and work goals at odds. In addition to being philosophically opposed to their employers' management practices, these NEPA practitioners approach the project work from a heavily scientific perspective. The pure science perspective believes that an environmental assessment will simply run some studies of the environment and put them up for a "yea or nay" consideration. This focused practice sees the natural environment as an object of study. Such a view underestimates the number of decisions and assumptions that go into how scientific studies are designed. Decisions seemingly as simple as the extent of the project boundary can be different for the air quality analysis than it is for the soil survey. This scientist frame also downplays the processes necessary to manage the public reaction, motivate the political decision makers, and steer the tradeoffs and cost-benefit analyses that will get a project done.

Environmental science is only one frame of reference in NEPA, and is a major reason why the concept of NEPA is somewhat thorny. A report that looks at an issue at a single point in time is static, while the environment is dynamic, and it is difficult to adhere to the spirit of the NEPA legislation, or to effect real environmental protections, when producing a stand-alone assessment. NEPA has a dual existence as an administrative process and a scientific assessment. If that is multiplied by the number of interest groups—government, consultants, the public—then NEPA has many states of being. Legally NEPA is a procedural statute, which means that the overarching management and governance views it as a procedure to be completed, a.k.a. "a hurdle." The practitioner will view the same project as a process of coordination and communication to be managed delicately, while the technical field personnel mainly view it as yet another government intrusion on the environment. Each party has its own roles with differing allegiances. The management of NEPA projects was once relegated to bureaucratic functionaries who marshaled projects through to completion so they could check the box that said done. It turned out, however, that some specific skills can help or hinder the process. After enough blunders over the years, resulting in busted project budgets and schedules, there is now an increasing professionalism within the field in all employment arenas. There remains an undercurrent of interested practice, with government managers, planning consultants, and environmental engineers each having their own interests. People still struggle to decide the appropriate noun to put after NEPA and it depends on their perspective; sometimes it is a NEPA *study* or a NEPA *analysis*, other times it is the NEPA *process* or the NEPA *document*. The reality is that a NEPA process with any level of complexity is all of these things at once and the reflexive practitioner will need to manage each in its own right at the same time.

From a legal perspective, NEPA was designed vaguely in order to be adaptive. Since the Act was passed 40 years ago the professional practice of environmental consulting has been a turbulent evolution of procedures, measures, and tactics attempting to satisfy the ideal. Like all fields, some best practices emerged as well as accepted standards of quality. However, many of the accepted actions are not scripted, they are simply the long-held process that developed over time. When challenges arose, perhaps a lawsuit from a nongovernmental organization, the solution was to plug those gaps with more analyses and procedures. From the legal frame, the main interest is avoiding lawsuits. Consequently, the expectations of a NEPA analysis have been slowly additive, the practice has built itself up, learning from mistakes and reacting to institutional inputs—a new federal regulation here, a new corporate management approach there. I like to say the practice of environmental assessment is *accretionary*.

Perhaps the most difficult element of professional environmental practice is the continuously shifting base of information, concerns, and even legal requirements. The Obama administration has acted rapidly to reinterpret the applicability of an Endangered Species Act ruling, dusted off the Migratory Bird Treaty Act, and reaffirmed the standing procedures for consulting with Indian tribes as independent sovereign governments. The EPA is revising mandatory reporting rules under the Clean Air Act, which is one of the dark green laws and a rare example in which environmental professionals apply strict measurement methods and standards. The Recovery Act funded many new federal projects in 2009 but came with new NEPA reporting requirements as well. There is an initiative to better integrate cultural and historic resource evaluations on federal projects within the NEPA process, even though those resources are managed by state agencies. And this is all in the first seven months of the new administration.

Environmental practitioners need to know legal requirements that apply to their efforts today, but are well served if they can see what is coming on the horizon as well, recognizing mismatches of practices as well as opportunities for correction.

Amid the shifting environmental policies are many decision points. Collective decisions are not easy to reach among practitioners, and harder with public stakeholders. The project team must engage the public properly and, even if done, the team cannot expect consensus decisions. The need for a highway bridge replacement or a new railroad spur may be acknowledged as vital by the public, but local citizens will be skittish about large government projects. Consequently even if they want what the project offers, they will be critical and antagonistic. This dialectic is part of framing the environmental standard that will be applied on a project. Locals live close to their environment, and public involvement often identifies very valuable planning details such as which street always floods during storms or how many feet deep farmers typically bury their drainage systems. The local public has the best information on historical resources, so their concerns about the corner house where someone famous was born, the school that was the first in the state to integrate, or the battlefield that they'd like to make into a tourist attraction often become the frames that add to the project. Additionally, a successful and vibrant project is one that has a vocal opposition to provide a counterpoint. When a multimillion dollar infrastructure project has a political champion, that person usually has a political rival who might seize your project as their opportunity to spotlight differences of opinion.

The public forum sometimes adds only localized context but can also raise major concerns. The public comment and review process provides valuable information but even if approached efficiently and proactively the public component always reframes project perceptions which can complicate the NEPA process and send it in different directions. Decisions about mitigation hinge on the relationship of public and political variables—we will route the pipeline under that river because it has been designated as scenic and contains an endangered mussel species, but we will trench through this other river and place the pipeline along the bottom because it will save us some money and no one seems to care. These kinds of tradeoff decisions must be made, but if the project team is clumsy in presenting their materials, or if stakeholders sour on the project for any reason—real or perceived—that can become a negative frame to the process that must be dealt with in its own right.

Public awareness of environmental concerns has grown immensely in the last decade, well beyond the "feel good" recycling programs and double-sided printing initiatives. Science steadily increases our knowledge of the natural environment, including climate causes and effects and the linked nature of biodiversity among many natural and technical processes. In addition, we are becoming more acutely aware of the human place in the environment and how limits on energy, water, and other resources may impact our lives. Between the natural and human considerations are many of our social institutions that try to mediate and balance divergent interests. The consequences of environmental decisions can be very expensive and are not without their winners and losers. Suffice it to say most things "environmental" are infused with political opinions, economic choices, and regional differences of opinion, a situation that makes every environmental assessment highly politicized.

## Growth of the Practice

In May 2009 I was optimistic about the climate guidance that I had concluded and its ability to improve environmental work on aviation projects. NEPA makes no mention of greenhouse gases or climate change as a type of environmental impact, and most agencies have no formal policies for dealing with climate issues. It is a veritable blank slate for practitioners to deal with, and my guidance memo therefore has major potential to shape the field. A few questions remained, such as who should have authority over flight emissions at altitude, or how to calculate international fuel sales and their emissions, but those seemed solvable. The chief reviewer to whom the draft went has a Nobel Peace Prize on her office wall and was one of the scientists on the United Nations panel that produced the Fourth Assessment report on climate change in 2007. Many months later, however, we have not been able to move the policy forward; such is the tangled web of bureaucratic implications, interagency working groups, federal rulemaking procedures, and other red tape.

As an organic practice with a tendency for accretion, the environmental field requires some reflective consideration of the applicability and relevance of its actions. Government agencies are slow-moving and wait on risk-averse lawyers who tend toward whatever practices have worked in the past. That leaves only the consulting and engineering firms to go out on a limb, but they too don't exactly *like* new or unproven methods and practices, and only take risks when they are impressed to do so by the collective decision-making group.

The average practitioner recognizes that a NEPA assessment is complex in two primary ways. First, no two projects are ever the same. The project and its assessment must be conceived uniquely. Every project has a distinct justification and cost-benefit argument behind it that is an arrangement of needs and opportunities combined with funding and politics that shapes the scope and extent of analyses. Each large project is in a distinct place and will have unique environmental variables to consider, including public concerns.

The second way that a NEPA project is naturally complex is the shifting criteria by which the process and its quality are judged. How the work is valued has a ripple effect on the practice, and the primary variables of the NEPA process are time and money. From the environmental consultants' perspective, the absolute minimum standard on a project is to get paid by the client, which means producing an analysis that is legally justifiable and acceptable to the client. The consultants and engineers, if they are lucky, will get a letter of recommendation that they can use in soliciting the next project proposal. The young scientist types who often perform much of the base fieldwork can have differing motivations, but their main rationale is generally to get the government to pay for more and more research so they can continue doing their scientific analyses. The rational practitioner and even the principled professional would like to think that there are key variables somehow based on environmental characteristics; however, they are contracted for the project through a business relationship and that is judged upon satisfactory completion—the time and the cost. There are better and worse practitioners, of course, and the parties involved recognize and appreciate when your decisions turn out to be correct most of the time. They may recognize that it is a convoluted process in which not all factors can be controlled completely, but they don't want their career to go down with the ship. It is easy for management to point to the time and the cost.

Every few years or so agencies go through a process of "streamlining" NEPA, conceiving of it as a process that will yield to efficiency improvements. But NEPA is a practice, a set of relationships among the various parties, a triangulation of agency staff needs and the recommendations of their counsel and consultants. Streamlining efforts are usually initiated by government agencies and result from a perceived gap between the policies, the practice, and the product. Streamlining efforts are a type of reflection, but they tend to focus on trimming the effort, time, and money within the extant environmental process. Such a narrow focus is doomed from inception not to find the efficiencies sought. Having witnessed several different environmental "streamlining" initiatives, it is clear that the reformulated practice tends to reinvent the same issues, relationships, and process. That result should come as no surprise, since the environmental practice is an adaptation, a reaction to situational variables.

In most cases environmental assessment is not a federal agency's direct mission or authority. With the exception of the EPA, FWS, and a few others, agencies have little expertise, facility, or even interest in expanding environmental assessment capabilities or initiatives. This is changing somewhat, but the allocation of resources to this area is often to "safety net" programs such as expanding the environmental law division. The final quality control measure is the legal department, which often receives the document at the end of the process and decides what else needs to be added. While legal review is crucial, there is a long process leading up to that point during which the scientific analyses are developed, decisions about project engineering and mitigation actions are made, and the document is compiled and written. The burden of quality assurance throughout that time is on the practitioners.

The last thing the federal environmental process needs is more patches to symptoms. There are, however, some overarching considerations that cross-cut the practice frames and the disciplinary spheres of influence and, with only a little effort, can be taken to a more dynamic level. The accumulation of atmospheric carbon dioxide and its effect on climate change have already challenged the American process for design, review, and approval of large federal infrastructure projects, and not just because climate change is a complex global problem. Climate change is a complex and evolving field of environmental interest. NEPA says nothing about it explicitly, yet the oversight agency, the White House Council on Environmental Quality (CEQ), has made it clear that nothing about NEPA precludes the inclusion of climate as a type of environmental impact, and that it should be included in an assessment if it is appropriate. Thus the priorities of the general public affect the scope of environmental assessments and are a driving force behind adaptation in practice.

## Opportunities

For existing federal programs where proposed actions are similar to other past projects, conceptualizing the environmental process is only "normally" complex. In such cases the established environmental practice will involve all the decisions and difficulties of a standard environmental review. Such normalized practice has an underlying assumption of stasis, or at least only incremental modifications. But in this new era of energy independence, clean technologies, and federal leadership on mitigation, many agencies are being asked to go beyond incremental improvements and to find larger efficiencies and synergies in their operations. One such program is the FAA's Next Generation Air Transportation System (NextGen). The goals of NextGen, in brief, are to enact a wholesale reinvention of U.S. airspace organization and management, a process that calls for changes in ground facilities, navigation methods, aircraft technologies, and nearly everything else related to commercial flight. When new agency programs are striving for complete transformational change, practitioners applying old methods of environmental assessment will lead to delays, repetitive or redundant analyses, and needless costs. A reflexive practitioner will see beyond the mere project challenges and begin to recognize where structured problems and differing ideological frames begin to interact.

The public is demanding more robust environmental considerations and decisions. The structural problems with federal environmental work, such as differing goals among the parties, the ambiguity in the laws, static reports done on a project-by-project basis, varying management expectations, and employee mismatches now find themselves under the microscope of attention that is reframing some of the objectives. "The very notion of what is best is in motion and in play" (see chapter 2). On October 5, 2009, President Obama signed Executive Order 13514 titled *Federal Leadership in Environmental, Energy, and Economic Performance*, and it states that "It is therefore the policy of the United States that Federal agencies shall... reduce their greenhouse gas emissions from direct and indirect activities...." This is good news environmentally but draws into focus some examples of at-risk practices.

Kent Myers related a story that illustrates how "good practices" can lead to unfortunate consequences. U.S. Customs and Border Protection (CBP) was told to hire 7,000 new agents, and a team of construction managers and engineers was assigned to plan more than a hundred new buildings to house the expanded workforce. Treating this crash construction program as a single superproject was intended to promote better use of expertise and insight and yield better results under complex criteria. The planning team espoused an interest in creative options. They even agreed that it would be wise to include at least one project that tried something distinctively different. The CBP planning team expected to use the Army Corps of Engineers (ACE) for construction, and a representative was included in the discussions. The Corps presented a stock building design which could be repeated at almost all locations. The eventual plan simply plugged in this design, which resulted in a huge number of ugly and minimally efficient buildings that would saddle the agency with high and rising energy consumption.

Several times there was a general call for different ideas. None of the suggestions were taken seriously, even though many members, when approached individually and in private, admitted that the ideas were realistic, proven, and beneficial. Three illustrations will suffice to demonstrate the fractured deliberation on this CBP initiative. First it was questioned whether some of the buildings were needed at all. In some border locations, the new hires would be on patrol almost all the time and would not need office space. What would be needed, instead of a new building, was a change in supervisory practices and laptops that agents could use at home or on the road to send in their paperwork. The planners, as construction engineers, felt obligated to meet a completely arbitrary engineering standard of office space per employee, and to not ask questions about how that space would be used. The second idea was to point out that many of the structures would be in remote areas of the desert Southwest where costs for cooling and electric hook-up for the Corps-recommended structures would be very high. A concrete dome construction technique was proposed as a structural design option. It had been used often in the region and had remarkably superior performance on all relevant criteria such as speed of construction, cost, longevity, sturdiness, and especially cooling. Self-contained geothermal or solar power sufficient for cooling a dome could be added at a fraction of the cost of supplying a conventional structure from the grid. These options were dismissed without discussion. A third idea was to begin immediately several EIS studies that were surely required, where construction was a top priority and where no alternative sites were available. Members unanimously agreed that starting these EIS studies right away would reduce high costs for temporary leasing. Yet the team decided to take no action for months in order that a complete package be assembled "for decision"—but this was needless delay as there was no possibility that these EIS projects would not be conducted.

This CBP program was a hopeful opportunity where planners were given wide discretion, ample support, and encouragement to do something better. Policy was one of those encouragements. Since the 1970s federal agencies have been under regulations to reduce energy consumption. Just as this project was starting in 2007, the Energy Independence and Security Act was nearing passage and had stronger regulations. It required little imagination to see that the agency would soon be required to demonstrate facility energy savings beyond minimal standards. Opportunities were clearly raised during the planning process and would have resulted in savings and efficiencies in the overall program, but the team instead recreated a "safe" consensus with only a ritual effort to examine alternatives. But in a fast-changing situation it was not safe at all, resulting in an expedient building program that was out of step with emerging national priorities. The result will take decades to correct and will harm the CBP's mission.

Every government agency has a similar story, and the tendency of at-risk practitioners to refuse to read what is new about a situation and to find opportunity should not be underestimated. Federal agencies, in particular, experience a serious pull toward "proven" methods and procedures and it often takes an act of Congress or Presidential order to move them in different directions. Most practitioners understand that they can't change the systemic issues of the environmental planning process in the course of a single project. Those avenues can be pursued through participation on research steering boards and policy development groups which move at their own pace. As the government takes on more mega-projects, ideally they can go beyond baby steps to fit the environmental process to climate and other new environmental challenges. There will be hundreds of environmental projects carried out as part of NextGen, which gives a rare opportunity to design an environmental review process holistically.

## Environmental Modernization

If there were a silver-bullet solution to the multitude of issues wrapped into environmental assessment it would have been done long ago. But there is not a legislative fix, and it is impossible to codify every possible outcome of environmental work in clear formal policies. The best NEPA can do is to specify which disciplinary spheres will require some study and decisions. The amount of "decision space" in a NEPA analysis is great, and ever-changing, which puts a lot of faith back onto the practitioner to execute. Consultants dream up project alternatives while the government agency staffs suggest mitigation measures or license conditions that worked for them on other projects. These feedbacks inform the project design, and may cause redesigns, which change the frame again. The reality is that there is no stable background or floor and the environmental practitioner must always continuously adapt. Obviously project scenarios will differ, as will the environmental considerations. The structural variables, such as state statutes, regional political views, or a community's economic condition will always vary and the practitioner will never be able to eliminate this turbulence.

There are, however, some unknowns within the environmental assessment process that can be influenced or minimized more easily than others. Most ripe for this is the culture of the project team, the active engagement of public dialogue, and potentially the development of performance standards. An irony of the federal environmental process is that most practitioners disdain the public components. Interaction with the public tends to be sloppy and disorderly. Everyone has been to a public hearing that wasn't run well, or seen a special interest group go off on a tangent that didn't seem relevant to the subject. Nevertheless, the public components are the more malleable elements of the environmental process and can be quite powerful in what they deliver. Many pieces of the environmental process—the legal statutes, agency organization, even the science in a way—present the practitioner with apparently fixed structures. Elements of the project culture that involve interaction, including the project team's attitude and their ability to engage the public dialogue, are the areas of environmental assessment most conducive to creative transformation based on the abilities of the practitioner. These are the elements that can create positive momentum for a project and rein in secondary support factors such as approval of public financing or permits. The challenge is that working the public dialogue requires professionals to have their fingers on the pulse of society. In addition to knowing the environmental policies and staying current on environmental sciences and applied uses, the practitioner must have a sixth sense for public sentiment and the vectors of concern and power that go along with a project. There may be history within a community that has shaped their outlook on the government or that left undercurrents of distrust about certain agencies or actions. Knowing how to ferret out these sorts of circumstances in order to defuse or counteract them can be a real art, and is a personality characteristic that isn't necessarily selected for within the discipline.

In addition to a nose for relevance and linked issues, the other portion of the public piece that practitioners have control over is education. The practitioner works with environmental topics every day but the stakeholders at the project level don't, and to have any chance at facilitating key decision points they need to be brought up to speed. This preparation includes crash courses on the policies and the environmental review process, how it is likely to unfold, and what the stakeholder's role is in it, and that is all in addition to the supporting data on natural environmental conditions and potential effects of the project. The largest educational hurdle is the general public, but education must take place across all levels of a project. Each group will have legitimate concerns but little policy experience. Each group finds the process crazy, but for differing reasons, and the practitioner must explain why things have to be done the way they are. When a practitioner "briefs" senior administrators it is educational outreach about a project designed to align expectations, clearly describe options, and many other variables beyond environmental effects.

Organizing the public arena has shown several creative successes. For a large bridge reconstruction project in the Washington, D.C., area it was clear that the original environmental analysis was inadequate, and an objection raised early on was that there was no way to know so far in advance what the true environmental impacts would be. Some of the interchanges and overpasses hadn't been developed by the engineers beyond a 10 percent design stage and weren't scheduled to start for another ten years. Public interest groups don't like to agree to intangibles, but in this instance the environmental team developed a process that all could agree to that laid out how emerging issues would be dealt with, how the plans would be developed and reviewed, which parties would be responsible for which parts of the approval process, and how monitoring and follow-up actions would be implemented and tracked. On another project, this one a rocket launching facility in New Mexico, a similar agreement was reached that included an annual meeting of the stakeholders to review the project performance and look at upcoming activities that may require new or different strategies. The group who signed the agreement was quite varied, and included a number of federal agencies, several state agencies, Indian tribes, nongovernmental organizations, and local landowners. The running joke was that we were planning the plan for the plan. Call it what you will, these are examples of engaging the public head-on. By highlighting for stakeholders what is known and demonstrating what isn't known convincingly, it becomes possible to devise a path forward buoyed by positive buy-in. These agreements were initiated because the path could bring unknown environmental challenges, and they worked for the superficial reason that stakeholders could see their role in the process and where it was going. But there were larger forces at work, and the fact that such differing groups could agree to anything was, I believe, from the appeal these projects had to a sense of logic and intelligence that made all parties see the greater opportunities with full knowledge of the tradeoffs.

Another area of potential change that could help environmental practitioners manage uncertainties is more concrete targets on the environmental side of the argument. Each NEPA study has to argue the science of the environmental impacts, but also must re-argue the context of why they are or aren't significant in each particular case. Some projects have employed creative mechanisms to set performance goals and review the application of them. This is a fundamental practice question: should environmental management be guided by scientific interpretations of what's best for the natural environment, or should it be a local community's decision, or economic realities, or something else? The process for environmental assessment integrates many differing interests making it easy for the average project to be driven by multiple purposes and goals. If the Presidential administration or Congress wanted to take a more active role in matters, they could have real positive benefits for the environment. Establishment of a national strategic framework with environmental performance standards would provide an independent measure of what NEPA projects are working toward. Certainly too much federal regulation can have its drawbacks. Every industry has unique environmental considerations and will need to explore solutions for minimizing environmental effects in their own way. The fallback position so far has been to point out that agencies have common but differentiated responsibilities under NEPA. If the overarching objective is environmental protections, a set of standards would add clarity by stressing the parts that are common. Each political administration has its own interests which are prone to fluctuations but gives the freedom to set its own agenda. Fixing the environmental variables through policy would remove that flexibility from the politicians, and also remove a bargaining point practitioners currently navigate within the project dynamic. It would limit some of the "democracy" by adding weight to the environmental side when balancing the interests of stakeholders.

Executive Order 13148 was signed under the Bush administration directing agencies to develop "environmental management systems."

The premise was to weave environmental considerations into all government actions. Instead of treating environmental assessment as a one-time hoop to jump through, the idea was to integrate environmental considerations upstream in the planning and management process such that environmental effects are being examined at every juncture in development and well in advance of problems. The process was a little too utopian. It has been interpreted by the agencies as only applicable to their internal operations and not to be extended to the actions and programs they oversee or regulate, a serious limitation on its reach and potential.

There have been some upgrades to the standard mechanical tools of NEPA. Most large projects now host a website that provides information. These "electronic dockets" allow somewhat more access and visibility to the process. These changes have improved the project operation considerably, including the administrative process for the agencies. Documents are posted on shared websites for ease of access by agency leads, consultants, and the public. There is no doubt that the electronic document systems have facilitated agencies with maintaining an administrative record of their proceedings. Additionally, there is the potential for these systems to further democratize the environmental review process by allowing interested parties to more easily see and monitor what is taking place. However, many of these systems are so confusing and opaque as to defeat that purpose.

Recent success stories don't result from these mechanical tools but from dynamic practitioners. One example regarding climate is the environmental impact statement for the Corporate Average Fuel Economy (CAFE) standards.[3] A Ninth Circuit court decision found that a previous analysis of fuel economy standards for automobiles ignored climate change impacts that could result from the ruling. The new study was a massive effort of the National Highway Transportation Safety Administration (NHTSA) and the firm ICF International. For political reasons related to the change in U.S. presidential administration the new document had to be prepared at breakneck speed. The real story, however, is in how the project team crafted an assessment of climate effects at a national level. Everything environmental is political, and there is no policy or guidance for dealing with greenhouse gases. In addition the scale of the CAFE analysis was a national technology standard that touched large stakeholders including automobile manufacturers. Most of the technical creativity in the CAFE analysis was in how the study scaled its discussion of the environmental impacts to a level that mattered to most people. The study estimated a social cost of carbon, and extrapolated their vehicle recommendations from analyses of technology synergies based on emerging capabilities, economic practicability under different scenarios, and a national need to conserve energy. Making a nationwide environmental decision regarding climate change meaningful and understandable for the average consumer or bureaucrat is no small feat. Other studies have done pieces of this, but none had sewn them all together in this way with environmental protection as a primary goal linked into broader U.S. economic and political initiatives.

## Conclusions

There is a call to organize environmental planning and management on a broader scale, but what form that would take is debatable. It is the environmental practitioners role to raise up the "social conditions of possibility."[4] Those frames include the institutional aspirations but also the critiques, the arguments against a method or a project embodied (usually) in the public component of the project but sometimes in the principled environmentalists, too. The reflexive practitioners will find themselves navigating all environmental frames, including the critiques, and extracting from that dialectic an improved frame of reasoning to apply in an overarching manner to environmental issues such as water rights or climate impacts.

The environmental practice, with regard to the NEPA process in particular, is a continuous co-evolution (see chapter 3), and theorists like Stephen Jay Gould always stress the fact that evolution is not linear and does not have an inevitable conclusion. Instead it is opportunistic—a dynamic of differentiation and change that explains how a diversity of options persist or not through time. The environmental field is an example of survival of the fittest within an ecology of interaction and competition, and it requires a rich collection of ideas from which evolutionary opportunities can arise. It is agreed that complex environmental concepts such as sustainability and climate change are global and can not be addressed piecemeal or be resolved by a one-time evaluation of the circumstances and the application of a few stock mitigation measures. Climate change presents environmental professionals with "a novel and dynamic decision-making environment."[5]

A heavy government hand in planning and conservation is often derided by environmentalists as a cookie-cutter approach, and is viewed by the politicos as socialism. If the government were to designate areas of the United States as special corridors for pipelines, power plants, or transportation, that would begin to shape land use decisions and induce residential and business developments, and that is just the affirmative feedback loop they would like to avoid. The beauty of the example from Bali of water management through temples is sublime because disapproval and sanction in the afterlife is a singular unknown that many won't want to risk. Climate change now brings together a similar driving set of circumstances for Western society, proposing that catastrophic global warning will doom the planet in the future based on what we do about it now. It is an interesting moral question as well as a scientific one, since the cause and effect are decoupled and any rewards deferred. Action to reduce atmospheric carbon dioxide and global warming amount to hypothetical rewards only to be reaped by our generation's children or theirs. For both water in Bali and the global climate debate the relationship between subjective hopes and objective opportunities is intangible. This lack of clear linkage to immediate interests drove Daly and Cobb to speculate that those with a religious commitment will eventually be necessary participants in the long-term effort to change society toward sustainability.[6]

Focusing on the political arena, there is no question the control of resources equates to power, and that social power is volatile. In contrast to the cooperative nature of Bali water temples, another anthropological study of Asian water management, *Oriental Despotism*,[7] details a case in which control of water was used to coerce labor and political subservience from neighboring societies that needed the water for irrigation. At times the modern environmental process seems to be more politics and economics than environment or science. For those reasons, many elements of environmental conservation are most effectively managed at the scale of the local community. Improving or preserving environments should start small with communities revising zoning codes and other local policies, as well as participating actively in public hearings.

Many environmental professionals argue strongly against any changes in the policies associated with NEPA, claiming that it has worked for 40 years and the only thing that can improve it is exemplary practice. Another viewpoint is that we are facing increasingly complex environmental issues requiring new guidance and procedures. A long-time practitioner of environmental consulting recently took on the role of critic in a new book *Our Unprotected Heritage: Whitewashing the Destruction of Our Cultural and Natural*

*Environment*.[8] Author Tom King presented his thesis to a group of agency officials responsible for overseeing federal environmental and preservation programs. The audience was defensive at best, but most of King's points were made well. I have likewise taken a somewhat critical tone in this essay, but hopefully in a reflexive way. I have tried not to reduce the many players in a NEPA study to polemics or stereotypes but instead to pull out from the large pool of diverse perspectives and relationships what some of the major frames are. One of King's main points is about people—there will always be people involved in environmental analyses, and the whole intent of environmental regulations is to serve the continued interests of people.

With change as inevitable, and the admission that there is no foregone conclusion in the environmental field, the onus is put back on the practitioner to make a practice with known policy problems, structured deficiencies, and considerable turbulence come out all right. And the public seems willing to accept this even though it is our shared environment at stake.

# 8

# Reflexive Personality

*Eleanor Criswell*

Turbulent times call for professionals who are open, flexible, and reflective as opposed to decisive and resolved, traits traditionally valued. Termed "reflexive practitioners," these professionals are eager for the options created by ambiguity and variability, and do not try to hide the existence of options, suppress options, or prevent options. They have discarded thought processes, such as denial, distortion, isolation, acting out against colleagues, and unexamined responses to cognitive dissonance that favor quick, firm decisions. Instead, they prepare for more turbulence, indulge intellectual curiosity, and develop consensus work products arising from a transparent, collaborative process. They produce living products. They avoid closed door deliberations that crank out official responses and marching orders, but add nothing of value to professional dialogues and provide little support for growth. Reflexive practitioners see that understanding ultimately creates more potential than resolve. Reflexive practitioners value the quality of life fostered by use of an open process over short-term material gain. Openness and flexibility can create problems when applied to tasks needing decisiveness, but are instrumental in creating professional growth in turbulent times.

This chapter first considers at-risk practitioners who minimize turbulence, rely on a "feeling of knowing," and avoid self-critique. Next, this chapter identifies "ideal" psychological attributes, aspects of personality and thought, of an effective reflexive practitioner. These attributes are emotional stability, proclivity toward relatedness, open-mindedness and curiosity, tolerance of conflict, flexible goal orientation, qualities of intellect, and reframing. Each is described, and some are illustrated by using a "case in point." Finally, the chapter concludes with ideas about ways to foster openness and adaptability in professional life. These include continuous self-reflection, workplace training in scenarios requiring adaptation, consultation with a clinical psychologist specializing in workplace personality, and executive coaching by role models.

To those familiar with psychological terminology, a "reflex" refers to an unconditioned or involuntary response to a particular eliciting stimulus that, through a learning process, can become a response to other stimuli that previously could not elicit it. In this book, "reflexive" as applied to a professional practice, has much broader meaning. "Reflexive" implies a responsive practice, but a practice involving thought, reflection, a sensitive back and forth in a process of changing, of seeing or introspecting, responding with a more complex response, seeing another thing, responding more complexly, and so on. The reflexive practitioner is someone who responds to the immediate situation, yet who also reflects, uses multiple perspectives, is open-minded, and builds knowledge in professional settings capitalizing on the back and forth in turbulence.

## At-Risk Practitioners

This section sets the stage, describing some common professional behaviors and attitudes that will interfere with reflexive practice: attempts to minimize turbulence; practice based on "feeling of knowing"; and inability to admit mistakes.

### Minimize Turbulence

Routines and stability help people survive. People have an inborn tendency to apply routines to reduce chaos around them. We look for answers. We want to understand things, know what to expect, and how to make things happen. We extol knowledge gained scientifically through induction and deduction. We retain our hard-earned best practices and rules, things we have been recognized for. We develop unique and persistent views of ourselves and how we fit in the world, and we are able to operate safely within a relatively peaceful space.

On the other hand, there is also a competing human drive for the variability and openness that facilitate new learning and creativity.[1] Reflexive practice recognizes that ideas come from everywhere. "Remixing" of ideas leads to strength. A professional, and perhaps especially a senior professional, must continually strive to learn more, to put ideas out for consideration, accommodate revisions and more ideas, take more actions, learn from experience, accumulate knowledge, and change and grow until the end of life. Reflexive people do not advocate chaos, but have an insatiable curiosity and openness in professional life that addresses new challenges, variety in the environment, and uncertainty.

Extremes in doing either routine behaviors or highly variable behaviors can cause problems. The need for too much routine and predictability can constitute personal disorder. For example, people with obsessive compulsive disorder cannot tolerate some of the inherent uncertainties in daily life, and may take actions (mental acts or behaviors) over and over to make themselves feel more certain, effective for only a moment at a time, but nevertheless reassuring. Disorders along the autism spectrum are also characterized by routine, well-worn behavior patterns, even patterns of social avoidance to restrict contact with variability. Some people with autistic characteristics gravitate to the IT (information technology) field because computers offer routines, certainties, and resolution not to be found in more social careers.

By the same token, we can find personal disorder in people who seem open, flexible, and change frequently. For example, some people are extremely open because they have passive personalities and depend on others. Other people dart from one idea or person to another because they are simply distractible and have problems maintaining attention and focus. These are not examples of openness, but illustrate problems.

For Holmes, open and flexible people are often victimized in the workplace.[2] Holmes articulates a cynical view, that open and flexible people offer themselves up, but get cheated by people who exploit their openness or steal their ideas. People who are cheated or stolen from must try to resolve or avoid that disturbing outcome or they risk becoming resentful, suspicious, and closed off. Projecting the exploitation problem in the extreme, Holmes sees the abuse of flexible people as a ruinous downside to globalization. Even if a person is abused in the workplace, the alternative of not having a job may be worse.

A reflexive practitioner can't solve the problems of global inequity, but can at least generate value under the conditions of change that globalization presents. Giving freely and allowing others to use one's products should in today's professional environments, more often or over time, benefit both givers and recipients. Because information becomes more valuable the more often it is used, strong ideas become more precious than money or commodities that wear out, disappear, or become obsolete through the advance of technology or of style.

## Rely on "Feeling of Knowing"

As Burton makes the case, professionals often fall into traps set by the "feeling of knowing."[3] Burton explains that the "feeling of knowing" is that feeling you get when you think you know something, you feel certain you are right, you just know you are right, but you are unable to explain it completely or understand why. This is similar to a gut feeling. "Gut feeling" is not "intuition," which is a cognitive act. In fact, in the "ideal" reflexive personality profile presented in the next section, being "intuitive" supports complexity much better than being "sensory." In some cases, the feeling of knowing attaches to a masterful and intuitive synthesis and insight, but sometimes it attaches to an opinion that feels right but is plain wrong. Any professional could find it hard to tell the difference; turbulence confounds matters further by invalidating judgments that would be sound in more settled environments.

Burton argues that professionals in fields across the board (medicine included; Burton himself is a medical doctor), make mistakes all the time and don't even realize it. Burton attributes this to a confluence of two bedrock assumptions held to in the professions, both of which are actually seriously flawed.

Burton says our first mistake is the flawed assumption that we become better, more capable professionals by virtue of experience. We all want our clients and patients to get better. We expect that we provide better and better service to more and more people as we gain in experience over the course of our careers. We would have trouble letting this belief go. But this bedrock assumption is flawed because not all experience is equal. The main reason for this is that we typically learn the effects of our actions only in the near term, and only as measured by our own standards. If we are doing something very wrong, we see that immediately. But if we are doing a job well in our own minds or according to an abstract standard that others are expecting us to use, and no mistakes are visible over a short period of observation, then our practices have been reinforced, and we will be likely to apply the same practices again later. This is where the problem gets magnified. How could you tell if what you are practicing is actually associated with improvements? We don't consider that. We just assume we are learning from experience, and that's good enough.

In professions such as medicine and clinical psychology, the dubious worth of unanalyzed experience can be harder to expose than it is in professions with quantified rankings, such as professional sports.

Yes, we do have to help our patients, but sometimes they go away with limited improvement or some degree of dissatisfaction, and we might never know it. In contrast, the professional golfer plays golf on national TV for all the world to see, wins sums of money that are tracked in the press, and moves up or down in quantified rankings. But in medicine and psychology, as long as patients don't stay extremely ill or die or feel that their mental condition is worse for having worked with us, we may never get any feedback. In our minds, we have gained in experience. But in a turbulent environment, there is no stable background, so we must examine all aspects in our casework that influence outcomes. This means that we need to seek feedback and evidence in areas where it is not naturally forthcoming, and to continue to question our standards and assumptions. We also need to let others evaluate us, even to let the system evaluate itself, to provide additional perspectives.

Burton writes that a second flawed assumption is our rightful pride in our "sixth sense" in parsing difficult situations and deciding on best actions. This sixth sense is each professional's unique offering to his clients and patients, his or her own spin on how to get best results. Yet, our professions rest on large bodies of research that support best practices. The value of a single practitioner's unique sixth sense is certainly not something that could become an independent variable and subjected to empirical validation. The value of your sixth sense may be your own illusion, or it may not. It has advantages, but intuition without perpetual adjustment is a drawback.

The ambiguous value of experience and problems in relying on a sixth sense may create even more risk in government consulting, where standards of professional practice are less articulated than even in medicine and clinical psychology. Military and intelligence consultants provide advice based on their experience. Their solutions may meet with rewards such as quick improvements in efficiency, strong endorsements from clients, or exciting new ways to do things. The best consultants can at least articulate the reasoning for their suggestions, though unfortunately those who are most articulate are not necessarily those with the best judgment.

### Avoid Self-Critique

One common way high-minded professionals do damage is to answer a question incorrectly, or with a lie, or develop a flawed course of action but be unable to self-critique and say they were wrong. The squirrelly "mistakes were made but not by me" defense offered up by professionals, notoriously by politicians, usually seems like thinly veiled self-protection. But instead, Tavris and Aronson blame this defense on the powerful need for self-justification, which can be achieved by reframing something bad into something good.[4] Note that the at-risk "principled" practitioner excels at self-justification: his principles cannot be wrong, and he is highly adept at rationalizations. Many of the "mistakes were made" people really don't think they made mistakes, despite contrary evidence. The need for self-justification compels the mistake-makers to say that whatever they previously considered as "bad" is now "fine." Endless examples of politicians doing this draw jeers from most of us, but illustrate that the personality capable of delusional spin can star in politics. Recently South Carolina Governor Mark Sanford accounted for his breach of public trust and marital infidelity as a "love story," attempting to invoke honorable principles to salvage understanding from those he deceived.

Cognitive dissonance is the uncomfortable state a person feels when he experiences conflict between what is expected and what is achieved, and this psychological discomfort is resolved by self-justification and denial of evidence. Professionals caught up in self-justification cherry-pick evidence. As Tavris and Aronson point out, they see only evidence of their own correctness, and do not see or look for evidence of failure. In essence, they are completely unscientific in approach and never look for disconfirming evidence. Any negatives are quickly redefined as positives or ignored.

Yet, because of turbulence, revision is often needed and improves products. Official iterations of professional practice standards typically aren't current, so interim review of products and practices within a changing professional environment can offer timelier self-critique. To their credit, some noteworthy professional disciplines, such as military operations and corporate bid and proposal departments, both with life, death, and money on the line, have committed to break through the reluctance to analyze results and connect them with actions. The "After Action Report" and similar review techniques in process control, knowledge management, and morbidity and mortality boards, can be instructive and even cathartic experiences, although they can easily devolve into inauthentic exercises.

A reflexive practitioner then needs to continuously look at his process and outcomes for signs of self-justification that deny reality. Reflexive practitioners will be those people who can actually do that, who do not have a personal need to be right all the time. A reflexive practitioner accepts that outcomes can be both positive and negative, that negative results are not necessarily serious problems that have to be spun as positives. By using objectivity and a scientific process, the reflexive practitioner builds a basis for growth. He is not building on delusions.

Ariely, a behavioral economist, provides compelling evidence of a different kind of professional mistake, namely dishonesty.[5] He cites evidence for a widespread decline of professional ethics across many fields, including law, medicine, and petroleum geology. Dishonesty covers such acts as overstating one's own abilities, cheating the public, racking up charges for unnecessary services, and making "professional" judgments and choices while taking pay from someone under consideration.

In a simple experiment with MIT students, with assumed intelligence and honor, Ariely experimentally compared three different methods for paying students for their number of problems solved: number solved according to a proctor's check of the answer sheet, number of problems solved based on self-report, number of problems solved based on self-report but also with a pledge of honor. Ariely found that students cheated by overreporting their number correct if no honor pledge was required; this group reported the highest number of problems solved. However, number of problems solved in the honor endorsement condition equaled number solved as checked by a proctor. So for Ariely, bringing back the practice of signing professional products with an oath of honesty and an assurance that there has been no conflict of interest might help remind us all of our professional oaths.

The concept of reprioritizing professional honor can be extended to a more personal basis. Because reflexive practitioners seek relationships, they perforce take on personal responsibilities to each other. Trusted personal connections form in the course of working together, if not face to face, then virtually. Refreshing the meaning of personal honor, trustworthiness, and responsibility among individual professionals could help attenuate any loss of ethics due to reciprocity or unexamined practice within the professions.

## Profile of Reflexive Practitioners

This chapter uses a psychological definition of a "reflexive practitioner" as containing seven characteristics of personality and thought. The characteristics related to personality derive, broadly, from a widely used personality model called the Five Factor Model of personality,[6] and the characteristics related to thought derive broadly from a model of intellect underlying the widely used Wechsler ability tests.[7] The profile was developed by considering how these factors would or would not apply to a reflexive practitioner. Each factor was then elaborated and modified to better describe what we mean by reflexive practitioners. This analysis yields a set of seven characteristics:

- Emotional stability in the face of turbulence
- Proclivity toward relatedness
- Openmindedness and curiosity
- Tolerance of conflict with others
- Flexible goal orientation
- Intellectual abilities
- Reframing

These seven factors also apply to the main pillars of Myers's generic model of practitioner cognition presented in chapter 2. That model is composed of two dimensions: gather/release and inward/outward orientation. The "gather" side is supported by the personal characteristics of openmindedness/curiosity and flexible goal orientation. The "release" side is supported by the reflexive practitioner's intellectual capability and cognitive reframing. "Inward" orientation is supported by emotional stability in the face of turbulence, and "outward" orientation is supported by proclivity toward relatedness and tolerance of conflict. As Myers posits in chapter 2, "Reflexive practice is a kind of intelligence." The seven characteristics in this psychological model of a reflexive practitioner further refine that view.

The Five Factor Model or the "Big 5" is a widely used, broad model of personality. The five factors in the model are neuroticism (problem with emotional control), extraversion; openness; agreeableness; and conscientiousness. The Big 5 model was developed through factor analysis of many personality traits and characteristics, has been extensively studied, and has been found to be both descriptive of personality and predictive of performance. An international project continuously studies and improves on the specificity of the factors.[8]

A personality assessment inventory using the Five Factor Model has been commercialized in a self-report, multiple choice format (e.g., "NEO-FFM," and a short version called the "NEO-PI-R"). The commercial inventories can be administered and scored by untrained personnel, but interpretation must be done by a trained psychologist. Based on extensive experience using and interpreting commercial inventories, we expect that the "ideal" reflexive practitioner will score low in neuroticism (be emotionally stable), high in extraversion, high in openness, average in agreeableness (agreeable, but not conflict avoidant), and average in conscientiousness (having high work energy but not overly concerned with plans).

A similar personality inventory, the Myers-Briggs Personality Inventory, contains four factors: introversion/extraversion (I or E, similar to the Big Five extraversion); sensing/intuitive (S or N, similar to the Big Five openness); thinking/feeling (T or F, similar to the Big Five agreeableness); judgmental/perceptual (J or P, similar to the Big Five conscientiousness).[9] The emotional control/neuroticism factor in the Big Five is not represented in the MBTI. Millions of people have taken the MBTI for workplace use (no psychologist required for interpretation) to understand how their own and coworker personalities will best synergize for improved communication and working relationships.

Each of the four factors in the Myers-Briggs has two possible polar values, yielding 16 personality types. None of the 16 types is maladaptive if it suits a particular job, and an assumption is made that workplace synergy improves if coworkers understand each other's personality type. Of the 16 possible personalities, the "ideal" reflexive personality seems most aligned with the "ENTP" or inventor/strategist personality; this type accounts for about 5 percent of the general population. The E for extraversion indicates a preference for people over being alone. The N indicates a preference for intuition (e.g., thinking) and projecting into the future (is open to the future) over sensory or descriptive information about the present. The T indicates a decision-making style based on thought and logic over feeling. The P indicates a perceptual outlook, one that keeps options open, rather than using judgmental evaluation and approaching things according to plan.

The reflexive practitioner also needs intellectual capabilities. Intellect is viewed (at least in the Wechsler concept) as consisting of verbal comprehension and perceptual organization (e.g., nonverbal reasoning, fluid intelligence), supported by working (very short term) memory and processing speed (speed of thought as well as motor speed). The reflexive practitioner also requires another type of intellectual or cognitive capability, that is the capacity for self-reflection and cognitive reframing.

## The "Ideal" Profile

Only a rare person would score optimally in all seven factors in this profile. Echoing Myers in chapter 2, these characteristics are not related to education, ethnicity, or social class, but would more likely be found in people who have done well with turbulence in professional sectors of the mainstream national or global economy. We expect that the more similar a person is to these characteristics, the better that person can perform as a reflexive practitioner. Although to some extent the factors in the profile are enduring and stable qualities of a person, some of these qualities can be improved or enhanced through learning. Ways to become more reflexive are presented in the next section.

Table 8.1 compares and contrasts psychological characteristics of reflexive and at-risk (as presented in chapter 3) practitioners, emphasizing how they perform under turbulence. The figure also mentions how the reflexive personality can be misfit in stable conditions. The discussion following the figure takes these characteristics one at a time.

### Emotional Stability

Emotional stability enables a reflexive practitioner to take turbulence and unknowns in stride. Doubt and uncertainty don't bother reflexive practitioners. When problems arise, reflexive people can listen and take on challenges without getting upset, lashing out at others, or blaming themselves. As a member of a work group, a reflexive practitioner can be counted on for positive outlook. They hear problems but do not get emotionally overwhelmed by them.

In the extreme, too much emotional stability, being overcontrolled, has downsides. An overcontrolled person can fail to read people and situations, fail to see urgency or hardship. Others who see looming problems that need urgent attention might be bewildered by someone who fails to show appropriate concern. Thus, there can be a distant, nonresponsive, or clueless quality to someone who is always calm. Some people who appear to be well under control actually are inflexible and can rage from time to time when control is lost (in common parlance, the "control freak"). The overcontrolled person is quite stable as long as things go his way. Another extreme that may look like emotional stability but is actually emotional flatness may result from inability to perceive social cues and ills,

Table 8.1 Characteristics of reflexive versus at-risk personalities

| | Reflexive personality in turbulence | At Risk personality in turbulence | Reflexive personality is at risk in stable conditions |
|---|---|---|---|
| Emotional control in turbulence | Stable, positive Tolerates doubt and uncertainty | Overwhelmed by complexity Rattled by uncertainty | Slow in a crisis Distracted by small matters |
| Proclivity toward relatedness | Common good Social networks | Good ideas Individuals | Any and all ideas Social butterfly |
| Openminded; curious | Uses ideas Tolerates being wrong Thoughtful, intuitive; sees ahead Multidisciplinary | Decisive Self-justifies in resolving cognitive dissonance Theoretical | Indecisive Unconcerned with errors Frequent changes of mind |
| Tolerance for conflict with others | Cooperative Responsive Approaches conflict | Competitive Partisan Conflict avoidant | Makes nice, doesn't get to work Distracted; nosy |
| Goal Attainment | Flexible, varied aims Shifts focus comfortably, agile, can act quickly | Driven to single goal, single issue (e.g., money) Focused on a plan; compulsive | Unclear what he really wants Doesn't stick to a topic |
| Intellect; reasoning | Reasons especially well nonverbally; broad conceptualizer; uses fluid intelligence to develop new ideas | Quickly seeks bottom line Drives products top down | "On the other hand" Unclear what he really contributes |
| Capacity to reflect and reframe | Lifelong learner Uses experimentation and what-if Accountable, open loop process | Well trained in specific domain expertise Resolute; closed loop | Wastes time on questioning, reading, when should be doing Endless tweaking |

perhaps symptomatic of Aspberger's syndrome or something along the autistic spectrum.

The converse extreme, being highly neurotic and easily upset, is nearly always a problem in the workplace. We've all had problems in the workplace with extreme worriers, gloomy, suspicious, or angry people. Widespread neuroticism is actually a public health problem.[10]

Positive mood is related to cognitive flexibility, adaptability, and creativity.[11] Findings from Baas and coworkers' large meta-analysis of studies in this area indicated that positive moods produce more creativity than neutral or negative moods. Putting an even finer point on it, positive mood related to happiness and approach was more associated with creativity than positive mood related to relaxation and avoidance. Related to this finding is research that shows that happy people value a task for its creative potential as well as its pleasantness.[12]

Ease and comfort with doubt and uncertainty contribute to the stability of a reflexive practitioner. Traditionally, though, many practitioners seek to quickly unburden themselves of doubt and act with resolve. These professionals will be more comfortable in work where protocols and laws can be followed (e.g., some physicians and surgeons, the military, engineering, accounting, some types of law).

*Case in Point*
This case in point is from fiction. Sister Aloysius, protagonist of the tragic play "Doubt: A Parable"[13] is a professional educator, principal of a Catholic boys' school, a job requiring maintenance of order and rules, but also surely requiring reflexive responding within in a turbulent environment. Sister Aloysius, though, has some "at-risk" personality factors, such as premature deduction and reliance on intuition (e.g., falsely accusing a colleague, a priest named Father Flynn, of giving wine to a student), selectively gathering only evidence that supports her prior intuition to distrust the priest, and steadfastness in spite of unfolding contradictions and pleas from others to amend her conclusion. For Sister Aloysius, the anxiety involved in admitting doubt is more than she can bear, so she uses resolve and principle as self-justifications. The play ends tragically, and when she finally admits her doubt, her actions have already changed lives for the worse. The tense dialogue below illustrates "at-risk" characteristics doing their destruction:[14]

> Flynn: ... *Why do you suspect me? What have I done?*
> Sister: *You gave that boy wine to drink. And you let him take the blame.*

*Flynn: That's completely untrue! Did you talk to Mr. McGinn?*
*Sister: All McGinn knows is the boy drank wine. He doesn't know how he came to drink it.*
....
*Flynn: So that's it. There's nothing there.*
*Sister: I'm not satisfied.*
....
*Flynn: ...You've got it in your head that I've corrupted this child after giving him wine, and nothing I say will change that.*
*Sister: That's right.*
*Flynn: ...You had a fundamental mistrust of me before this incident!...*
*Sister: That's true.*
*Flynn: So you admit it!*
*Sister: Certainly.*

## Proclivity toward Relatedness

Reflexive practitioners gravitate to other people and tend to trust and respect others. They like people, excitement, and stimulation. They use social networking tools. They draw strength from others, recharging their batteries by being with and talking to others. Although needing some time alone to reflect, they would never be described as loners. Within a work group, they can welcome, interact, and lead. Their proclivity toward relatedness extends to their view of community; they place great value in the common good. The good of a few is too limited in scope for reflexive practitioners.

The extraverted personality does not do well in work environments where quiet reflection is continuously needed to come up with solutions to familiar problems. If you put an extraverted reflexive practitioner in such a situation, he will likely take more time than is available, soliciting inputs from others instead of doing it himself. He may wander off with a solution, trying to encompass too much. He will appear to be dependent.

### Case in Point

This case, a composite from clinical practice, illustrates a reflexive practitioner working in the wrong job. On the one hand, the case shows the value of an extraverted person working with turbulence, but on the other hand shows a job misfit problem created by a desire for flexible goal orientation and desire to reason collaboratively.

A young, smart, outgoing IT professional provides short-term consulting services to private and government organizations about critical back office software systems. This is lucrative work done in turbulent environments, with variety, responsibility, discretion, and frequent interaction with important but stressed-out CFOs. The work requires analysis and people skills. This very level-headed, bright, energetic young woman, though, is miserable and ready to leave her job. As it turns out, the misery stems from a terrible mismatch between the results-driven compensations offered to her, added on to strong pressures from family to make good money, versus her own personal quest to develop her unique potentials. For example, she values ideas and long-term relationships far more than software products and computer code that compiles, but she gets rewarded for products. This is the sort of young woman who likes to absorb ideas and will become a reflexive practitioner, but needs an organization that lets her interact frequently with other people, build consensus products that evolve over time, and reward her for improving professional process. If her company does not recognize her value in being reflexive and move her to another position, she will leave.

Not all professionals need to be reflexive in order to be effective, especially in situations that do not require discretion, but many more professionals do need to be released to develop in this direction. The role is in demand, and doing it successfully will demonstrate its usefulness, and perhaps attract others to a new, legitimate pattern of practice.

### Openminded to Points of View; Curious

The openminded person is curious about the world and likes to explore. This person enjoys the diversity in the world, seeks novel ideas from many quarters and disciplines, and is willing to try new approaches. The openminded person experiments. He gathers data on his own ideas, is accountable, and self-correcting.

When faced with contradictions, the openminded person does not try to deny them or reframe opposing data as actually similar to the data already at hand. He does not use self-justification, explaining why some mistake he made is not actually a mistake. This quality of openmindedness is similar to Kegan and Lahey's "self-transforming mind" which is characteristic of a person who actually looks "at" diverging information instead of "through" it.[15]

Within a group, the openminded person really shines. He wants to listen to all points of view and make sure the base of support is broad. He is not interested in having his ideas win. He does not propose solutions based on a theoretical position, such as liberal or conservative, especially if it has no special relevance to the situation at hand. An openminded person, though, can run into trouble in situations where protocols need to be followed or decisions can safely be made unilaterally. Even in routine situations, an openminded person will tend to generate idea after idea, listen to absolutely everyone, and by default have the problem solved by others. Openminded people can have trouble getting closure.

*Case in Point*
SAIC is an $8 billion corporation that grew to that size within 25 years without a Grand Plan.[16] Robert Beyster, SAIC's founder (and CEO until recently) writes:

> My emphasis was on growing the business by trying out different ideas, not by excessive planning [page 106]. [As a result:] Unlike many companies where managers have to encourage their employees to innovate and 'think outside the box,' SAIC sometimes had the opposite problem. There were so many people with so many good ideas that my challenge was getting them to focus on existing targets rather than new ones [107].

The SAIC Grand Plan was more of a Grand Strategy, e.g., "Hire the best people." These people came to SAIC with ideas about succeeding in a wide variety of application areas. They created a company that surprised industry observers by anticipating and expecting changes in government priorities, not staking out an area and specializing. So, after doing well in the Reagan defense years, when defense spending decreased during the Clinton years, the company was ready. In this author's experience over the past 25+ years, I remember grousing from some that the company was too scattered, not focused, too "mom and pop," that Beyster was too fickle, the company could not make up its mind if it was a big or a small player. With the sharp acuity of hindsight, though, it seems that having an openminded company that welcomed people who could be creative and flexible was indeed a contributor to SAIC's success.

Another hindsight about SAIC's success with being openminded: for a long time it was noted as a place where people stayed many years, yet the clients and topics changed a lot. This showed that people continued to retool. SAIC did not immediately cast them aside just because there wasn't a "tight fit" in that mindless way of matching a resume to a task order. The people seemed to come first, then product development resulted from their skills.

## Tolerance of Conflict

Reflexive practitioners are able to tolerate conflict and even seek it out. Reflexive practitioners are comfortable approaching others and listening to their ideas, even when those ideas run counter to their own. A person who can handle turbulence seeks opposing or refined points of view in an effort to improve group products. When someone disagrees, this is framed as an opportunity to get new inputs. The challenge becomes how to incorporate alternate points of view, not how to avoid alternate points of view.

Within a group, a reflexive practitioner does not smooth things over. While remaining emotionally stable and flexible, he can sit with conflict around him. He does not get overwhelmed by argument. He does not compete to win, instead he accommodates others in developing consensus.

On the downside, accommodating others can be done poorly. Sometimes expertise is needed that others don't have, so polling others wastes time. In addition, time can be frittered away in pointless discussion or silly arguments about arcane or irrelevant points. Another problem attributed to accommodating others in the workplace is the manager who polls others because it is required to let people feel like they have been heard, but in truth, the decision has been made unilaterally, and consulting others is done only to comply with corporate guidance. Employees can tell when this is happening, though, and eventually rebel.

Conflict with others makes many people uncomfortable. In fact, some people avoid interpersonal conflict at all costs; they agree with anything as soon as a difference of opinion arises. They can acquiesce in important professional situations and everyday personal situations as well. There are various psychological rationales for agreeing in order to avoid interpersonal conflict: thinking that one's own ideas are poor, inadequate, or even failed; thinking that the other person's view is so widely divergent that accommodation would be difficult or impossible; feeling an insecurity that if a heated discussion would develop, things might be said that would be regretted later; having an intuition that the conflict will end badly; being resigned that one's own ideas will be rejected so it is a waste of time to argue. People who are conflict avoidant will work better alone, perhaps submitting their inputs to someone else, but not working with others to incorporate conflicting points of view.

Conflict avoidance is a common clinical problem. In the workplace, people who do not speak up for themselves can eventually feel resentful. In addition, many people who prefer to work alone become irritated by being treated as someone with potentially important inputs when they have no desire to discuss their ideas. They only want to submit their ideas in response to a problem given to them. Many people grow to hate meetings, and if they cannot be let out of them, may engage in passive-aggressive sabotage, such as chronic lateness to meetings or "forgetting" them altogether. Professionals can improve in their ability to tolerate conflict and approach it better, for example, by learning how to be less catastrophic in their assumptions about conflict and how to be clear in expressing themselves without being unpleasant. (The last section of this chapter describes the usefulness of clinical psychology in improving skills for reflexive practitioners.)

Approaching and accommodating conflict is critical professionally because extremely tough problems have to be dealt with by people who hold opposite points of view. For example, what does this country do about climate change when overwhelming scientific evidence still does not convince key people who are responsible for dealing with climate problems? What does the country do about a woman's legal right to choose when a vocal minority opposes it on religious grounds? How does the society move forward with new programs when small-government activists oppose any new spending? Burton (2008) suggests that we as a plural society could better accommodate points of view by agreeing that whatever we know is "provisional knowledge." Assuming such a cognitive stance helps us to remain open to conflict rather than avoiding the other side completely.

*Case in Point*

President Barack Obama is famously and effectively openminded to rivals, as exemplified in this excerpt. The use of approach to conflict, what-if testing, and multi-disciplinary collaboration is a feature of Obama's style.

> Obama, a former law professor, encourages debate among his advisers, asking them to stake out opposing positions and often pushing rivals to argue their points further as he listens. He listens to everyone in the room before presenting his own view and decision. "(Only) then," the adviser (Valerie Jarrett, longtime Obama colleague) said, "the meeting is over."[17]

## Flexible Goal Orientation

Reflexive practitioners enjoy variety in their strivings. They shift focus and multitask easily. They are not compulsive and do not insist on using the same behavior patterns over and over. They are able to go off a timetable. They can modify plans if necessary. They can invigorate.

In contrast, though, there is a downside to too much flexibility. Within a group, a person with a flexible goal orientation can be frustrating if schedules and adherence to plans really are required. Excessive multitasking prevents progress because energy is too diffuse and projects don't develop findings.

Sometimes a delay or overrun is overemphasized as evidence of failure. The failure may exist only in the perception of those who define success bureaucratically, placing high priority on meeting a schedule, even an arbitrary one. Some great successes were finished late and with many changes in plans.

Within today's turbulent professional environment, though, where shareholders press so hard for profits, are there really other plausible business goals besides profits? Can an organization, then, provide reflexive practitioners with other incentives besides money? Can a business be successful if it reprioritizes profit?

## Hedonic versus Eudaimonic Happiness

Research on happiness helps with this question. Waterman reminds us about the important differences between hedonic happiness and eudaimonic happiness.[18] Hedonic happiness is achieved through acquisition of pleasures and is accompanied by a feeling of relaxation and forgetting your cares; eudaimonic happiness is achieved through efforts at developing your potential and produces a feeling of invigoration. While the two are correlated, there are differences in their sustainability.

In the pursuit of hedonic pleasure, the more pleasure you get, the happier you become. Traditionally, pleasure means material pleasure, like money and what it buys. Who can deny that money makes life easier and more fun? According to Waterman, though, the big problem with equating amount of pleasure with amount of happiness is that once a pleasure is acquired, there is a need for more pleasure in order to get even happier. Such a dynamic sets up a treadmill effect, where each pleasure acquired leads only to a step toward another pleasure. Can professionals and our corporations escape the hedonic treadmill?

In contrast, eudaimonic happiness is achieved through a life well lived. This is Aristotelian happiness, the quest for fulfillment of personal potential that gives meaning to a unique individual life. As Waterman writes, reaching for eudaimonic happiness creates a staircase effect, not a treadmill. Once one part of your potential is fulfilled, you step up to fulfill even more of your potential. Even if you reach beyond your potential, and aim higher than you can achieve, you can still take pleasure in effort, according to Waterman. For Waterman, hedonic happiness is only sustainable if accompanied by eudaimonic happiness. Professionals break out of the hedonic treadmill by also aiming for eudaimonic happiness.

Happiness research provides support for inclusion of flexible goal orientation as a desirable trait of the open and flexible personality. In turbulent times, high profits are going to be harder to see anyway, so an adaptive practice could achieve satisfaction albeit with less profit. While the attainment of money and material success does make people feel happy, a more sustainable and satisfying environment can be created for reflexive professionals if developing their personal potential is an explicit part of the organization. Some professionals may be uninterested in this, and if so, fine. But if your profession or service excludes development of personal potential in reflexive practitioners, you may lose them.

## Intellectual Abilities

Reflexive practitioners reason well in a variety of ways, for example, verbally and nonverbally. People who have succeeded at higher education are typically good at verbal learning and can use words to communicate about concepts with peers. Verbal learners are often good with reasoning based on facts and verbal concepts. However, common verbal reasoning strategies relied on in college such as reading, making outlines, and writing position papers will be helpful but inadequate for thinking through the problems tackled by reflexive practitioners.

Nonverbal learners are visual and capable of broad visualization, able to find and make meaning in pictures, graphics, and objects. Nonverbal reasoning is fluid, on the spot, not relying on memory and facts. Someone with poor (or even just average) nonverbal reasoning capabilities might have difficulty with the big picture aspects of reflexive practice and not be able to think well or visualize things changing that is needed in reframing. Strategists and other reflexive professionals must be able to visualize a big, multidimensional, multidisciplinary picture and conceptualize the various parts within the scene as things change. Visual thinking and fluid intelligence will be needed.

What about memory? Must a reflexive practitioner have special qualities of memory? Assuming normal memory functioning, no special attributes of memory seem required to be a reflexive practitioner. A professional must, of course, have studied, learned, and mastered the domain knowledge of their field. A reflexive professional must keep current and refresh and expand memory through continuing education. However, someone who over-relies on rote memory and has gaps in understanding his subject matter or someone who crams a lot might not be a good reflexive practitioner. Fluid, on the spot reasoning is still required.

Kent Myers notes that Professor Emeritus Russell Ackoff (recently deceased) of the Wharton School frequently took a mathematical approach to solving problems, but did not rely on rote memory of formulas, such as the quadratic equation. He would actually freshly derive the quadratic equation when needed. This is obviously beyond most people's analytic ability, but gives a glimpse of how one creative mind was organized. Everything in Ackoff's mind was subject to redevelopment, and all the skills and energy were there to do it.

What about speed of thought, another aspect of intellect? Professionals typically have normal (or faster) processing speeds. Interestingly, though, sometimes, a very bright person has a slower than normal processing speed; this can be caused by trying to understand something fully before responding, rather than rushing through. This person may not have memorized things, may truly understand things, so is trying to fit new data into existing mental models. Someone who thinks too quickly runs the risk of premature decision making. Drawing conclusions too quickly is going to be a problem if the job is to think things through collaboratively.

We assume that strong general intelligence is required for reflexive practitioners. General mental ability (which psychologists often refer to as "g") comes in handy for just about everything! However, not every intelligent person can handle, or even wants to handle, the intellectual task of collaborative, adaptive reasoning in turbulent environments. There are even findings that general mental ability can be a drawback in certain types of cognitive adaptability, as Lang and Bliese found in a difficult military tank battle simulation using a "task change paradigm."[19] Under this paradigm, a subject is confronted with a reflexive and difficult task that unexpectedly changes and requires adaptation. Lang and Bliese distinguished two types of adaptation: transition adaption or "immediate loss of performance following a change," and reacquisition adaptation which is the learning of a new response over time. Interestingly, Lang and Bliese found that general mental ability actually detracts from transition adaptation. They found that under changed conditions, bright people simplified the task and focused on too few features. One implication for this finding is that high g, smart, reflexive practitioners need to be taught how to adapt to change better. Another implication is that personality characteristics, such as openness, could be used to select practitioners who can become good adapters.

*Reframing*

Reframing is an ability to use inputs from others as well as from oneself to review, expand, and see a situation differently. Being able to think with a work group and reflect upon other points of view is an important facet of reasoning in a reflexive practitioner. Diversity, and swarm or collective intelligence, are resources that the reflexive practitioner is prone to employ. A person who prefers to think alone or is uncomfortable debating will struggle with complexity and turbulence.

Let's compare some "at-risk" practices to see how they fail to reframe with contradictory points of view. The "interested" practitioner is all rhetoric all the time because he must win for his special interest. The "rational" practitioner wants to bludgeon people with unassailable logic. The "focused" practitioner deluges the workgroup with more and more facts and details. The "principled" practitioner trumps all with his righteous truths. None of these practitioners listens to the others.

The reflexive practitioner does not eschew any of those advocacy strategies completely, but uses them in the proper place and sequence within collaborations. The resetting of agreements and understandings must occur at such a high rate in a turbulent environment that the emphasis has to be on collaborating at multiple levels simultaneously, very quickly, constantly, with more people and concepts in the mix. An "at-risk" practice extracts too great a cost in wasting time with single-minded communication, excluding points of view, achieving a skewed solution, and then holding on to its biased result too long simply to protect its win. The reflexive practitioner has to keep people, emotionally and logically, moving to adaptive regions.

Another important aspect of cognitive reframing in reflexive professionals is insistence on hypothesis testing, what-if analysis, and self-critical thinking in evaluating professional outcomes. Tavris and Aronson make the point that some professions, such as the confidential private practice of clinical psychology or analysis of intelligence data in classified environments, are "closed loop" because results of their work are not scrutinized in public.[20] In contrast, other fields, such as practice of medicine in today's managed care environment, are scrutinized by insurance companies, and physicians veering from expected procedures are not reimbursed. This situation creates professional dissatisfaction and ethical problems, although patients/consumers do have the right to compare the treatment they receive to other options. Clinical psychologists, physicians, intelligence professionals, and other professional advice-givers, though, have an obligation to evaluate their own practices. However that is accomplished will depend on circumstances, but nevertheless, it is a professional obligation. Just feeling that you know your advice is wise or having intuition based on experience is not adequate intellectual justification to continue unexamined professional practices.

The term "evidence-based practice" refers to the use of practices that have basis in research, typically in the fields of education and medical or mental health care. How these tested practices migrate into any professional's practice though is variable. Many professionals strive to use only experimentally valid practices, avoiding alternative practices that have not helped people when tested under experimental conditions. Other professionals are most willing to use alternative treatments. Midgley describes three practitioners with respect to how they handle evidence-based practices: improvers, adapters, and rejecters.[21] Improvers and adapters support the use of evidence-based practice, although they find that applying these practices requires some discretion when applied to any given individual. However, rejecters find evidence-based practices exclusionary and harmful. They cannot reframe their own ideas with inputs from research. "Rejecters" would have trouble being reflexive practitioners owing to their negativity and disdain of objectivity.

## Becoming Reflexive

This section describes several ways professionals can become more reflexive, that is, improve in their ability to handle turbulence, work better collaboratively, and push for adaptive strategies and solutions. As mentioned earlier, it is unlikely that many individuals possess all the "ideal" characteristics in the psychological profile of the reflexive professional. Many professionals possess some of the desired qualities, but also have areas where improvements would be valuable. As described here, better adaptability can be gained through continuous self-evaluation and through specialized workplace training. Attitudes, relationships, and emotional responses (e.g., "comfort zones") can become more adaptive and reflexive through one-to-one work with a clinical psychologist. Reflexivity can also be learned from role models, from executive coaching, and through practicum education with master practitioners who have the appropriate orientation.

## Continuous Self-Evaluation

One way a reflexive practitioner could approach continuous self-evaluation is to assess oneself against the seven characteristics in the psychological profile:

- *Emotional stability*: Am I generally remaining calm and stable or becoming upset, lashing out, or acting in passive aggressive ways?
- *Proclivity toward relatedness*: Am I reaching out regularly and meeting with others?
- *Openminded and curious*: Am I reading broadly and asking others what they think or insisting on my own way?
- *Tolerance of conflict*: Am I seeking inputs only from like-minded people and shying away from conflict or am I seeking inputs from those who would disagree?
- *Flexible goal orientation*: Am I evaluating my work as to the quality and value of its process as well as its outcomes?
- *Intellect*: Am I visualizing the problem space I work in and looking ahead as it changes? Am I relying on facts I already know about the problem and forcing new data to fit in my old mental model? Am I keeping current with my domain knowledge?
- *Reframing*: Do I listen to other points of view and try to push myself into new thinking? Am I evaluating my own work or seeking quality assessments from others?
- Continuous review against these characteristics provides useful self-assessment and suggests avenues for improvement.

## Workplace Training

Workplace training can help employees to improve at handling novel and turbulent circumstances. As an example, the military needs large numbers of adaptable people in order to succeed in the turbulent fight against international terrorists. Adaptability to turbulence underlies the work of counterinsurgency, for example, the need to develop long-term trust relationships in foreign cultures, engaging in economic development and peacemaking, and conducting combat operations. As mentioned earlier, though, bright people (high "g") especially tend to simplify immediately following change rather than remain open.[22] Routine domain knowledge possessed by smart people is not sufficient for adaptability. More needs to be done to support their success in turbulent environments.

Mueller-Hanson, White, Dorsey, and Pulakos operationally define adaptation as an "effective change in response to an altered situation."[23] To develop workplace training objectives, they go on to describe four types of adaptability applicable to military personnel (but in some ways "generalizable" to other career fields): mental (adjusting one's thinking in new situations), interpersonal (adjusting what one says to make unfamiliar interactions go smoothly), physical (adjusting to tough physical environments), and the ability to teach others to be adaptable. Mueller-Hanson and associates provide evidence that these abilities can be taught and improved in military officers, finding that two factors emerge as especially important in teaching adaptability. The first factor is acquisition of domain expertise, gained through classroom work and real-life experience. The second factor is training, which includes repeated opportunities for practice under scenarios of change with provision of feedback. Mueller-Hanson and associates find that some characteristics related to adaptability are more trainable than others; these include communication skills, situation and self-awareness, and adaptability applied well in a range of scenarios.

Krynski and Tenenbaum suggest a different, possibly complementary, approach to training people to make better decisions with limited data.[24] Following a series of experiments, they found that people can be taught logical ways to use probabilities in drawing conclusions from incomplete data, such as "does this patient have a cancer or a benign tumor?" People—in this particular case, medical personnel—often use only intuition and overestimate the likelihood of a problem instead of calculating the probabilities related to all the evidence at hand to arrive at a conclusion. Professionals mismatch the evidence to the causal model; typically people fail to consider the base rate of occurrence, such as the likelihood of cancer in the general population and the likelihood of false positive mammograms in the general population. Krynski and Tennenbaum found that people can be taught to better map all the evidence to their causal mental model and arrive at more correct conclusions.

Understanding of bias, a line of research within the vast areas of "cognitive human factors" and "behavioral economics," helps us to develop training to improve decisions in complex environments. But correction of bias is not enough. It still must be put within the context of reflexive practice: need to continually scan for signs, make tentative conclusions but remain open to correction, reframe, test, and read feedback, be sensitive to weak signals of underlying dynamics, and choosing to approach threats instead of avoiding them to gain advantage without a confrontation.

Active learning is a workplace teaching method that fosters adaptability.[25] Bell and Kozlowski note that traditional training such as the lecture method fosters acquisition of routine expertise, but not adaptive performance under changing conditions. Active learning places students in difficult (usually computer-based) simulations that require self-regulation in turbulent environments. In a series of experiments, the authors developed simulations to provide practice in cognitive, motivational, and emotional aspects of performance under stress. Getting the students to use exploration improved the cognitive aspect of training and produced more adaptive transfer than proceduralized instruction. Encouraging students to experiment and feel free to make errors improved the motivational aspect of training and also improved adaptability. Encouraging students to remain calm improved the emotional aspect of training and helped students report lower stress levels, but did not improve adaptive performance.

## Clinical Psychology

The methods of clinical psychology (a professional practice requiring state licensure) are much different from training or simulation experiences provided in workplaces. Clinical psychology addresses the personal characteristics of professionals, their intellect, gifts, thoughts, attitudes, feelings, and typical behavior patterns. Many personal characteristics addressed by clinical psychology are thought to be attributable to "nature," but "nurture" (e.g., life experience, study, practice) plays a large role in how these characteristics are manifested within any individual. Clinical psychology and psychotherapy provide ways for reflexive practitioners to clarify their capabilities and improve in their professional effectiveness.

Clinical psychologists are trained to provide assessment, psychological interventions, and follow-up to individuals with a broad spectrum of concerns in daily life as well as concerns that could be diagnosable psychological disorders. Many clinical psychologists specialize in topics related to workplace performance and executive personality. Developing personal characteristics such as better emotional control under stress, friendliness, and acceptance of others' ideas, improved ability to approach and resolve conflict, and smarter ways to think all fall in the domain of clinical psychology.

Two important processes in clinical psychology are increasing personal awareness and making changes in cognition, emotions, and behavior. If a reflexive practitioner consults with a clinical psychologist, the process starts with the professional describing his problem areas (e.g., trouble getting along with multiple bosses, doesn't like being rushed, doesn't like being criticized, dissatisfied with others' performance, wanting to quit job but concerned about finding another one, all work no play, need to make more money). Through free flowing and guided conversations, perhaps also using personality profiling or cognitive testing, problems are clarified. The professional's self-awareness of how he sees himself, others, and the world, and how others might see him are up for discussion. A professional can deconstruct a workplace problem, and analyze his own role, the role of others, and the role of involved institutions. A professional comes to identify his or her own personal tendencies of emotions, thoughts/attitudes, and behaviors. They come to see what mistakes are made every time (e.g., Do I tend to side every time with management? Do I always ally with underdogs? Do I always make light of financial concerns? Have I gotten away from my values? Do older female supervisors remind me of my mother?). Another equally important area to clarify is what the professional gets right (e.g., Why do people seek me out? What do I offer? Do I have allies? Do I know who or what to stay away from? Do I keep current?).

Following problem clarification, the professional starts identifying things to change. This includes their own attitudes, feelings, and behavior, not trying to change others. Even if you are management, you can do little to change the personalities of others in the workplace. Then methods for change in work behavior are pursued. Examples include cognitive behavior psychotherapy for stress management; acceptance and commitment psychotherapy to commit to self-experiments with new behaviors; and bibliotherapy or study of recommended readings.

As an example, a practitioner might be a professional who succeeded in college and career for many years by setting goals, developing schedules and milestones, and producing final products, pleased to be a sole author. But now the professional finds himself in a more turbulent environment where analysis and consensus products are valued more than delivering final products on time. In working with a psychologist, the professional could try self-experiments with new behaviors. For example, he could determine to find value in working with others, could become better at checking in with others, could teach himself to be more interested in what others think, and could undertake stress reduction activities in his personal life. Sometimes behavior changes can be done readily.

Other times, though, behavior change isn't so easy, and the professional may need to look more closely at himself to find out why. Maybe collaborating with others creates too much uncomfortable stress. Using cognitive psychotherapy, he might examine underlying beliefs held about other people, perhaps finding, as an example, that he assumed at some level that others seek to cheat him. Previously, this might have been unknown to the professional. He can work to become more confident about the motives of others and search for ways to share better. Alternatively, the practitioner's problem might be that collaborating with others seems too divergent from his own professional value to create products of his own. He may benefit from reviewing and clarifying his own life and career goals, possibly reframing them to learn to find satisfaction in the process of learning instead of taking satisfaction only in final products.

The clinical psychologist providing the psychotherapy needs an awareness of reflexive practice. A reflexive practitioner would not be served by a psychologist who encourages a client to control turbulence, rather one who encourages a client to work within it. A psychotherapy approach that emphasizes me-first or establishment of the client as an authority might tend to foster "principled" professionals who are more didactic than interactive. Psychotherapy that fosters strength, persuasion, and competitiveness could foster "interested" professionals, who seek to beat the opposition.

Clinical psychology cannot create reflexive practitioners. It cannot change an introvert into an extrovert, or take a curmudgeon and turn him into a charmer, but clinical psychology can teach motivated people to become more interactive and reflexive. Sometimes work with a clinical psychologist will lead to a realization that one is in the wrong field, and a better work match should be sought.

## Executive Coaching

An executive coach specializes in working with business leaders. Often, executive coaching uses the processes of mentoring or role modeling. For example, an executive who had worked successfully within turbulent environments could be employed as an executive coach. The advice he gives will arise from his own experiences and thus could be very valuable and inspiring. The coach could be a good role model and mentor.

Some executive coaches, who may not be experienced executives themselves, use goal-setting processes. They help their clients to identify problems, set their own goals for better workplace performance, and set up schedules to attain the goals. The coach helps the client to track progress and develop remedial plans for missed goals. Such a coach might be an adjunct to a role model or mentor.

If an executive client finds goal attainment difficult using coaching, a consultation with a licensed clinical psychologist could be in order. For example, personality characteristics such as excessive need for control, extreme worry, poor stress tolerance, inability to handle conflict, or difficulty sustaining focus on the tasks at hand may interfere with the coaching process.[26] For those executives, clinical psychology may be more advantageous.

# 9

# Reflexive Practice on the Global Scene

*Kim Forss*

The purpose of this section is to illustrate global organizational practices and examples of reflexive practice (even if that concept is not known to the actors that are described here). These cases raise questions about the concept of leadership and the current discussions around what constitutes a good leader. In some of the cases there is no "leader" and in others traditional leadership is not particularly significant. It is more relevant to see these case studies as illustrations of collective action with many individual roles.

As a starting point, I would like to refer to the current debate on global leadership and in particular the devastating criticism of the present Secretary General of the United Nations. Indeed, there are many things that he can be criticized for, in particular what appears as a passive stance on many global challenges. A different interpretation is possible. The Secretary General paid a visit to Sweden and (amazingly) he also visited some schools and met with students. The whole visit was covered on TV and some students were asked what they thought of the Secretary General—arguably one of the most influential and prestigious jobs in the world. A 15-year-old girl said, "I think he was nice. He was an ordinary kind of person. It makes me think that I could also get a job like that if I study hard and work for peace and security." When the Secretary General's leadership is discussed, one should not forget the ability to inspire common people to do good things, though the style is perhaps not as flashy as that of many other leaders, and not what we have come to expect.

Perhaps expectations need to change. These following cases examine the evolving middle management roles, professional practices, learning organizations, and problem framing in substantive fields. I'm not only interested in the concepts of management and organization, but also how people actually work, despite what the formal accounts say. What I hope to show is that organizing for peace and reconciliation in, for example, Liberia or Sierra Leone, is more worthy of our attention for understanding how people can succeed today, more worthy than belabored refinement of industrial processes (cars, refrigerators, toothpaste, etc.) that are a mixed contribution to social development and adaptation at best. We need to address not only how things are managed, but also what it is that is managed—the purposes to which skills in organization and governance are put to use. The four cases reflect different social realities and different issues:

- Concerned Parents Association in Uganda (peace and security)
- China Council for Technical and Scientific Cooperation (environmental management)
- MAMTA/SRIJAN network for sexual and reproductive health and rights in India (health and well-being)
- Export of organic products from Africa (economic production and trade)

## Concerned Parents

Uganda has had a troublesome history over the past 40 years and the northern parts of the country have been hit hard by civil war beginning in the early 1990s. The fighting is not over yet, even though a tentative peace process between the government and the rebel group "The Lord's Resistance Army" (LRA) was initiated in 2007. The LRA has been a particularly grim enemy; it has become globally infamous for its atrocities against civilians and for kidnapping children to become child soldiers. It has also been a difficult group to engage with for peace talks and political negotiations as it never had any political agenda.[1] You can't easily negotiate with people who have no other aim than to plunder, destroy, kill, and rape.

On October 10, 1996, a group of LRA soldiers attacked the village of Aboke and as always went on a rampage massacring people of every sex and age, burning houses, kidnapping children, and then taking to the forest quickly. This attack was not much different from thousands of other attacks. The LRA took 136 girls who had been at the St. Mary's College. As the surviving villagers gathered together, some of the parents of the abducted girls decided that they should pursue the LRA group and try to get them to release the girls. Most people supported the idea and a small group of parents set out on foot after the LRA group.

The LRA bands were known to move rapidly through the dry forests and savannas of northern Uganda. Even though it is a thinly populated countryside, farmers and cattle-keepers are there to observe. With their aid, the pursuing parents were able to track the LRA group for weeks. At some points they even managed to contact them, sometimes by having meetings mediated by people in villages who were sympathetic with the LRA or who had relatives fighting for them. Through such pragmatic and tenuous means the parents could establish sporadic dialogue with the kidnappers. They eventually reached areas far away from home, in some cases in Sudan and in Congo where the leadership hid and where the groups got their arms and supplies from sources in Sudan.

Here the group of parents visited the LRA bases and they got to see how many children were kept there. It has later been estimated that as many as 50,000 children were kidnapped by the LRA. Young boys were trained to be soldiers or used for various errands and the girls were kept for household work. Most girls were sexually abused.[2] The negotiations, or rather the pleading and persuasion from the parents from Aboke, were lengthy (they did not have anything to negotiate about, they could just ask for mercy for their children). However, they gradually had their children released and by 2006, 100 of the 139 abducted girls had returned to their families. It is, of course, terrible that so many have been lost, but it is a victory for the parents that many were released.

This is a remarkable achievement and a remarkable story and it is hard for me and probably for most readers to imagine what it means to survive such an attack, to mobilize and set out in pursuit of savage kidnappers, to track them for weeks and months and establish contacts, to enter into their bases completely at their mercy, and to return again and again over many years. It is not this achievement, however, which is the point of this case.

When visiting the LRA camps these parents from Aboke realized that they were not the only parents whose children had been stolen. Given that the LRA is estimated to have kidnapped some 50,000 children there would be 100,000 other mothers and fathers—not mentioning brothers and sisters and other relatives—who had suffered this loss. So they decided to work not only for themselves but also for other parents. They built on the contacts they had established with the LRA and over the next ten years they kept negotiating for the release of children and for their return home. The LRA kept up with its murderous attacks and the fighting did not diminish, but throughout, the groups of parents maintained contacts and got large numbers of children released.[3]

Soon after the attack on Aboke the parents there set up an organization called "Concerned Parents Association." Their aim is to promote peace and protect the rights of war-affected families in Uganda through advocacy, psychosocial support, and community empowerment. They have developed a network of Parents Support Groups in more than 500 locations in northern Uganda (much like what they themselves started out with). Once the peace process started, their work shifted—not so much pursuing the LRA but more to provide continuous help in resettlement. Many children have been away from their families for ten years or more and it is not easy to come back into the communities (many of which have dispersed and remaining relatives may live in refugee camps). But the Concerned Parents Association continues this work and they have skillfully extended their networks, supported other communities, and set an example of courage, initiative and practical skills when it comes to defending human rights.[4] Table 9.1 sums up the case with respect to general features of reflexive practice.

Table 9.1 Reflexive practice in the case of Concerned Parents Association

| Feature of Reflexive Practice | Characteristics of the Concerned Parents Association and the Environment It Works In |
|---|---|
| Turbulence | Extremely turbulent environment in the civil war in northern Uganda; long-lasting, shifting alliances, informal and formal conflicts, different tribal groups moving in and out of the armed conflict |
| Complex | Motives for action unknown, rapid changes in logic, random violence and also random acts of mercy and reconciliation |
| Reflexive | The action of organizations change the logic of the conflict and every actor and his/her activities are embedded in the conflict |
| Judgment is uncertain | The role of theory in understanding social relations limited for the actors described here |
| Unanticipated effects | Concerned parents started with one simple logic, to get their children back, but it soon grew to a large organization with long-range development objectives |
| Development potentials | Their experience can be a source of inspiration in less evil situations and can also serve as a practical guide when violence and civil war break out again—as it unfortunately will do. |

## China Council

The environmental problems caused by economic growth in China are enormous, and if there is any single factor that would jeopardize peace, stability and continued growth (and probably democracy as well), it would be the inability to manage environmental deterioration. This case is about an effort to address the political will of the government and, through advocacy, get it to address environmental issues and to provide the scientific basis for action. The China Council for International Cooperation on Environment and Development (CCICED, or the Council) was set up in 1992 as a high level advisory body to the government of China (formally on the initiative of the State Council of China). The Council's stated purpose is "to further strengthen cooperation and exchange between China and the international community in the field of environment and development."

From the very beginning, the Canadian International Development Agency (CIDA), has been a key supporter of the CCICED. The government of China provided support, in cash and in-kind. Later, Canada was joined in funding the Council by other bilateral aid agencies, such as Norway's Ministry of Foreign Affairs and Swedish Sida. A self-assessment of the CCICED was conducted in 2000 and the exercise sought to rethink some of the Council's components and operations. These changes were implemented in order to ensure that the CCICED continued to respond to the needs of China in an efficient and timely fashion.[5]

The project's objective was to provide the government of China with recommendations on sustainable development and environmental protection, allowing policy makers to be better informed. The Council provided more than a hundred recommendations annually to the government. Many of these were timely and relevant, and there was also evidence that several of them have had an impact. It is possible to outline five major categories of impact coming from the recommendations: (1) use in the policy formulation process by the government of China, (2) new legislation on environmental issues, (3) new organizational structures set up to work with environment and sustainable development, (4) continued research on technical, economic, and other issues, (5) implementation of projects based on suggestions from the Task Forces and the Annual Meeting of the Council.

The quality of the recommendations varied greatly. Some were rather general and obvious, others were technically very narrow. Some recommendations do not reflect a full understanding of the Chinese context. At times, the focus of the Council was out of phase with the development plans and the rallying concepts of Chinese policy-making. There was a need to improve the quality of the policy recommendations in order to optimize project effectiveness and long-term results. But by and large the creation of the Council and its work over the past 17 years was a useful example of leadership on an issue of global concern, and the Chinese environment is likely to have been significantly worse if the China Council had not been initiated. So it is interesting to see how the Council works, as that displays what some forms of organizational solutions to address a global change may look like.

- *The Council and its membership.* At 54 members the Council is a large organization and such an organization needs to be large. It was a great advantage to have many members but the organization had to struggle with confusion over the roles played by government members as they are both on the giving and receiving ends of policy advice, but that could hardly be avoided.
- *The Executive Bureau.* The Council is managed by an Executive Bureau which has approved its present structure, function, and membership. It is the Executive Bureau that manages the operations of the organization, funding the different research programs, monitoring progress and organizing feedback to the government.
- *The Lead Expert Group provides strategic direction to the Council.* The Lead expert group has a flexible composition with core members to be complemented by short-term members whose expertise is needed to handle the specific focus of the Annual General Meeting. There are both Chinese and foreign members of the group.
- *The Task Forces.* The actual work of scientific cooperation occurs in task forces that focus on rather short (two-year) research projects, with a clear, practical and policy- relevant focus. Each task force is composed of a team of Chinese and foreign researchers, and the projects take the form of bilateral cooperation between Chinese and foreign universities/ research organizations.
- *The Annual General Meeting.* This is the crux of the matter. The research of the task forces is presented at the Annual General Meeting of the Council, where high level representatives of the government take part (ministers, parliamentarians, municipal governments, etc).

Since its beginning the Council has provided advice on a number of critical environmental management issues. As an example, the Council financed research on watershed management, in particular on the organization issues of managing water resources and especially along the Yang-tze-kiang valley. More than 100 million people live in the surrounding areas and depend on the river for many aspects of their lives, from power generation to water for consumption and transports up and down the river, and inevitably the river system has become highly polluted. Efficient and effective use of the resources are hampered by fragmented decision making in organizations that have mandates built on a sector-specific logic. Hence the well-known problems of free-riders has made it impossible to mobilize any action to protect the river as a resource for sustainable use. The research has provided knowledge on how to set up cross-sectoral agencies, how to build networks among agencies, and how to develop transparent and responsible governance structures. These changes take time, but the China Council had an impact on policy-making and legislation.

Table 9.2  Characteristics of the China Council and the environment it works in

| Feature of Reflexive Practice | Characteristics of the Concerned Parents Association and the Environment It Works In |
| --- | --- |
| Turbulence | Politics, environment and rapid growth change by leaps and bounds and when the system collapses, as it does occasionally, the effects reverberate in unpredictable ways |
| Complex | Large numbers of actors, at national, regional and communal levels affect the system, with different interests and objectives and changing relations to each other |
| Reflexive | The advocacy work creates its own logic and the provision of evidence on problems and on solutions get the actors on the Council further involved in policies and in management |
| Judgment is uncertain | The role of the research is also to point to uncertainties and advice on cautious paths of action, thus increasing rather than reducing the level of uncertainty in the system |
| Unanticipated effects | The aim of the Council was to affect policies, but it could not predict exactly which policies, when and how, when it was formed. Many years later, it can be found to have had much more and more diverse impacts than the originators of the Council could have imagined. |
| Development potentials | The Council presents an example of policy advice and international cooperation which both has continued relevance in China and that could be a workable model in many other fields and in different countries. |

The Council has addressed a large number of other issues such as desertification and land use in dry areas of Western China, socially responsible mining operations, and effectiveness of legal systems of environment protection. The Council has been successful because of its long-term commitment to environmental issues, its constructive engagement with issues, and the focus on policy relevant research and practical recommendations, and thus it has for long also had the attention of the highest levels in the Chinese government and much of its advice has been followed up in action.

The next case is another example of policy development, practical action on social development issues and the defense of human rights, but it starts at a more basic level and it does not take the concerned organization as far into policy development as the China Council went.

## Sexual and Reproductive Health

This is the story of an organization that was initiated in the late 1980s. Contrary to the other cases, it is possible to speak of a founding entrepreneur who saw a social need for action and responded to that. The cause for concern was the sexual and reproductive health and rights in India. What does that mean? Young people were deprived of their rights (and still are) because of uneven educational opportunities, compulsion to work at home and outside, poor nutrition and lack of access to adequate food, and increasing stress (of both school-going and out-of-school adolescents) and violence—all leading to a range of biological, social, and psychological problems. Early marriage and childbearing before attaining full physical development were universal and the incidence of spontaneous abortion among girls aged 15 to 19 was higher compared to the general population.[6]

The sexual and reproductive health and needs were poorly understood and ill served at all policy-making levels—national, state, and district. Adolescents have very special and distinct needs and these were consistently overlooked. They did not receive the attention they deserve. The existing public health system services provided services for married adolescent girls only and none for boys. Moreover, the declining sex ratio was in itself a disturbing indicator of gender discrimination, also to be seen in the low nutritional status of girls, selective abortions of female fetuses due to the "dowry system" and "son preference," and early marriage resulting in early pregnancies, high fertility, and high maternal mortality rate among teenage girls.

The psychological concerns of adolescents were accentuated by parental discord, rapidly changing social and cultural values, increasing exposure to global media, different life styles, and exposure to different cultures. Characterized by high-risk behavior such as substance abuse, premarital sexual activity and antisocial behavior on the one hand and lack of adequate knowledge of sexuality, contraception, sexually transmitted diseases including HIV/AIDS, and reproduction on the other hand put the young people in a vulnerable situation. There was a clear need for effective counseling, information, and health services specifically—but none were provided by the government services and only a small percentage of those in need were reached by a few scattered nongovernmental organization (NGO) projects.

The newly founded organization thus had many things to address. The main focus was (and is) on young people—male/female, married/unmarried, and in/out of school—in the age group of 10 to 24 years and from poor and disadvantaged sections of the society. The overall goal is to create an enabling environment for improved health and development of young people through an integrated approach to sexual and reproductive health and rights, especially of poorer sections of society by promoting gender equality. While it all started with the organization MAMTA, this has now expanded to being a network of Indian NGOs named Sexual and Reproductive Rights Initiative for Joint Action (SRIJAN), with partners in seven states.[7] The project rests on six broad strategies of advocacy, research and documentation, informatics, networking, phased interventions, and global partnership in development. Each of the six above-mentioned interventions has its own specific objectives:

1. *Network*: a strengthened network of at least 200 NGOs in 10 states along with enabled youth
2. *Advocacy*: policy environment for young people that reflects and supports reproductive and sexual health and strategies
3. *Research and Development*: support base on specified issues and systematic documentation to feed into project initiatives
4. *Informatics*: a strengthened resource and training base at national and state to capacitate young people and related stakeholders
5. *Phased intervention*: successful implementations and developed models for future replicability and scaling up
6. *Global partnership in development*: a forum for global partnership in the development of reproductive and sexual health of young people

By the end of 2009, MAMTA was a well-established organization in India. The organization has played a major role in affecting national legislation in several fields, for example by advocating for and providing advice on how to develop a curriculum on reproductive health for schools. The organization combines research on projects at village levels and also in urban slums, and it interacts with the government on policy issues. It combines field work where experiences of real living conditions are needed to inform research, policy development, and international operations.

The network is also significant. India is a vast country and MAMTA could not possibly be everywhere. Besides, when the organization started work it was not alone. Several others were doing similar work all over India, but none did so at the policy level. So MAMTA gathered many others together in the SRIJAN network. It started informally but has since become a formal network with a governance structure (constitution, board, annual meetings) and a set of joint activities, such as common training, soliciting finances together, and sharing experiences of best practice.

Table 9.3 Characteristics of the SRIJAN Network and the environment it works in

| Feature of Reflexive Practice | Characteristics of the Concerned Parents Association and the Environment It Works In |
|---|---|
| Turbulence | Political issues, in particular fundamentalist religion, plays a major role in the development of reproductive health and rights of young people—boys as well as girls |
| Complex | Large numbers of actors, at national, state and village levels affect the system, with different interests and objectives and changing relations to each other |
| Reflexive | The advocacy work creates its own logic and the provision of evidence on problems and on solutions get the civil society organizations (MAMTA and SRIJAN network) further involved in policies and in management |
| Judgment is uncertain | The actors have to be very cautious in judgment and must treat the other actors very carefully given the ethical and moral sensitivity of issues and the deep cultural conflicts that can arise |
| Unanticipated effects | The aim of the MAMTA and the network was to affect policies, but they could not grasp the resistance that would be met, nor the support that emerged from many locations. |
| Development potentials | The rights and responsibilities are global and the experiences of MAMTA and SRIJAN in India are of relevance in many other locations. |

## Organic Agriculture

The fourth case takes us back to Uganda but now in another region. The events described here also took place in the region shared by Tanzania and Zambia.

In the early 1990s the cash crop economies of these countries faced several problems. In many places the cash crop cultivations that were introduced during colonial times were damaged by misguided policies, land reforms, shifting patterns of trade and cultivation, and by lacking inputs, such as fertilizers and pesticides. It struck some agricultural extension workers and some consultants from the Netherlands and Sweden that this opened up new opportunities. Many of crops exported were sold at regular prices, as for example, cocoa, coffee, tea, cashew nuts, dried fruits and fruit juices, sesame, vanilla, spices, cotton, lemon grass, and other products. But many of these products also had an organic market, and if you could sell on the organic market the prices would be significantly higher—often 20 percent higher. If the African exporters could sell their products as organic they would be much better off. The organic markets are growing much faster than the markets for ordinary products and the demand is very high.

An initial group of enthusiasts started a program that they called EPOPA—export promotion of organic products from Africa. It is a private sector program, developing markets on the local and international levels through business, and in doing so it is expected to benefit rural communities by increasing agricultural production and smallholder farmers' incomes. The export projects under EPOPA started by identifying a crop where there is a demand for organic products. It then proceeded to identify exporters and to solicit their interest in getting access to the market for the organic products. The exporter should be an already established firm, for example a coffee trading company, which sees a competitive advantage in the organic coffee. If the exporter is interested in the business proposal, the firm is assisted in setting up a system for buying organic products; that is, registering, contracting, and certifying farmers, buying the organic crop, and establishing contacts with importers of organic products. This entails an investment in capacity within the firms, and in training and supporting farmers, as well as in certifying the process. Through EPOPA, there is a cost-sharing model whereby EPOPA contributes to training and systems development—a support that is phased out over a period of three to four years.

The overall goal of EPOPA was to improve the livelihood in rural communities and to increase export volumes and value of organic products from Africa, benefiting rural communities, while the agricultural sector is exposed to sustainable farming techniques. During the 13 years of the project, a total of 11 full export projects were initiated and completed. In addition, a number of smaller export projects were also implemented, where EPOPA helped solve specific bottlenecks, but where it was not necessary to go into a full project.

Impact studies of each completed project confirmed that there is a considerable impact on livelihood in rural communities. Approximately 31,000 farmers have additional annual incomes of an average of 500,000 Ugandan shillings. This represents an additional net income that can be used for housing improvements, school fees, new lands, or consumption. In total, the export value of the EPOPA projects amounted to US$5.3 million in 2006, and the total extra amount of money paid into rural communities because of the organic and quality premium was US$932,000 in 2006.[8]

When EPOPA started in 1995 there was no organic sector in Uganda. A few exporters had started pilot projects in cotton and sesame, but that was all. There were no organizations of organic sector stakeholders, no policy documents, no recurring training program, and no certification facilities. Uganda did not participate in international trade fairs. In 2007 the organic sector was estimated to have a turnover of US$15 million, and there were 85,000 registered small-scale farmers and many more programs under conversion but not yet delivering certified organic products.

The rapid growth of the sector has obviously not been caused by EPOPA alone. A number of committed Ugandan businessmen and women, people working for NGOs, officials in the Export Promotion Board, and many others have shaped the sector. There has been support from other funding agencies. But it is doubtful whether that would have been possible without the pioneering efforts of EPOPA. A list of organic producers in Uganda is more or less similar to a list of projects that have received support from EPOPA, either as full export projects or in the form of limited support to exporters. EPOPA has been involved in setting up trade organizations and in developing a certification company, it has participated in the development of an organic agriculture policy, it has organized participation in trade fairs, and has helped in many other ways. The country management team of EPOPA has a wide network of contacts and appears to be involved in most of the significant events and developments in the sector.

The brief exposition here suggests that EPOPA has been reasonably efficient, highly effective, with a high and sustainable impact, and relevant in the light of development issues as expressed in Uganda's development strategy. The program was a pioneering effort and that has made implementation more difficult and it has faced more resistance both in Uganda and in Sweden than expected, which is one of the reasons for the somewhat lower "score" on efficiency. Consequently, effectiveness and impact could also have been higher in theory. On the other hand, resistance and doubt always face pioneering efforts and the question is, could any other actor could have achieved what EPOPA has done between 1995 and 2008? Many lessons can be learned, but this case taps some potentials that remain dormant in many other projects. More projects might benefit from these potentials if professional program designers understood what the right conditions were for them to be engaged, and set about to create those conditions. A reflexive practitioner will be sensitive to these options which others have overlooked as mere noise scattered about the "fundamentals" of economic development. We present here a preliminary list of these features:

- *Private and public sector contributions.* First of all, and most important, the program shows that it has been possible to work with the private sector and with different firms, from multinational trading companies to small private exporters, and to generate substantial and sustainable income increases for rural farmers.
- *Program objectives.* The program did not fall into the trap of setting quantifiable targets where that is not appropriate. Many programs fall into the trap of setting easily quantifiable but inappropriate targets. They measure what is measurable rather than discuss what is significant. The rather general purpose and targets have lent the program flexibility to respond to different situations and to move to institutional development, learning, and sharing activities in the latter phases.
- *Program design.* The most important lesson to be learned on program design is that the design has been evolving. New activities have been added, the first flanking activities in the late 1990s and early 2000s, others being added later. The balance between export projects and flanking activities gradually shifted. The concrete experience of the export projects, and their success, paved the ground for and increased the need for institutional development. It would probably have been disastrous

to start with the institutional development activities and bring in the export projects later—although that would be a general approach that is not uncommon in development cooperation.
- *Program management.* Having two consulting firms, one Swedish and one Dutch, jointly managing a program over 13 years in a rather difficult environment would seem very risky and would lead to unnecessary and overlapping work. However, in this case it has worked very well. The companies have complemented each other and the fact that they were two firms has meant that someone has been present to solve problems and provide backstopping support. EPOPA shows how the balance between change and continuity should be established.
- *Project concept.* While the overall program purpose is clear but rather general, the design of the export projects is specific. The systems for registration, certification, contracting, and purchases are very clear. There is a clearly described and easily comprehensible division of labor between actors. There are sound incentives built into contractual relations for the actors to perform their roles. The results are recorded and can be accumulated across exporters to a program level. There are well-established training programs for field officers as well as for farmers and these training programs have found a form that can be replicated. When the exporters expand, they repeat the systems development and the training.
- *Results.* The results show that it has been necessary to channel funds to the exporters so that their commercial risks are lowered. Risk capital is not easily available in Uganda, although it is necessary on projects such as these. It has also been necessary to assist with the system design and to provide training for the control system and to reduce the initial costs of certification. The need to absorb some of the risk for exporters remains, particularly when new organic crops are developed. Full export projects have been supplemented by specific export projects, also called flanking activities. As the organic sector has grown, the demand for such flexible and quick sources of problem-solving funds has increased. In the future, it is likely that smaller amounts of funding, quickly responding to specific needs to solve bottlenecks in trade, will be more in demand than full export projects. Furthermore, grants may have been justified in a situation with limited competition and few actors. As the sector grows, such grants risk distorting competition and it is necessary to find other ways of financing such needs, as, for example, through a system of revolving funds.

Table 9.4 sums up the main points of this case in terms of reflexive practice.

Table 9.4  Characteristics of the EPOPA and the environment it works in

| Feature of Reflexive Practice | Characteristics of the Concerned Parents Association and the Environment It Works In |
|---|---|
| Turbulence | Crops have ups and downs and the markets are extremely volatile, it is not unusual for prices to go up and down by hundreds of percentage points—depending on natural disasters and human disasters |
| Complex | Many tropical crops involve several middlemen between producer and consumer and there are many organizational interests, all with open and hidden objectives and vested interests |
| Reflexive | All actors can have systems impact and whole communities rapidly follow suit if they see good and profitable practice |
| Judgment is uncertain | The actors have to be very cautious in judgment and must treat the other actors very carefully given the commercial importance of crop decisions |
| Unanticipated effects | The organic agriculture project had many unanticipated social effects, shifting incomes in families and leading to new patterns of expenditure |
| Development potentials | The organizational experiences spread, but so do the practice of organic farming—witness the growth from zero to 200,000 registered farmers in about a decade |

## Conclusions from the Four Cases

What is it then that unites these four cases, and what are the implications in terms of network organization, leadership, communities of practice, and organizational learning? There are certainly differences among the cases and there are features common to some, but not to all. The following list summarizes some of the emerging themes:

1. *The speed of change.* The "problem" never stays the same and is continuously reinterpreted by participants. In all the four cases we see how the activities have shifted, how one problem was embedded in another, and how the problems first identified and confronted changed character and thus how the people and the organizations changed their approaches and the means by which they pursued their ends, shifting ends as well.
2. *The ethics of motivation.* The actors started these organizations and identified their areas of work out of real concerns with ethics and

morality and our basic human rights—be they derived from the right to a livelihood, to safe and secure living conditions, to a sound environment, or to sexual and reproductive rights. Friendship between the actors, solidarity between groups, and a strong sense of being engaged in moral causes bound them together and made the organizations extremely successful.

3. *Responding to emergencies.* The activities described started in direct response to emergencies. There were no formal strategies or processes to plan action initially—the events can all be seen as emergent. Later on, some adopted more formal planning processes in order to have access to finances, but I would say that the core of activities, the fundamental nature of the processes, retained their emergent characteristics.

4. *Grasping opportunities.* An aspect of this emergent nature is that the organizations changed in accordance to needs and opportunities. MAMTA formed the network and developed its activities at national levels. The concerned parents moved from their own children's safety to that of all Ugandan children. The China Council diversified its approach to environmental issues and tackled them in new and interdisciplinary ways.

5. *Building and sustaining networks.* What started as a small organization in each of these cases rapidly developed into large networks with hundreds of actors. The objectives were mostly fuzzy, but grounded in a clear sense of human rights and in right livelihoods. The networks were basically informal and kept together through many loose ties rather than a few strong ties.

6. *Breaking traditional management prescriptions.* There was seldom any clear leadership, mostly an overlapping division of labor, vague objectives but strong ethics, and often weak financial stability.

7. *Strong reflexive practitioners among professional staff.* This involved a culture of questioning, tremendous professional substance, prevalence of performance data, accountability, and sense of service, and much volunteering work.

Strategic uncertainty remains high in these networks and their future course is open. On the other hand, people in the organizations do not always worry over what comes next. The networks and the organizations are not ends in themselves and the people who work there now could equally well work for different reasons—or the same—in other organizational contexts. Organizations come and go, and while ingenuity in organizational solutions is important, as the example of both the China Council and EPOPA show, the real issue lies in the action to solve practical problems. There is an art of problem solving here that Ackoff might have recognized.[9]

# 10

# Building Reflexive Practice in Graduate Education

*James T. Ziegenfuss, Jr.*

Questions about the capability of the education system are quite common. Critical commentary has ranged from curriculum to faculty to teaching strategies to relevance. We have come to recognize several national challenges—namely, that education systems at all levels are in need of redesign and that our future generation of leaders must be given greater opportunities to be engaged at earlier points in their learning. There is emerging consensus on these simple but difficult issues. If we skip ahead to acceptance of the need for complexity in thought and action (a large skip for some), we move to the point of considering when and how to introduce this style of thinking about and responding to problems. In this chapter, I will present several modest attempts to introduce reflexive practice in graduate programs directed at mid-career professionals from a variety of fields. We begin with the necessity in the education field, nicely stated by Russell Ackoff and Sheldon Rovin:[1]

> A basic requirement of moving into a new age is creative thinking. But schools stifle creativity, particularly in children, by insisting that they conform to standards of behavior and belief, and by teaching them to respond to questions with answers that are expected of them. Answers that are expected cannot be creative, precisely because they are expected. Creative answers are necessarily surprising, unexpected. The current American educational system can be characterized as having students memorize known (expected) answers to predetermined questions. In an effort to please their teachers, students memorize predigested material selected by their teachers or others, material that fails to inform students about the changing nature of society and what the changes mean. Parents often reinforce the conservative efforts of teachers.

In a limited way, teaching reflexive practice skills begins the process of transformation, meaning implementation of successful strategies for a wide range of social system problems.

## Challenges

The challenge is to rethink our approach to teaching and to problems. We need new conceptions of purpose and process, i.e., a reframing and incorporation of multiple perspectives aimed at the common good. If change were easy, it would have been done—elements of the need for change in pedagogy theory and practice have been recognized by educators for some time. To begin to understand the barriers in this field, we must address at least several outstanding challenges:

- Efforts to open the process of teaching generates fear and resistance.
- Much of our education efforts continue to rely on rote memory as the learning strategy.
- Active participation by students, while increasing, is still not widespread at colleges and universities and is delivered with a shortage of proven methodologies.
- Distance education has emerged as a potentially disruptive technology.
- A culture of entrenched professionals has been at work in the same ways for many years/decades.

Viewed in this context we need to change the culture of the educational system while we address the development of new approaches (e.g., reflexive practice) to teaching students at all levels. We can best initiate the discussion by considering a topic for teaching—the creation of America's future in whole and in parts. Rather than address "constructed exercises," students are asked to tackle redesign of some part of America (in an effort to contribute to thinking about America's future). Why have we chosen a country level subject and why America in particular? Inside America today we find the following troublesome situations ( a short illustrative set):

- Employers face the fear of constantly changing business environments, seemingly unable to control their own destiny, hobbled by taxes and global competition.
- Employees individually and in teams struggle to balance the competing demands of quality and costs in fields from health care to transportation.
- Safety of products and services from foods to transport to security is suspect, but we move reluctantly to acknowledge and act on the deficiencies.

- Despite the most advanced medical technologies and personnel in the world, millions of citizens are without health care.
- Citizens live in cities and rural areas scavenging for food and shelter, too often in survival situations.
- Leaders are failing to find problem solutions yet seem uninterested in teaching new generations about new approaches.
- Citizens are angry; some are willing to actively confront unfriendly public and private organizations, while others prefer to passively accept the degradation of the country.

Meanwhile, there are considerable contextual challenges lodged in America's external turbulent environment.[2] Here are several outstanding pressures facing current leaders:

- Competition between country blocks pursuing common strategies
- Sustainability of the environment and overall quality of life
- Political will to openly identify and confront longstanding problems of a global nature
- Citizen support and recognition of world-wide interdependence, exemplified by the recent financial distress

These problems are connected, complex, and in need of interdependent, coordinated responses. We can use "America's future development" as a target for teaching reflexive practice and simultaneously contribute and test fresh ideas for some longstanding issues that have not yielded to conventional approaches.

## Maladaptive Practices and Failed Reforms

Reforms have been underway at various levels of the educational system from K-12 through college and professional programs. We have experimented with active learning and field projects and most recently technology-assisted delivery and performance portfolios. At the college level, the reforms have exposed several weaknesses:

- Use of sterile exercises—problems with little relevance to students and outside the classroom
- Cases presented complete with the problem defined and all data required to address it included
- The ongoing presence of "one best way" thinking—how to solve problems in 4, 6, 8,... steps
- The limited use of scanning beyond existing and comfortable boundaries of the university's departmental/disciplinary structure

- Continued acceptance of win-lose solutions generated by partisan/advocacy groups
- Fears of philosophical and values diversity in the academy
- The use of rational approaches to the process

The educational literature is quite full of "current status diagnoses" but has far fewer reports of successful innovations and the methods by which the innovators conquered resistance. For business schools, current teaching/learning approaches have been savaged by several critics.[3] We continue to experiment but the successful efforts are limited and widely distributed so that evaluation and diffusion are most difficult.

## Progress and Change Efforts—Redesign Thinking and Practice

Reflexive practice promises a new approach. For our purposes here it is considered an attempt to capture opportunities for change and improvement by leveraging networks to initiate change for the common good. Reflexive practitioners create dialogues between participants in a social system, building hope for new developments by reframing the conceptual base of the target problem. Incorporating multiple perspectives from diverse stakeholders is the means by which emergent situational issues are confronted and addressed. Where can we look for some of the innovation and for some beginning teaching of reflexive thinking approaches to managerial and policy problems of a national scope?

Several recent publications have considered aspects of education reform in K-12 and in colleges and universities.[4] The innovators have suggested that we address several issues: why and how we learn; how we transmit information into knowledge in ways that are customized to fit individual students' interests and abilities; the longstanding barriers between the academy and the community; the resistance generated by decades of standardized practices; and the loss of excitement about learning—the passion for both primary and life-long learning. There seems to be strong consensus that students are stripped of their freedom to choose both the topics and the methods of their learning experiences.

As a doctoral student I read *Redesigning the Future* by University of Pennsylvania Professor R.L. Ackoff.[5] His systems thinking approach caught my attention then, and some 30 years later I find myself deeply fascinated by social systems problems but simultaneously intimidated by the challenge. For my own part, I have encouraged political leaders to plan, using strategic vision and consensus to move forward on a wide range of public administration issues, including health care.[6] I have also contributed to the thinking about the design of health care services in developing Latin American countries.[7] These efforts were just enough to introduce me to the task of country level design, convincing me of the enormity of the challenge. Any of us with this interest would welcome committed partners from both political partisan bases who want to find a way to replace the advocacy-oriented win/lose approach. At this time we are confronted with several leading examples which we could see as opportunities to think differently:

- Health care reform
- International affairs strategy from war fighting to diplomacy
- Financial regulation
- Public education reform in K-12 schools
- Environmental control and conservation—forests to climate

For example, in an effort to move America forward in one area—proposals for health care reform—it has been difficult to embrace the technical challenges of a new design while incorporating significantly different ideological positions. Both parties are reluctant to put down their "battle axes" long enough to consider the advantages and disadvantages of various complex solutions (even when they are billed as interim, implying a need for continuous redesign going forward). Again we hear from Ackoff and Rovin:

> None of the proposals for so-called transformation of the health care system offered would provide the incentives that would change the behaviors of its two most important stakeholders: the recipients and providers of care. And just as crucial, they would not make the kinds of change most needed to focus the system on the maintenance of health rather than on the treatment of sickness and disability. Furthermore, they would not significantly reduce the system's cost because they do not address excessive administrative costs, unnecessary testing and treatment, those aspects of the current system that encourage abuse. Meanwhile, more and more hospitals and practitioners are going out of business, and the number of those who are uninsured is increasing.[8]

The struggle with large country-level social and technical issues such as health care is but one example in a set of fields. We complain that we continue to confront problems in the same old ways yet we spend little time growing future leaders with new styles and approaches.

There has long been some experimentation with redesign thinking in university courses as a learning strategy.[9] Some professional schools have explored alternative approaches. The following is a brief presentation of one ongoing pilot effort in a graduate studies department.[10] In graduate public and health administration programs I am giving students the opportunity to redesign "parts of America." This is assigned to adult graduate students (mid-career, average age 38 years). In a strategic planning course students may choose their redesign task from some 15 "parts (or subsystems) of America" including education, transportation, health care, international affairs, environment, commerce, housing and urban development, arts and humanities, science and exploration, agriculture, and law and justice. The diversity of topics allows for individual and team interests. Students are instructed that their task can be completed with one or more of these design options: *continuous incremental improvement* of the existing system, *radical reengineering* of the current system, or presentation of an alternative *vision*. These three options (*incremental improvement, radical reengineering,* and new *visions*) can be developed for any of the "parts of the subject system" but each part must be related to the whole and to relevant other parts (a synthesis). In this course we are focusing on the whole country (America in this case, but other countries could easily be used as the redesign subject). Students are asked to address five points in their redesigns:

- External environmental analysis of threats and opportunities
- Internal assessment of the current systems structure, processes and outcomes
- Design of a desired future
- Gap analysis—a comparison of present with future
- Choice of strategies for moving toward the future

On beginning their research, students immediately grasp a sense of the complexity of the challenge both within and between such systems as international relations and international finance, or politics and health care. Some students, especially undergraduates, constantly ask for more direction on the scope and direction of the task (this was noted by Kent Myers as well in his efforts with undergraduates and alternative approaches). The instructions are kept purposely lean, suggesting students choose topics and teams according to their interests, and that they use the available creative space. The assignment has been used in three courses: strategic planning, health care strategic management, and organization theory.

As I have many health care students, I use an example in medical care to illustrate the complex redesign task. Medicine treats heart disease in aggressive ways. We have become highly skilled at bypassing blocked arteries to the heart. Our coronary artery bypass operations have gradually become quick and safe as procedures have standardized, infections are reduced, and hospital discharge is quickened (*continuous incremental improvement*). We have also *radically reengineered* by adding stents to prop open clogged arteries, reducing the need for bypass. Finally, some communities are instituting new *visions*—healthy communities that encourage exercise and good nutrition—cutting off the growth of heart disease and the corresponding need for either bypass operations or stents. Implied in the assignment is that the student bring a perspective to the problem—a reframing. Many draw on previous training and experience from multiple disciplines, for example, economics, political science, psychology, medicine.

In each field, *incremental improvement, radical reengineering,* and *new visions* are design strategies students could employ in the context of their own perceptual set. For example, students from the business school often see the problems in economic and financial terms as they are grounded in economic theories of strategy and interorganizational relations. In addition, students are asked to include a stakeholder mapping to present the "perceptions of problem reality" from various points of view. Students are to assume they have a truly "blank sheet" with no hidden criteria for them to be evaluated against. They conclude with a "white paper" and group presentation to their fellows, with the instructor just one among them. The white paper is not meant to be a detailed diagnosis that proves a result, or a plan that guarantees a solution, but an appreciation of the situation and a vision of feasible development paths that will help others see the problem differently and elicit further creative response during the presentation, not nit-picking. But the manner of presentation is up to the team as well, and we learn from discussion of the different approaches that were taken.

In a second example, doctoral students in public administration enrolled in an organization theory course are given an assignment designed to link schools of organization theory with an organization experience. In organization theory there are various schools of theory which compete for dominance in the field—classical theory, human relations theory, economics, systems theory, power and politics, culture, and so forth.[11] Each school has its own principles, research practices, and adherents that promote the "correctness" of its view of the organization world. Each school becomes, in effect, a lens by which we can view the nature and functioning of organizations (an organizational systems reality, if you will).[12] When we focus on issues of importance—health care reform, financial regulation, educational reform, transportation development, homeland security—we tend to define the problem through the lens of our training and that of our colleagues. In this course, we try to develop sensitivity to reflexive practice, that is, the ability to "see through multiple perspectives." No one lens is defined as correct; all are accepted as part of the view of the world. In a series of short papers, doctoral students are asked to summarize the basic assumptions of the target school (e.g., human relations), then link them to an actual experience in an organization of their choice. Thus, the financial distress could be viewed as a breakdown of the economic system or an overabundance of greed or a failure of regulatory review or a dominant political philosophy or.... The exercise encourages students to think in terms of complex perspectives, acknowledging the interactive effects of many aspects of the problem, and highlighting the many dimensions needed for resolution.

In a third course, health care strategic management, students have the task of health care system redesign. Here they follow the same path as above but their choices within health care are diverse. For example, hospital-based management students may consider redesign of acute care settings. Practice managers can address the "practice of the future" in their specialty from orthopedics to oncology to cardiology and primary care. Long-term care students are concerned with the obvious demographics of an aging population and an intense interest among the elderly in "aging in place." Again the design options are incremental improvement, radical reengineering, or a new vision, all presented in a white paper that begins with a stakeholder mapping.

With this orientation toward graduate teaching I have supervised two dissertations that explore alternative approaches to the education of mid-career military professionals at the Army War College. In the first research Susan Myers explored the capability of distance education approaches to the development of cognitive strategic thinking: are distance education approaches able to enhance military professionals' abilities to think beyond operational concerns (in a broader and multiple lens perspective)?[13] The second paper by George Woods explored the mechanisms by which War College faculty have reorganized to stimulate cross service thinking: joint command perspectives in senior leaders—Army, Air Force, Navy, and Marines.[14] The War College is incorporating faculty from services other than the Army on its staff and recruiting students from other services as students.

The natural diversity of service perspective creates several "lenses" by which leaders confront military problems of planning and operations. Both researches illustrate the military's attempts to think beyond traditional lenses in both methods and outcomes.

## Conclusion

How does this ongoing experience map to reflexive practice and the development of professionals who think differently? Here are a few of the linkages in the context of the health care problem:

- The opportunity for and the assignment of redesign needs in health care makes the student fully confront turbulence in the system/organizational environment—the connectivity of outside forces in economics, politics, technology and demographics. There is no escape by means of cutting the problem down to size "for educational purposes."
- Complexity is viewed through varied lenses, often beginning with different disciplinary approaches—economics to politics to culture—but then moving on to cross-cutting formulations and linkages unique to the situation, e.g., malpractice concepts in tension with longstanding medical oaths.
- Reactions to change proposals are surfaced, e.g., insurers can be viewed as "evil rationers of care" or as "protectors from financial tragedy."
- Common sense solutions seem too simple, e.g., we cannot just expand Medicare without significant interactive effects.
- Interventions we propose will create unintended effects, some positive, some negative—e.g., insurance premiums will rise.
- "Once and done" solutions are viewed as ineffective as the intention is continuous improvement now and forever (meaning continuous design/redesign).

Collectively, the use of educational experiences like this by many colleges and universities would greatly expand participation and engagement of our future citizens and would also sensitize younger professionals to their power to work with others in more adaptive institutions.[15]

How is this approach different? Reflexive practice recognizes that what is rational to some is irrational to others. Organization and individual boundaries are overlapping and permeable. A guiding principle is stakeholder inclusion in the process of reframing of problems and solutions, i.e., interest groups are free to present their perspectives in ongoing dialogues. As we move toward the teaching of new processes in our educational institutions we should begin to see change in practice.

What will be the benefits of the student effort in our current subject? First, country or regional level redesign is a stimulating and relevant topic to students. I believe it is attractive and suitable for all ages. The younger set is gradually being allowed to learn how societies work and is being asked to work in groups, take their own initiative, and present different perspectives using multimedia and unique approaches not dictated by the teacher. This is a hopeful trend. Conditions have changed from the 1970s when Alvin Toffler had a contract to develop grade school curriculum that provided anthropological modeling techniques for learning about world cultures. The contract was canceled during a panic over "relativism" in the schools.

In time, the effects would spread. On a local basis, and as a group of academic organizations, we would increase the policy and public affairs participation of our younger students and mid-career professionals. Students could channel their engagement in the critical system design issues of our current time and our future. We would build interdisciplinary thinking and teaching in our colleges and universities, asking faculty and students to reach across departmental boundaries (or, following the lead of several schools that currently produce superior practitioners, merge, scramble, or abolish the departments). We may realize some fresh ideas and creative proposals for some of our most intractable problems. And, we may increase the number of students willing to invest in public service leadership or volunteer activism. In this way we are moving back toward Thomas Jefferson's values regarding citizens, both young and old:

> I know of no safe depository of the ultimate powers of the society but the people themselves; and if we think them not enlightened enough to exercise their control with a wholesome discretion, the remedy is not to take it from them, but to inform their discretion.[16]

In other words, teaching reflexive practice and problem solving to students is one way to build tomorrow's leadership and simultaneously tap into the creative energy of those not old enough to be narrowed by limited options and those not yet cynical after having been fed answers that everyone knows do not work. This task is challenging for all but most needed by our young citizens because it is *their* system and *their* professional future they can shape.

# 11

# A Behind-the-Scenes Scenario with Reflexive Practitioners

This chapter tells the story of four fictional colleagues:

- Mark Redd, an engineer for large energy projects
- Sally Black, a military officer working at the CIA
- John White, a management consultant
- Larry Green, an economist with an international development agency

All are reflexive practitioners engaged in a many-sided global crisis involving energy, environment security, economy, and much more. These professionals use their discretion and seize opportunities to scan, elaborate, reframe, potentiate, and prune. They are frequently unsure of themselves and in tension with their institutions. Together, they may be creating coherent social adaptation that others cannot.

Mark Redd works in an engineering consulting firm in the Washington area. Colleagues at his company were passing around an article explaining how the global energy system could, as a technical matter, be transformed from the consumption of natural capital (i.e., fossil fuels) to the consumption of current income (i.e., sunlight and its various forms, such as air movement, water movement, and plants).[1] But they had also been reading the vast literature on how this transformation *cannot* be accomplished due to economic and institutional factors. Some of his colleagues muttered about how obtuse politicians are—they are either all for drilling and burning, or all against drilling and burning.

Redd is seeing a different image. His fellow practitioners, not the politicians, appear to him as pins holding institutional factors in place. Professionals, by staying in place, are driving their institutions and connected systems into oblivion, confident that they are playing their responsible part and saying what is expected of them. Redd considers his role in this predictable drama. What if he were to loosen his pins, rather than tamp them down? Maybe if he were to loosen the right pins at the right time, he may actually have a chance to influence an alternative outcome. He doesn't have a plan, but that's OK because nobody is prepared to hear a plan or become committed to one—except perhaps inadvertently as a victim. Any doubts that his fellow practitioners may have about their roles are drowned out by the noise of immediate pleadings and needs, which must be heeded. Redd is unable to formulate his concerns into a problem that his at-risk peers would accept as either legitimate or solvable. All he has is an aimless dream. No controls are available to make any good happen.

Redd calls up John White, his management consultant colleague and tells him about the situation. White agrees that there are no controls, but evolutionary potential is available. Redd can recognize that as a resource, even locally. So what they talk about is not a solution, but elements of a strategy. The strategy will not guarantee anything, but it will address cognition, where Redd appears to have some leverage. The strategy may not even be particularly strong, in that he and his colleagues haven't been asking questions about their practice and won't want to start. He knows that he will have a tendency to revert to engineering thinking that will please Redd's peers. They are used to the rhetoric and it flows easily off his tongue. It is what they think is convincing. But Redd will now have to change his approach. Stop convincing and start changing.

Redd may have to do what his friend Susan Black did. She deals with some mighty rigid people in the military and intelligence community who don't like to deviate from the concepts they are told to use. She puts her arguments in three columns: conventional, sophisticated, and reflexive. If a nonreflexive argument comes to her first, she writes it down, in order that she may effectively examine it for why it hasn't worked, then thinks of a reflexive alternative different from the other columns, then gives it a whirl.

Meanwhile, over at Larry Green's international development institution, FundX, he is expected to think big about development and to have a few innovative projects in his group's portfolio, in order to maintain the group's reputation and legitimacy as a practice leader. They call themselves economists, but in their field, to be a leader means to not be limited by that label. Also, they are no longer expected to pursue the Washington consensus uncritically. They influence investment decisions among their many alliance partners.

Green's group at FundX realizes that the world is changing rapidly. That's exactly what Green wants to be more aware of, but his colleagues consider it a burden. They don't want to read tedious reports, and they don't want to prepare them either. Yet the team is curious about what others are thinking, what others know about the situations they face overseas. Green sees that as an opening. He ponders how to open them to their potential and their leverage, beyond what they have been doing. He figures that the most flattering thing he can do is to ask them for a little piece of their expertise, then return to them a gift that incorporates their expertise while adding connected knowledge that was not necessarily obvious to them. Once they see the results they will want to influence each other's thinking further and put their knowledge on display to others. They will be hooked. This will have to be a globally integrated scan with connections to many institutional levers. But Green is not sure whether the fears of his colleagues might be correct, that any effort along these lines will bury them in information with no way to use it.

Rather than pull back, Green reaches beyond his normal orbit. He had a great time last night at the get-together for international professionals where he met Susan Black. She was pretty interesting but from a different world—U.S. military and intelligence. That's not the kind of person he ever meets. It would be fun to hear more of her ideas.

Black enjoyed getting a call from Green. She said that her group just received an interesting presentation on a technique that might help Green. She explained that at her office they see new decision-making techniques all the time. Vendors think they can get a research contract or make a sale, but her group rarely buys or uses any tool. (Those who work in the intelligence community are lucky if they can exchange emails.) At these presentations, the old-timer intelligence analysts won't even talk, out of some misguided notion that valuable secrets may be disclosed. Anyway, she told Green that he should check out a technique called Spire.[2] It takes as input simple statements in the following form:

*If environmental variable* **A** *changes, it will influence variable* **B, C** . . .
*And to the extent there is influence, it will matter to decisions* **X, Y** . . .

Pick lists of environmental variables and decisions can be maintained that keep the statements at an appropriate level of generality. The point here is to arrange strong associations, not get fussy about definitions, feedback, or the relative strength of associations. A group of participants should generate 150 statements that include links across domains. Too few statements, and the results after processing will be too obvious. Too many, and changes to the inputs won't create an interesting changes in the results.

Green tries the Spire technique. He asks his team members to give him statements about influences in international development, on the promise that they will get something back that will stimulate thought in their area of interest. They realize that it is fairly easy to write input statements and they agree to humor him. The activity relies on what they know and care about and doesn't bog them down in documentation. Green runs the collected statements through a simple synthesis routine that specifies a diagram. The diagram is easy to read but is not oversimplified. It shows some surprises and unanticipated implications. Figure 11.1 is his first diagram. It is vague but is enough to get everyone interested. As one colleague said, "Let's help poor Mr. Green, who just doesn't seem to know how to build a proper strategy product." Green encourages them to think that he needs their help—which of course he does! The purpose of this first round is to stimulate a learning process that becomes compelling to participants. The point is not to get the finished diagram, but to continue with rounds of review that track with changes in thinking and changes in the environment.

Green led them through an interpretation of the first diagram. Since terrorism is to the left of trade, Green reads that as meaning that terrorism has more downstream effects, one of which is a contribution to trade wars. An implication is that if FundX could get some control on terrorism, it would have some positive multiplier effects on trade and other downstream variables. If instead FundX put priority on water supplies, that would have somewhat less of a multiplier effect. Of course, FundX may still want to do that, because it can be effective at it, and because that activity saves lives, but it has less impact on the other variables. For example, increasing water supply in the Sahel desert region of North Africa isn't going to influence terrorism much in either direction. Terrorism, on the other hand, could end up disrupting water infrastructure rather quickly. But note that this relationship wasn't directly stated by anybody previously. It is just an hypothesis that arose from the synthesis and inspection of the diagram. In the inputs, the participants as a group said more often that terrorism influenced other variables, which resulted in it being placed toward the left.

Green suggested to his expert panel that FundX's priorities might change to take on some of the upstream variables and decisions where FundX projects might have more leverage than had previously been

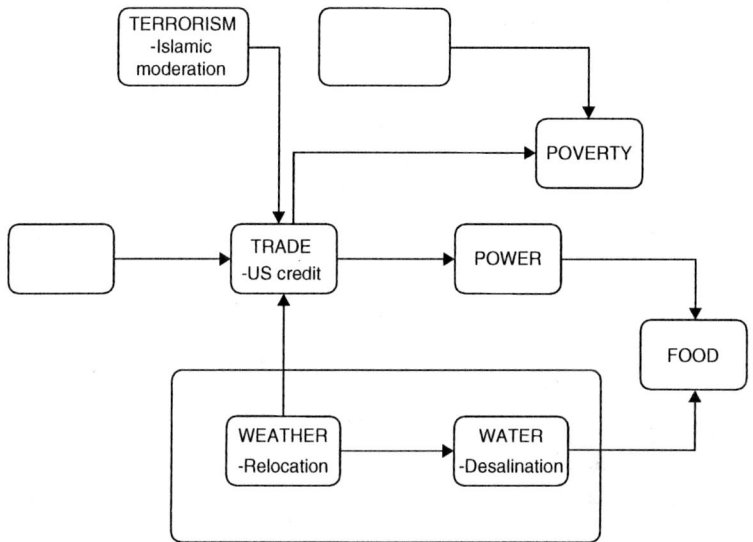

**Figure 11.1** First-round cognitive map.

considered when assessing projects. Some of these questions had not been asked before, nor had they been asked at the same time and in a broader context, but now that they have been asked, with the help of a reflection technique, somebody is likely to come up with a creative response.

But things don't proceed smoothly. The expert on Bangladesh is incensed that Green's panel members did not seem to grasp the importance of water. Himalayan glaciers are disappearing, and people in his region are in imminent danger.[3] Water needs to be a priority! In the next round he writes new statements emphasizing water and gets his friends to write additional items. The next diagram looks different. Others on the team object to this hijacking of the process, everyone has to explain himself, and the panel ends up with an interesting record of dialogue and more elaboration of what variables and decisions are involved, all nicely documented and summarized, all current, all ready to change in the next round as enthusiasm and thinking waxes and wanes. Every participant can use the results to lend context, precision, and legitimacy to his own points. Or the process can at least clarify conflicts and link them to specific disagreements over framing.

Green sees this model as a map of the group's cognition. He can use it for guidance for placing strategic nudges that make sense to the group, but he also needs a criterion beyond financial return, one that encompasses potential on the global scale. Instead of "democracy," he reframes that aspect of potential as something more culturally neutral, such as "justice supported by the people." The point would be to place new projects that will, as a byproduct, tend to unfreeze structures of thought or politics that fail to incorporate interests or respond to needs as they arise. Green checks what the Open Society Institute is doing and he sees that they failed miserably in their project in Congo. He can learn from that. To his team's cognitive map he links source material describing the context and this example, and he also starts generating a bank of project ideas that score well on potential.

The Spire technique and diagram struck some of his colleagues as excessively loose. Of course, that is exactly what Green wanted, in order to keep a direct perception of the whole, with vagueness that powerfully elicits ideas about possible changes, system responses, and interventions. Basically it is a tool for surveillance and for generating perspectives. It is brief and also holistic. A Spire diagram is not something to be believed or not, but a foil for sensemaking. One is led to consider: "If these are conclusions, and they differ from what I first thought, what accounts for the difference, and am I moved to change my views as a result of how others are making sense? If we agree to differ, why and in what way?" These questions are often bypassed when one drives toward an "accurate" model, where one allows data, principles, or a model—all of which are supposed to be "objective" and relatively timeless—to decide the outcome. But they necessarily fail, and in ways that are obscure. Why not keep humans in the loop throughout, as sensors, sensemakers, and judges? One can then interrogate them about their observations and also keep assumptions in play. One is required to interpret with varied perspectives and assumptions. This is no guarantee that the group has been thorough or has somehow avoided the ignorance of each member or the group as a whole, but by being open, they have a better opportunity to correct. By being aware of and able to speak on behalf of everything in the group's cognitive map, participants are in better stead as actors and interveners, continuously sensing, and making sense as they act and interact with the world of which they are part.

Green knows that soon after the group becomes accustomed to the Spire technique, either their attention will wander or they will be tempted to start polishing. He wants to keep them learning instead. He observes that there are many additional resources at hand in Washington that haven't been tapped yet. The U.S. government, many foreign governments, and nongovernmental organizations (NGOs) are all around. FundX could incorporate the seasoned judgment of many experts in all fields, including some that may not seem on the surface to be relevant. In particular, how do things seem to those who worry about U.S. national interests overseas, rather than international development in general?

Green asked Black to nominate some people from the intelligence community who might want to participate in FundX's scanning efforts. Black suggested the long-range staff at the National Intelligence Council (NIC) who had just finished some unclassified futures intelligence in which U.S. national decisions are arrayed against influences and outcomes in turbulent world environments.[4] Many such analytic products are unfortunately difficult to incorporate in a Spire model because of their relentless recourse to prediction, elimination of cross-domain influences, and lack of clarity on how decisions are affected. Green had also hoped to uncover "structural" features that would remain true for a long period, but then he realized that he was backsliding. In a turbulent environment, such information is an illusion. It would be better for him to not bias his attention, especially in a way that would discourage reframing under varying assumptions. He uses the NIC materials that Black recommends but adds perspectives from elsewhere, sometimes from controversial blogs that tend to make mistakes, doubt themselves, and occasionally offer breakthrough ideas. The Spire process has its own biases, of course, but everything is visible and can be disputed and modified based on both information and judgment.

After working with his group, he found that his on-going scanning model had these advantages:

- Helps him augment decision making on a range of new small projects by framing the issues strategically and coherently in context
- Shows how the group perceptions can evolve and be updated transparently without unwarranted closure or simplification
- Can quickly produce low-detail assessments, avoiding lengthy work on a large product that suffers from obsolescence and poor linkage to the dialogue of decision makers

The group continues to elaborate projects and ideas for action with the aid of this schema, emphasizing:

- Release of cognitive, cultural, and institutional impediments to social adaptation
- Opportunities to build potential
- Use of open-source, crowd-sourced, and locally sourced knowledge

- The selection of projects that can learn and change after launch (i.e., potential intrinsic to the project)

Green's recognition of contextual uncertainty is enhanced. He is now looking more creatively at risks that he has brushed off before as just part of doing business overseas. Maybe something could be done about them, even though Green isn't able to prove, any better than before, the benefits of any action. Outcomes will be mixed and will depend on unforeseen events.

It was now clearer to Green that one of FundX's normal practices is unwise, attempting to prove, at the outset, that a project had indisputable worth. Something like Grameen Bank, which pioneered microloans to poor people, would have been disqualified. That idea sounded very bad to FundX when they first heard of it. What possible good could come from lending a few dollars to poor people who cannot repay? Luckily, the eventual investors realized that they didn't need to rely on their faulty judgment to decide beforehand whether the project was a winner. Rather than judge the proposal, they held their noses and funded a test. This example had implications for FundX's learning design. Previously, FundX took decades to conclude that some of its big dam projects were poor investments. The original plans had been closely analyzed, but they grossly underestimated the risks that eventually doom these projects. Yet no amount of improvement in the initial planning and evaluation of projects could uncover such problems. FundX simply has to build in tests, generate benefits and reinforcements along the way, and find ways to stop or change projects when they go off track. Projects will be evaluated holistically, but the conclusions will be tentative.

Some projects may fail conclusively in one place and still make sense elsewhere, because conditions, partnerships, cultures, and other factors change. Grameen Bank, a success in one setting, didn't work in the United States. But with some adaptation, something similar does work in the United States and has worked better than ponderous bureaucratic approaches. For example, the Small Business Administration, which attempts to do all checking on project proposals at the beginning, ends up delaying project funding when it will matter the most, thereby imposing costs that lower everyone's chance of success.

Green found Black to be charming as well as helpful. He decided to ask her out on a date. They went to go see the Jim Carey movie, "Yes Man," and they really enjoyed it. Carey is an unhappy loan officer. He takes a life-altering course in positive thinking and begins approving all loans, including frivolous purchases by unemployed borrowers. The borrowers are so encouraged by the show of confidence that they get jobs, succeed, and pay it all back. An executive takes notice of this burst of crazy loans. Carey thinks he will be fired, but he is instead promoted because his portfolio was large and profitable. Green and Black talked about the movie over drinks. They wondered, "Were the banks acting like Jim Carey when they started offering-no-money-down 'liar loans' for inflated real estate? If so, why wasn't that just as hilarious?" They discussed the differences and ended up concluding that a little trust and positive thinking might not be such a bad idea, considering the alternatives.

Green's colleagues were happy with what happened in the Spire exercise, but they were convinced that it was just luck and they now wanted to get "serious." Their first complaint to Green was that the scanning diagram doesn't depict their favorite influences and feedbacks. They complained, "It isn't accurate!" Green considered explaining to them that the point is to look at the problems differently, based on the combined attentions within our institution as it relates to the world. But he decided against saying that. Doing so might prove him a fool and induce a crackdown on his "bad professional practice." Is there a way to avoid a showdown between these two different cognitive approaches? OK, he thought, I'll let them tweak the inputs to get a "correct" diagram. There is some sense in that. But at the same time he would insist that FundX's involvement in the climate change mitigation business be explored, especially since it potentially affects so many other actions that the institution is involved in. One of his colleagues had mused that shoreline slums that were invested in and improved over the years were now threatened. Massive migration could ruin a generation of incremental advancement.

Green was really in over his head now. He asked for help from his friend Redd, who has been doing his own scanning. Redd suggested that they dive into some project ideas that might score off the charts in terms of potential. Redd said that if the group at FundX is worried about a large migration of people away from coastal areas, which will be a disaster under conventional assumptions, then they need to look at the restoration economy movement.[5] There are many instances where a community has organized itself around depleted resources. Abandoned land often has residual value, and investing in its restoration often turns out to be a better investment target than finding new resources to deplete. What Green sees in this concept, that Redd didn't notice, is that such projects are potentially game changers in his field of international development. FundX can set up processes that are aided by the natural inclinations of local forces, principally the inclinations of both the ecology and the community to heal themselves. Simply, there is a lot of wasted land that has potential that can start to work for the community instead of against it. Green is surprised to discover that many restoration projects align the interests of real estate developers, ecologists, social activists, and the locally unemployed, all the groups who usually fight each other over scarce resources.

On their next date, Larry Green and Susan Black talk about Green's strategies. It occurs to Black that the same sort of try-and-test approach that Green was discussing at the level of the project can also be achieved at the level of policy over at CIA, where Black has been struggling. The rational practitioners she works with assume that policy must be made once and perfectly, with solemn incantations as to its probity, then held to for lengthy periods, because policies supposedly can only work if adhered to strictly. That this argument sounds an awful lot like religion appears not to occur to its proponents. It is an attempt to impose stable conditions, which make sense only until one checks and finds that conditions are not holding. Black tells Green about some of her dubious policies. For example, it is forbidden to "remix" secrets from one document into another. This is the essence of what occurs on the web and in every medium today. It also occurs every day in the President's Daily Briefing, and every day there are waivers from policy!

While Black recognizes the advantage of having some rules, she will argue that policy should explicitly and intentionally maintain variety. By implication this includes a readiness to move to capture new opportunities that may not have been anticipated and may not have fit one's preconceptions, even at the level of policy.

But how do you actually "try" a policy? Isn't that too expensive, and aren't the results too murky to make conclusions, and who would actually go along with a temporary policy? This is difficult but Black, the reflexive practitioner, is not without her resources. Black doesn't just change the message, but also changes the medium to one in which such messages are more palatable. She knows that it is now possible to simulate policy in a world in which many can participate and can experience the difference. You don't have to prove your argument before trying, but let people live through it. The experience will be realistic and sufficient for learning, and it will also put supposed sure-fire principles in doubt. They will confront simulated reality as well, and will not be allowed to escape squeaky clean to their hyper-idealized, rational, top-down, "proven" world of management.

This simulated world where you can try policy will need to be big. Getting the texture right will be hard, and it doesn't have to do with graphics or IT-generated immersion so much as whether the players are imagining reflexivity and turbulence. She figures that Medard Gable is on to the right design in Earth Game 1.0. He has continued to develop interactive gaming workshops since his start with Buckminster Fuller's World Game workshops in the 1970s. At the beginning, the emphasis was on playing out the physical consequences with engineering realism. More and more of his variations, however, have incorporated continuously changing background conditions and social contingency, more live choices and more players, and institutional features that complicate play in interesting and instructive ways. This same aspect of gaming is getting more interest lately in national security, where battles used to be played out with "accurate" engineering results of combat decisions, but now the professional advisor role can be played as well, not just "injected" from the game controller. So Black figures that she can claim to be reinforcing that trend, and claim that her World Game is "just like" the others that are approved, though she knows that it is different and will give her a stealth platform for changing minds and finding adaptive policies. An attenuated representation of the physical world, it turns out, can reduce distraction from the crucial aim of developing skill and insight into managing institutions through turbulence.

Black wanted to try something out. Redd would have to help her with this. She recalled that in May 2007 the U.S. National Intelligence Council quietly ran an unclassified game with 23 senior analysts and outside experts representing the United States, Europe, Japan, China, and India.[6] They simulated negotiations at the December 2009 Copenhagen climate change summit. This offered a great opportunity to learn something. Black arranged to replay the game, this time tracking with what actually happened. Then she compared the perceptions and dynamics of the group that played two years prior. (In fact, she got a few old hands to replay it, though most had dispersed. So much for institutional memory.) The prior game turned out to be fairly accurate in many details. Interests don't change that much, after all, but that's not where the value turned out to be. The players developed a visceral appreciation of what the pressure points had become, and the two perspectives from the two runs helped them understand in greater depth what all four parties were thinking, plus how they reacted to actions of others. For example, the Americans learned how much the Europeans were depending on them for leadership, and that's where the United States needs to step up its "whole of government" policy. That is spelled out abstractly in the U.S. National Security Strategy, and here was a new point of leverage that the U.S. government had been overlooking or misperceiving. Without needing to get the Senate to move, the military can act through the North Atlantic Treaty Organization (NATO). NATO operations consume huge amounts of fuel at high prices. Reducing consumption reduces a huge combat risk and huge costs at the same time, as has been spelled out in studies by the Rocky Mountain Institute. By leading through NATO, the rest of European governments and support systems follow, and that feeds back as pressure on the Senate.[7]

The game ended up suggesting several related follow-up moves, including ways to build confidence and a partnership with China that would head off resource conflicts in Africa. International negotiations are normally such a wearying process, but through gaming, Black got some surprisingly useful results and some understanding and agreement from the decision maker players at the same time. They gained insight into a true national security policy that added an increment of U.S. safety by making the energy and environment commons safe for all, starting a *virtuous cycle* that might continue. The military stance would no longer be just aimless toughness that tends toward a *vicious cycle* of mistrust. Insight into the common good mattered. Players saw that they could not gain anything from isolating themselves.

White had been watching. He wondered whether it would be possible to tune the simulation to exaggerate the rewards for playing like a reflexive practitioner. The more the practitioner bears down with an at-risk practice, in order to wrest control from the chaos, the more the practitioner and his client are punished. With that tuning, scenarios about global problems start to look different. There may be some quick or slow solutions to hard problems, but they won't be direct, and they will have to pass through some institutional thickets, not just through pristine economic or engineering models. Needless to say, this game will have an open architecture that facilitates participation in new scenarios, and it will challenge even the best players because it is so unpredictable—a little like reality.

Back at FundX, Larry Green was reflecting on what he left out. What would become a problem if he didn't jump on it now? He noted that FundX operates with partner organizations in many regions that use a broad range of expertise from many institutions. Hundreds of professionals are involved in all the steps, and they can either release or tighten their pins on adaptation. Any of these professionals might object: "I give up. Yes, there is a turbulence challenge in international development projects, and yes somebody has to deal with it. But what does that have to do with me, a lowly practitioner?" Just recalling the 2008 global financial meltdown, it is easy to see how rapidly the "unconnected" pieces are affected. News stories for the first weeks talked about how one group or another was relieved that it was only the investment banks, then only the insurance companies, then only the banks, then only the hedge funds, then only the United States, then only the car companies, but finally the struggling third world countries where FundX operates.

Another may argue, "OK, I may be connected to the global crisis, but there is really nothing I can do, because I am too weak, I must do as I am told, we must follow the rules, and I will lose my job if I step out of line." Green figured that these professional practitioners actually had more power to deviate and innovate in the interest of the common good than they think, at least compared to other players, including leaders (CEOs, boards), co-producers (partners, suppliers, support workers), and the served populations. This is because the practitioner is expected to bring independent expertise and knowledge. FundX pays to have such people, and FundX must on occasion listen to them, thus they have some authority. The practitioner has some leverage and the opportunity to deviate. That generates a kind of power based on reason, not on a constituency or economic influence. That reason may be rejected exactly because it is not a constituency or economic influence, but it can be an early warning of both, in time to avoid trouble or to gain a step. But if the professional chooses not to use his sensemaking capacity, then the opportunity is lost. The reflexive practitioner can claim some of this free space to maneuver. Green is going to have to find a way to change the thinking of all this extended chain of practitioners, not just his own group, and not just decision makers.

Green asks himself, "Instead of talking about solutions all the time—the ones that never work despite all the endless technical refinement—why not run some scenarios, or just plain tell some stories (true or not) that illuminate some opportunities? Could we do any worse than what we are doing now?" Green is beginning to believe that stories are the only way to communicate anything effectively. This is a shocking statement, given the amount of energy that is poured into reports and briefings. Some practitioners who have come to this realization and written about it have had to endure the criticism of their peers. After all, anybody can tell stories, so if professionals do it, doesn't that make them unprofessional? What about our science, our deep training, our project management skills, and our strategic planning process? Aren't they more important? This finding about the unique effectiveness of stories doesn't invalidate science, training, project management, or even planning—though it may invalidate briefing slides! It simply recognizes that the human brain accepts stories and changes because of them. It is the way we think? As psychologist-philosopher Jerome Bruner put it, there is a story-structure to experience.[8]

Green was reading Steve Denning, a promoter of story-telling for management. When Denning was at the World Bank, he was frustrated that no analytical report at the Bank ever seemed to make a difference. One day he told a story to an executive. The executive was struck and immediately began arguing for a change. Denning's prior laborious study had all the reasoning and had already been briefed but to no effect. The executive who was affected by the story retold it to everyone, who then told others, and the shift in attention by all the leaders, driven by the story, led directly to an important decision that the Bank had been avoiding for years.[9]

Green is wary because the training that his professional peers have undergone, and to which they return for "refresher" courses, reinforce the conceit that case studies need to somehow approximate positivistic science. The academics go through an elaborate charade of selecting representative cases and removing bias and announcing "findings." If it were only possible for organizational science to recognize that learning requires the use of narrative, development professionals might actually be able to get the story right, and also make it easier to identify their own biases by uncloaking them.

But story telling can easily be mishandled by those who push at-risk practice under the guise of quality, detail, rigor, and other typical limits on what may be said, such as the following:

- *Driving toward a preconceived "teaching point."* In novice teaching in many fields, the case is simply a disguised puzzle for which there is a "textbook" solution. The student is expected to detect stereotyped conditions, apply known procedures, and generate the correct solution. (The solution is a secret held by the instructor, but it can be obtained at a price from prior students.)
- *Reaching a conclusion.* An example would be, "Ten Reasons Why Bankruptcy at GM Was Inevitable." Such a work is not suitable because it suppresses the consideration of alternative developmental sequences. Further, it inserts arguments for or against these sequences. The student loses the opportunity to develop skills in discovery and in framing the situation from multiple perspectives.

- *Constrained to one point of view.* Examples are "My Time at GM," or "An Economic Perspective on GM." Again, the student is not given the opportunity to experience what he must face as a practitioner, which is a situation that is not preformulated by a discipline. The situation needs to be presented in a more naturally uncertain state that invites multiple interpretations, different valuations, and different conclusions about actions to take or not take. The case can present what others think and are recommending, but it should offer some information or contrary opinion that leaves any single perspective in doubt.
- Green was reading further in a curious book about scenario techniques and realized that, even if you get beyond these problems, one has to look more carefully at one's own role as an element of the system under study. The authors point out, "The scenario practice literature does not include a well-developed tool for understanding the socio-political context of a scenario project." In a rousing postscript they recommend that the reader pass beyond the "rhetoric of embracing uncertainty" and ask "whether we have the will to create and nurture the capacity for more effective (and therefore reflexive) future-mindedness, and whether we are capable of doing so rapidly enough and on a sufficiently global scale." But there is a troublesome constraint: "Decision makers still want certainty."[10]

Larry Green, Susan Black, and Mark Redd were all discouraged that the pins they were loosening might slip right back into place. The smallest threatening event might trigger, among their at-risk colleagues, a retreat to conventional practices. They call up John White and ask him to set up a group lunch. He tells them to meet at the Irish Inn, right near the Beltway where it crosses over the Potomac River. It is a lovely wooded area near the old canal and an amusement park, two relics that were briefly prominent. Susan Black pops over the river from the CIA. Larry Green drives up from K Street. Mark Redd comes across from his Bethesda high rise. Nobody knows where John White resides. He is more like an abiding spirit; he shows up when called upon.

The four talked about how they had used cognitive modeling, introduced potential as a criterion, tried things out in simulation, and introduced a new kind of sensemaking among their colleagues. Yet to do this well, they really needed to kick away at-risk practices. They would start here at lunch—by kicking away an agenda, pretense, and anything blocking an authentic encounter with the common good and with each other.

White said that he was reading Soros on the open society, where he explains that openness to a situation can easily be hijacked by the manipulative brain and inauthentic questioning and posing. Face-to-face meetings help, but how should they be run? White explained that everyone assumes that structure is needed for any meeting, workshop, or conversation. Something terrible is supposed to happen without it, but nobody can actually tell you what that is, because nobody has ever dared to find out. Everyone can point to bad meetings they have had, but come to think of it, they were all structured.

White tells of some facilitators he has met who insist on reducing structure. They get away with it, and clients usually are very pleased with the results, though they resent having to pay for what appears to take so little effort. The appreciative inquiry facilitators can get away with minimal interview questions, facilitators using search conference methods can run a free-wheeling discussion, but the ultimate deconstructor is Harrison Owen and his open space method.[11] He can start groups off with a single toss-up question and have them speak respectfully to each other (while passing around a talking stick). Often something surprising and creative comes of it, bringing to awareness what had been known or thought in private for years. Results also come much faster and engender commitment on the spot. Effective deliberation can be slow, but it doesn't have to be. As Thomas Hardy wrote, "Experience is as to intensity, and not as to duration."[12] When people ask Owen how they can become self-organizing, he tells them that, as products of evolution, they already are. What they need to do is get their minds out of the way and let it work.

The group decided to try it. Redd had the most urgent problem. He wanted to get his climate change mitigation work off the ground. The purpose of the lunch was not to solve his problem, but they did come away with a better idea of how to approach it. White tried Owen's approach. He didn't want to control or structure anything, just let the group find its way. But something has to be moving among the participants, and he gave them a starting point. White advised Redd to begin doing his project without fanfare. Don't plan it and then hope to raise interest and funding. If it is a good idea, simply doing it will end up being the best plan. Others will notice. His colleagues will then find the idea persuasive because it has begun drawing visible commitment. His project may not be accomplishing much at the beginning, but prospective supporters and funders want to see it before it succeeds anyway, before it is fully realized and no longer needs their help. Give the funders a creative challenge and an opportunity to see that they are really needed for a worthy cause. By beginning the work, the instigators and the growing team will learn and correct in ways that could never have conceived of if they had only planned without doing.

That's the strategy, but what might the project look like as Redd begins to do it? Black recalled some self-organizing activity on climate and figured there might be some ideas in it for Redd, but also for herself.[13] She explained that Steven Levitt, economist and co-author with Stephen Dubner of *SuperFreakonomics*, had argued in his book that global warming was solvable. Levitt said that experts were making it too hard and needed to think rationally, like himself. He argued that transforming the whole economy to low-carbon energy systems was not a conceivable project. Levitt's solution was to pump sulfur dioxide into the upper atmosphere. The gas will reflect sunlight and cool the planet. This solution would be cheap and quick, easily calculated and executed. This is what economic thinking can do for us, Levitt says, with the utter confidence of a rational practitioner. Just let the experts solve our problems and stop getting confused.

Black went on to explain that Levitt's argument really angered the climate experts, one of whom is Pierrehumbert, whose office is two blocks from Levitt's on the University of Chicago campus. Pierrehumbert wrote an open letter attacking the suggestion as not only irresponsible, but just plain wrong in its arithmetic. Elizabeth Kolbert, the *New Yorker* writer on the environment, was listening to the dispute and had an interesting response. She agreed with Pierrehumbert on the science, and thought that Levitt had a bad argument, but she went on to put this geoengineering option in context. There would be a way to do it, and it is not entirely out of the question as a last resort. In other words, it is a terrible idea, but if the situation become terrible, humankind may need to use it. By drawing attention to this dispute, Kolbert added a marvelous illustration of why the situation is terrible. By telling the story she raises the urgency of doing something else. All this was done out in the open, on blogs and in the *New Yorker*. It could also be retold as a case of rational practitioners fighting and getting nowhere, but Kolbert took the opportunity to draw out of it an advantage in public understanding that helps shift public motivation. The scientific evaluation of options needs to be done, but the significance of the analysis needs to be related to policy decisions, and that's what Kolbert accomplished. She was not exactly telling anyone what to do—she was herself uncertain—but she made it clear how the options could be sorted out and put in perspective, and at the same time inform everyone of the momentous decisions world leaders may be facing soon.

So whether Redd can use this story to help himself, Black was not sure. But everyone at the lunch did accept that several perspectives had been illuminated regarding one of the major geoengineering options. Perhaps opinion was not indelibly influenced and set, but at least for now the option makes sense as a poor but potentially effective emergency option that is not ready to launch technically, would have serious side effects, and would require constant maintenance for hundreds of years.

Then Redd got it. For his project, he needs his organization to perform Kolbert's role as the arbiter of sense, rather than as a promoter of a sure-fire solution. The role is essential, and can make the difference where many of the other roles cannot, toward approaching the common good in the global crisis.

It certainly felt good to talk about such matters with people who "wanted to go there," and who could refrain from throwing rocks of opinion at each other. They were all feeling pretty good. Especially White and Redd. White had ordered a Beefeater Gin on the rocks. Redd thought it looked beautiful in the sunlight and he ordered one too, even though engineers don't, as a rule, drink during the day. And he doesn't drink gin! He was willing to take a look at the world as White did, cockeyed.

Meanwhile, Susan Black and Larry Green took a short walk by themselves down to the canal. Black was recalling her childhood, when she and her father came to this canal every winter to skate. But the canal no longer freezes. Green kissed Black. They realize that they loved each other. But they were also struck by the impossibility of going further. They were from different sides of the Potomac. It would have worked if they had been a mixed-race couple, or even a same-sex couple, but the professional cultures that each called home would forbid the union. Green thought about what would happen if he invited Black to join him at the anthropologist's happy hour at the World Bank every Friday. If Black came in her uniform, it would be like throwing a stink bomb. Similarly, Black likes to go for a drink at the officer's club at the Pentagon. If Green tried to bicycle up to the gate with his beard and his Afghan hat, he might get shot. Maybe some day, but for now they would retreat into their separate professional cultures and keep the civilization game going, interpreting and constructing the world, themselves, and each other.

John White reflected on the day and everything that brought this group together. It seemed to him that no matter what position you find yourself in as a professional, it should be possible to start there and generate an adaptive response. The opening to do so may be small, and institutional structures may stand in the way, but you can move in that direction. The question becomes: How do you make use of the freedom and discretion that you have as a professional?

# Appendix

# C-SPAN: Window on Practice

*Margaret M. Nicholson*

This book has made the case for the effectiveness of reflexive practice over the at-risk practices: rational, focused, principled, and interested. To further explicate and compare the practices, several guests who appeared on C-SPAN's Washington Journal, a three-hour morning news program, are profiled. This program was chosen as a source over other news and magazine-type broadcasts because guests are allowed to completely answer questions from the moderators and call-in viewers, thereby providing sufficient content to determine a practitioner's type. In addition, moderators do not voice their own opinions or react with judgment, but simply help the guest and callers deal with the issues. On many other programs, responses are often restricted to "sound bites," and the host's interference may muddle rather than reveal the guest's views. Additional programs that might have been suitable sources are PBS' Charlie Rose or Bill Moyers Journal, but these programs have many fewer guests and the selection is narrower.

Over a six-week period, in situations where guests dealt with turbulent phenomena and were expected to demonstrate a practitioner's approach, an effort was made to type them. Given the purposes of this section, no attempt at systematic or comprehensive sampling was undertaken. In making characterizations, compliance on a number of features of one pattern was considered sufficient rather than a perfect match. Even with this relaxed standard, not all guests could be categorized. Sometimes questions from the moderator or those calling in did not elicit the kinds of comments from a guest that could be typed; other times a guest remained neutral on matters that would normally have disclosed a pattern. Of the 25 segments viewed in full, three did not demonstrate a clear pattern. A large proportion of guests are politicians or political strategists who were more often typed as principled practitioners (9), followed by interested practitioners (7), and a small number of rational practitioners (2) and focused practitioners (2). Only three were typed as reflexive practitioners.

See Table 3.5, Comparison of Practices, for a concise set of contrasting features of the five types: Reflexive Practitioner (XP) and the at-risk Practitioners: Rational (RP), Focused (FP), Principled (PP), and Interested (IP). (Materials below that are set in quotation marks are usually exact transcriptions, but some remarks have been paraphrased or condensed, always with the intention of conveying the guests' intended meaning.)

## Rational Practice

**Ray LaHood, Transportation Secretary,** used his time on the program to campaign to eliminate cell phone use while driving. He explicitly compared it to, and intends to use the same set of activities that were used in, the campaigns designed for reducing driving when blood alcohol level is beyond .08 and for increasing the use of seat belts. There was no question put to him by the moderator or a caller that elicited evidence of his having to reconsider the situation from another perspective or of looking outside his stated objective and the strategy he was certain would work. For the most part, he ignored aspects of questions that led him away from achieving his objective of selling his solution, policy, and practice as the best. No matter what he was asked, his answer (either directly, or after a sentence or two that at least alluded to the caller's question) ended with his conclusion that "texting is dangerous and has to be stopped." He repeated time and time again, "As soon as people get in their cars, they must put their cell phones in the glove compartment."

A caller questioned the efficacy of all such campaigns, given that drunk drivers are still killing people and that many people do not wear seat belts. Another asked, "Why wouldn't all distracted driving be punished, such as women putting on makeup?" His cognitive posture converged on one idea only: texting is an epidemic and must be the focus of the campaign.

LaHood gave the appearance of a management consultant who brings a theory on how to improve a system, uses a top-down approach to analysis (even if lip-service is given to employee participation), and concludes with a strategic plan.

## Focused Practice

Danielle Pletka, V.P. for Foreign and Defense Studies at American Enterprise Institute, in response to almost every question, provided clear "facts" based on AEI's detailed description about the government's approach to international conflicts. She demonstrated the FP tendency to be reductive, to simplify, and show a single or clear cause for a situation. Most FPs will allow their account of the situation to "speak for itself," allowing the listener to draw their own conclusions. But Pletka spoke with great confidence and eliminated any hint of complexity by stating the choice was between providing more troops to achieve success on the ground in Afghanistan, or to under-resource, which will result in stagnation and the possibility of failure.

Diane Rowland, Executive V.P. of Kaiser Family Foundation (KFF), maintained a neutral pose in discussing the demographics of the uninsured population in the United States and what effect the various proposals for health care reform might have. Without apparent judgment, she assisted the moderator in describing the detailed statistics that KFF collects. She was able to provide a complete account of the number of people who are not insured, along with their characteristics such as working status, income, and age. Sometimes, through her word choices, one discerns a preference for how the findings might be put to use, but this was never explicitly framed as an opinion. For example, she stated it is mostly children who are covered through Medicaid or subsidized programs, and that it was a "myth" that a large number of poor adults are covered for health services.

The moderator typically allows guests to remind the audience that they are "just reporting" if the caller complains about a guest's point of view. Therefore, it was notable that before taking the first call, the moderator was quite firm in stating, "This is an informational segment. The Kaiser Family Foundation is not an advocacy group, and Ms. Rowland won't take a position."

Rowland was committed to making an accurate account and in so doing was explicit in pointing out both sides of a question or the tradeoffs that have to be considered. In response to one caller, she agreed, "There is tension between the lowering of premiums and the rise in the deductible." In another case, she described a situation in which "given the cost of current insurance premiums, small employers are faced with a choice between hiring another employee or providing health coverage." She admitted that considering a public option is a controversial issue, and went on to describe all sides of the argument: It will provide more options for those going into the exchange, perhaps something modeled on Medicare; *but* the option was considered unfair by the insurance companies who have to compete; *but* having a public plan will create competition and may be an incentive for better coverage and price.

The moderator noted that Kaiser's materials "repeat over and over" that most uninsured are in working families. Rowland reminded him, "Our model for health insurance coverage is based on being employed; therefore, we either need to strengthen the connection between employment and insurance or provide a broader alternative." This relationship—employment and insurance—was reinforced when a caller cited his difficulty in maintaining coverage between jobs because he could not afford the premiums. Rowland calmly pointed out the contradiction in a government mandate that was supposed to solve this problem: "COBRA was set up to help an employee maintain coverage between employers by allowing the ex-employee to pay the full share of the premium, but it is unlikely that someone without a job can afford to do so."

One can find value in the facts provided by an FP, especially if one trusts the accuracy of the research. It seems such a loss that someone armed with such comprehensive information does not give an indication of a direction or frame the material in such a way that those facts can help shape the future. One does not need to lose neutrality to move toward an XP stance. The moderator, who rarely expresses any emotion, did not hesitate to show amazement in finding that "most uninsured are in working families." But in keeping with her neutral stance, Rowland did not express XP sentiments that one might have wanted to hear, such as, "We need to face these contradictions and tradeoffs head on instead of sweeping them under the rug and ignoring the unintended consequences that are likely to result with the current proposed legislation."

## Principled Practice

In categorizing guests, one must remember that it is the approach or pattern of thinking, not the content, that determines the type of practitioner. This comes across clearly, and seems especially strange, when guests, one following the other, argue opposite solutions to the same problem, but both can be typed as PP. Politicians will often be found to fit this pattern.

Phil Hare (Democrat) and George Lemieux (Republican) based their arguments for passing and for not passing, respectively, a health care reform bill by explaining how their own (and their parties) solutions were the result of applying the correct abstract concepts. They both claim the "desires of the American people" for their side.

By listening to the thinking pattern and ignoring the folksy asides, it can become quite boring to listen to politicians. Perhaps this is an overgeneralization, but it didn't seem to matter which specific politician was speaking, only which party he or she represented. Democrats (D) repeated certain phrases, while Republicans (R) favored others. A suggestion: tune into the middle of a joint interview after the guests and their parties have been introduced, listen and note answers for a few minutes, then look at the screen. If you heard "insurance companies are inhuman, they choose healthy people" and "reducing costs can be done by eliminating corruption" there will be a D under the guest's name. If you heard "health reform means substandard care because of gate keepers" and "tort reform is critical in reducing costs" there will be an R under the guest's name.

To decide by principle alone is to never allow evidence to draw the principle under question. Evidence, to the extent it is used, either provides confirmation of the principle or disconfirms rivals. This stance is not limited to political topics, economics, or other areas where there is a technical doctrine. Any issue can be solved based on a reference to an authoritative text, person, or belief. Practices, then, do not have to work, but simply be correct. The answer flows from a religious, economic, or constitutional doctrine that needs no further interpretation. To defend his view during a health care reform discussion, one politician said quite firmly, "Our Constitution is not written that way; it's not what our country stands for; it is a socialistic, Western European approach."

## Interested Practice

**Thomas Pyle is President of The Institute for Energy Research,** which conducts research and analysis on the functions, operations, and government regulation of global energy markets. He was unflinching in his support of the fossil fuels industry (coal, oil, natural gas). He reported no downside to the wide use and further development of these sources of energy. When questioned about the need to reduce pollution through the use of renewable sources of energy, he claimed that, "A growing economy produces efficiencies in the system and in tandem comes better environmental protection. In the 1970s we consumed 33 percent of oil in the world and now it is below 25 percent even though we have more cars, people, and homes."

An IP can make statements that sound like an FP. Responding to a caller who questioned the use of the term "climate change" vs. "global warming," Pyle said, "All sides use language to promote their agenda, but our goal is to provide the facts. We throw some information into the debate so policy makers, staff, and the media are aware of all the aspects of the issue and the impacts they will have." But the thrust of his substantive remarks was adversarial. He reframed all facts and statistics to support his interests. In discussing the development of renewable sources, he had the following viewpoint.

> [Renewables are] more expensive, less efficient, and only works when the wind blows and the sun shines. The biggest problem is that renewable energy sources are not compatible with the demand for electricity. Oil, coal, and natural gas are portable and can be turned on and off. In the U.S., natural gas must be used as back up in the wind corridor. You really have to ask yourself, If you are building wind mills and wind farms backed up with natural gas plants, where is the emission reduction? Just skip the subsidies for wind farms and build a natural gas plant.

Pyle brought up many concerns to clinch his argument—sustainability of alternative energy sources over time without massive government subsidies; much higher costs for utility payers if current efficiency bills are passed; cap and trade is perceived as a market mechanism, but is a national energy tax—that do, nonetheless, raise legitimate questions.

**Denise Bode, CEO of the American Wind Energy Association,** did not have to answer any of the challenges from Pyle and could start fresh with the material because C-SPAN had her follow rather than share a time segment him. In typical IP fashion, she reframed all the information at her disposal to her advantage: The recession is putting projects on hold, but growth is still beating previous years. The United States currently has sufficient wind power to fuel the equivalent of nearly nine million homes, up almost 23 percent from the start of the year. [*Author's note*: Nine million is approximately 7 percent of U.S. homes.]

As often as she could, Bode stated that wind is "free." She alluded to start-up costs, but these comments were usually buried in the rhetoric: Wind energy costs nothing once you get it online, no water is used, and it avoids carbon. During the entire interview she made no reference to any downsides or tradeoffs with this form of renewable energy. She clinched her argument as "pretty exciting stuff."

Her adversarial stance was not as obvious as Pyle's because she was not defending wind as the only energy source, but maintained that it needed to be added to a portfolio that also included fossil fuels and nuclear sources. Given the political correctness of supporting renewable sources, she continually referred to the support of the public: "People are looking at the U.S. to broaden the portfolio of electricity generation." In framing her answers to challenging questions, she also paired seeming benefits to people with the interests of the wind industry:

- *Why not development by public utility?* Private entrepreneurs are developing wind generation in a free market—this is the American way of doing things.
- *Is this the best use of tax money?* Government subsidies for economic development programs in factory conversions have been phenomenal for putting people back to work and helping a state's economy.
- *Given the abundance of gas and coal, what is the rationale?* The justification for wind is that it is free. Every time wind goes into the grid, it avoids fuel costs. It saves consumers money.

Pyle and Bode brought important concerns, such as costs to consumers, efficiencies in regard to pollution, and market versus government intervention, into their arguments to gain against the other, but little if any XP thinking that would help to untangle these complex issues.

## Reflexive Practice

Daniel Yergin, author of *The Prize: The Epic Quest for Oil, Money and Power,* did not try to simplify a complex issue and did not hesitate to state, "There is no clear answer to the fundamental question of limited resources. Technological developments will help; some we can imagine, some we can't. The world wants and will need more energy, because growth is inevitable." In response to a caller, he simply said, "It's a hard nut to crack. The peak demand is in the Western world. That will begin to decline, but there is a constant 5 percent increase in demand elsewhere."

Rather than a tight analysis or a complete account, he showed appreciation for the complexity: "Any solution to global warming, especially with the increase in development in India and China, is complicated and cannot be solved overnight." In response to a challenge about the legitimacy of global warming, he mentioned that "to even ask the right questions, one would have to become familiar with the evidence, which would require reading huge thick volumes of research." He maintained a questioning posture by stating: "There are legitimate scientific findings, but there are questions about the impact of carbon and clouds."

In reminding a caller that flexibility should be maintained in seeking various means to reach a specified end, he recalled that when China changed its basic economic policies, Deng Xiaoping was reported to have said, "I don't care if the cat is black or white as long as it catches mice." If rigid Communist politicians can move away from at-risk practices, Yergin seemed to imply, why can't the United States?

Yergin refused to be pulled into a "disaster is at hand" stance by callers. He reported that this is the "fifth time the world was about to run out gas." In terms of solutions, he explained that the cap and trade legislation of the 1990s, to reduce the acid rain in the Northeast caused by coal plants, demonstrated that a market-based effort can work faster and cheaper and could be used as "a guiding narrative for the current program." One would hope that learning from the past is possible, as long as there is a comparable situation.

Yergin is cofounder of Cambridge Energy Research Associates, an energy-consulting firm that advises governments and private companies on energy markets, geopolitics, and industry trends. He claims that the company tries to be a source of objective and independent analysis. From a few repetitive comments, he seems to believe that objective analysis can reach only so far and that unknown choices in the future will have significant effects. "Any steps taken in the near future will depend on what will emerge out of Copenhagen. These are big momentous questions, but they will touch every one of our lives."

**David Plouffe**, author of *The Audacity to Win: The Inside Story and Lessons of Barack Obama's Historic Victory,* and Obama's chief campaign manager, was invited to discuss his experiences. In recounting the events and strategies of Obama's successful election campaigns, Plouffe made numerous comments, too many to mention, demonstrating XP tendencies. He did have a clearly defined objective—to win the election, but the formulation for such an objective was that they had "an obligation to win" (for the good of the country). And instead of the typical political rhetoric that winning was a foregone conclusion, Plouffe maintained that the campaign team held out hope and that they continued to question their choices: "There was never a time we said we would win or 'when' we win." He made it clear they maintained a potential to learn, stating, "We perceived ourselves as a start-up company." He referred to using the Presidential primary as a laboratory for what could improve the main campaign. "In the primary, we learned never to look beyond the moment." He emphasized that the team avoided saying, "Boy, looks like we can win" or "when we win." We just kept our heads down. "We looked at the reality—when early votes started coming in, not spin or polls."

Plouffe spoke in terms of catching a wave that is emerging, rather than attempting to create it, and also continuing to probe for other aspects and opportunities, not just "staying on message." He was explicit in stating, "Our approach was to build a campaign and get momentum in different ways." Not only was he open-minded to the point of learning from the "other side," he actually admitted it: "We looked to Bush's 2004 campaign—not his administration—but his campaign." There were two things we learned and adopted: first, the expanded electorate (e.g., John Kerry had Ohio tied up, but lost because Bush's campaign found all the Republicans and turned them out for the vote) and second, maintaining a small, inner circle to manage the campaign in order that conversations could be kept confidential.

**Bruce Bartlett, author of *The New American Economy: The Failure of Reaganomics and a New Way Forward*,** demonstrates XP thinking in his examples of how policy implementers fail to take into consideration changing circumstances. First he gave a concise view of United States economic history. The Keynesian model, developed during the deflationary environment of the 1930s, was misapplied during the inflationary period of the 1950s and 1960s, which led to more inflation. A revised economic viewpoint was developed in the late 1970s during a period of "stagflation," referred to as supply-side economics, which tightened the money supply to reduce inflation and cut tax rates to encourage investment. "All conventional economists and Keynesians thought this was insane—as if putting your foot on the brake and gas pedal at the same time. But it was viewed as a success. By the middle 1980s, inflation was down and growth had been restored." But then in the 2000s, a misapplication of this approach was made. "What remains when people think of 'supply-siders' is a caricature—that there is no problem that more and bigger tax cuts won't solve. Groups try to ruthlessly enforce this view, although the economic problems of today are due to lack of demand, not supply."

Bartlett's research led him to observe that the conditions today are almost identical to the ones in the 1930s. Therefore, it is more likely that a Keynesian-type policy of government spending better fits the current situation. The information per se does not type him as XP, but statements such as the following do: "It is a mistake to think that one size fits all—to take something that worked under different circumstances and say let's do it again under completely different circumstances is ludicrous."

He provided another example of government repeating an unsuccessful activity, as he listed the instances that rebates were tried and summarized the results: "Government rebates have been proven not to work to stimulate the economy; people save the money."

A key characteristic of at-risk practitioners is that they are ready with a pat answer to any question. Bartlett demonstrated XP thinking when he comfortably responded to the moderator's question about stimulus spending: "I'm not sure. Perhaps give it to the homeowner or to Freddie Mac and Fannie Mae."

To be an XP does not mean one is lacking in concrete suggestions. Bartlett said, "A value added tax makes perfect sense and evidently the idea is not without merit because most congressmen agree with me. But the idea is so politically explosive that every one of them said if I quote them they will deny it." But Bartlett wasn't invested in protecting his suggestion as a fixed idea. He continued, "We need to have an open debate. It is awful that there are certain subjects we can't discuss."

## Conclusion

The focus of this appendix was to demonstrate by specific example the practitioner types as described in this book. It was surprising to find that all five types could so easily be identified after viewing only a few segments. Based on the premise that XP thinking is preferred (i.e., is more effective), one would have hoped to find a larger percentage of these in the segments evaluated. (A comprehensive review might have revealed a higher proportion.) Also, given that progress away from at-risk practice toward XP is the goal, perhaps exposure to guests such as Yergin and Bartlett on C-SPAN will encourage such movement.

Both practitioners and the lay public are exposed more than ever to important issues via "talk" media. But in much public affairs TV and radio programming, issues are packaged in a reduced form that is not designed to provoke better thinking, but rather to entertain and may, as a consequence, limit thinking. The attention here has been on the guests, but viewers—those who call in—have, at times, demonstrated their own practitioner types. Many seem to recognize the value in the opportunity to hear a less digested and more nuanced discussion of important topics. More than once, a call-in viewer has referred to C-SPAN as a "window" for the people. Two core issues of XP are the cognitive posture of questioning and dialogical reframing. When listeners—a politician, company CEO, management consultant, or ordinary citizen—are exposed to discourse in which, for example, a guest such as Bartlett says that he doesn't know and wants open debate, will they not come.

## Sources

Bartlett, Bruce. *The New American Economy: The Failure of Reaganomics and a New Way Forward*. New York: Palgrave Macmillan, 2009.

Plouffe, David. *The Audacity to Win: The Inside Story and Lessons of Barack Obama's Historic Victory*. USA: Penguin Group, 2009.

Yergin, Daniel. *The Prize: The Epic Quest for Oil, Money and Power & Power*. New York: Free Press, 1991/2008.

# Notes

## Preface

1. Albert Einstein, "Fund-raising Letter on Behalf of the Emergency Committee of Atomic Scientists," May 1946. In Otto Nathan, Heinz Norden, eds., *Einstein on Peace* (New York: Random House, 1981), p. 376.
2. Albert Einstein, *New York Times Magazine*, June 23, 1946.
3. Graham Allison, *Nuclear Terrorism: The Ultimate Preventable Catastrophe* (New York: Times Books, 2004).
4. Wikiquotes, Albert Einstein page, http://en.wikiquote.org/wiki/Albert_Einstein. Prior to May 2008, this Wikiquotes page included a collection of unsourced quotations from which we made selections. As of April 2009, "unsourced sections are no longer allowed on the main page." This editorial policy, while reasonable, is unfortunate because it eliminates support for the kind of social and cognitive analysis we are conducting here.
5. Robert R. Holt, "Can Psychology Meet Einstein's Challenge?" *Political Psychology* 5(2):199, 1984.

## I  The Turbulent Environment, Then and Now

1. Fred Emery, Eric Trist, *Toward a Social Ecology* (New York: Plenum, 1975).
2. Ibid.
3. James S. Moore, *The Death of Competition: Leadership & Strategy in the Age of Business Ecosystems* (New York: Wiley, 1999).
4. Emery & Trist, *Toward a Social Ecology*, p. xvi. Referring to Alvin Toffler, *Future Shock* (New York: Random House, 1970) and Donald Schon, *Beyond the Stable State* (New York: Norton, 1973).
5. Personal communication.
6. Taiichi Sakaiya, *The Knowledge-Value Revolution, or A History of the Future* (New York: Kodansha, 1991).
7. Donald Schon, *Beyond the Stable State* (New York: Norton, 1973), pp. 15–16.
8. Donald Schon, *The Reflective Practitioner: How Professionals Think in Action* (New York: Basic Books, 1983). See also Donald Schon, *Educating the Reflective Practitioner: Toward a New Design for Teaching and Learning in the Professions* (San Francisco: Jossey-Bass, 1986).

9. *William F. Ogburn on Culture and Social Change, Selected Papers* (Chicago: University of Chicago Press, 1964).
10. Karl Mannheim, *Ideology and Utopia: An Introduction to the Sociology of Knowledge* (Edward Shils translation) (New York: Harcourt Brace, 1955).
11. Elizabeth Kolbert, "The Sixth Extinction?" *The New Yorker*, May 25, 2009, p. 53.
12. Tom Friedman, *New York Times*, October 9, 2009, p. A25
13. Richard Florida, *The Rise of the Creative Class, and How It's Transforming Work* (New York: Basic Books, 2003). Paul Ray, *The Cultural Creatives* (New York: Three Rivers Press, 2001).
14. James P. Carse, *Finite and Infinite Games* (New York: Ballentine, 1987).
15. John R. Boyd, "The Essence of Winning and Losing," January 1996; Robert Greene blogs on how Boyd's work is a guide for thinking under turbulence; accessed at http://www.powerseductionandwar.com/archives/ooda_and_you.phtml.

# 2 Reflexive Practice for the Times We Live In

1. Gary Klein, J.K. Phillips, E. Rall, D.A. Peluso, "A Data/Frame Theory of Sensemaking." In R. Hoffman, ed., *Expertise Out of Context* (Philadelphia: Laurence Earlbaum, 2007).
2. George Lakoff, *The Political Mind: Why You Can't Understand 21st Century American Politics with an 18th Century Brain* (New York: Viking, 2008).
3. Donald Schon and Marin Rein, *Frame Reflection: Toward the Resolution of Intractable Policy Controversies* (New York: Basic Books, 1994).
4. Roger Fisher, Daniel Shapiro, *Beyond Reason: Using Emotions as You Negotiate* (New York: Penguin, 2006).
5. Karl Weick, *Sensemaking in Organizations* (Thousand Oaks, CA: Sage, 1995).
6. Gary Klein, B. Moon, R.F. Hoffman, "Making Sense of Sensemaking II: A Macrocognitive Model," *IEEE Intelligent Systems* 21(5):88–92, 2006.
7. Ikujiro Nonaka, *Managing Flow: A Process Theory of the Knowledge-Based Firm* (New York: Palgrave Macmillan, 2008). Also see Ikujiro Nonaka, Ryoko Toyama, "Strategic Management as Distributed Practical Wisdom (Phronesis)," *Industrial and Corporate Change* 16:371–394, 2007.
8. Paul C. Light, *The Four Pillars of High Performance: How Robust Organizations Achieve Extraordinary Results* (New York: McGraw-Hill, 2005).
9. Light asserts that his robust organization qualifies as a resilient organization in Hamel's terms, but that a resilient organization isn't necessarily robust. Several other works to be mentioned in a general review of resilient strategy include Karl Weick, Kathleen Sutcliffe, *Managing the Unexpected: Resilient Performance in an Age of Uncertainty* (Thousand Oaks, CA: Jossey-Bass, 2007), and Charles Perrow, *Normal Accidents: Living with High Risk Technologies* (updated edition) (Princeton, NJ: Princeton University Press, 1999).

10. Kent Myers, "Strategic Minerals," In Aron Katsenelinboigen, *Indeterministic Economics* (New York: Praeger, 1991).
11. Peter F. Drucker, "The Next Information Revolution," *Forbes ASAP*, August 24, 1998.
12. Mancur Olson, *Power and Prosperity: Outgrowing Communist and Capitalist Dictatorships* (New York: Basic Books, 2000).
13. Mihaly Csikszentmihalyi, *Finding Flow: The Psychology of Engagement with Everyday Life* (New York: Basic Books, 1997), p. 59.
14. Richard Thaler, Cass Sunstein, *Nudge: Improving Decisions about Health, Wealth, and Happiness* (New York: Penguin, 2009).
15. At *Wired Magazine* there was backlash on their blog from at-risk practitioners who wanted to use their own standards for the prize: http://www.wired.com/politics/law/magazine/16-10/sl_intro.
16. Russell Ackoff, "Transforming the Systems Movement," 2004, accessed at *http://www.acasa.upenn.edu/RLAConfPaper.pdf*.
17. Ralph Stacey, *Complexity and Creativity in Organizations* (San Francisco: Berrett-Koehler, 1996).
18. David J. Snowden, Mary Boone, "A Leader's Framework for Decision Making," *Harvard Business Review*, November 2007, pp. 69–76. Also see David Snowden, C.F. Kurtz, "The New Dynamics of Strategy: Sense-Making in a Complex and Complicated World," *IBM Systems Journal* 42(3), 462, 2003.
19. Bent Flyvbjerg, *Making Social Science Matter: Why Social Enquiry Fails and How It Can Succeed Again* (New York: Cambridge University Press, 2001). Mark Freestone, in his review of this book on Amazon, points out that Bourdieu contributed this blurb on the back cover: "This is social science that matters." That was momentous because Bourdieu, a famous sociologist, but also recognized as a leading theorist of reflexivity, had never before endorsed a book.
20. George Steiner, *After Babel: Aspects of Language and Translation* (New York: Oxford University Press, 1998). Steiner describes the general impossibility of having multiple "native" languages, though he was an exception and had three.

## 3  At-Risk Practices That No Longer Work

1. Thomas H. Davenport, "The Fad that Forgot People," *Fast Company*, December 2007.
2. Michael Hammer, *The Agenda: What Every Business Must Do to Dominate the Decade* (New York: Crown, 2001).
3. Nicholas G. Carr, "IT Doesn't Matter," *Harvard Business Review*, May 2003.
4. Robert D. Atkinson, "Digital Prosperity: Understanding the Economic Benefits of the Information Technology Revolution" (Washington, DC: Information Technology and Innovation Foundation, 2007).
5. Donald Schon and Marin Rein, *Frame Reflection: Toward the Resolution of Intractable Policy Controversies* (New York: Basic Books, 1994).

6. Deborah Tannen, *The Argument Culture: Moving from Debate to Dialogue* (New York: Random House, 1999).
7. Louis Kelso proposed such a plan for GM in 1981: http://www.kelsoinstitute.org/gm.html. John Menke recently updated the argument and pointed out that employee ownership saved Chrysler in prior years: http://www.kelsoinstitute.org/gm2.html.
8. Michael Gerson, "The Irony of Obama," *Washington Post*, October 22, 2008.
9. John M. Keynes, *Collected Writings*, Volume 4 (New York: Routledge, 2004), "A Tract on Monetary Reform" (first published in 1923).

# 4 Intelligence for Security

The views expressed in this chapter are my own and do not imply endorsement of the Office of the Director of National Intelligence or any other U.S. government agency.

1. Personal notes from meeting of Panel to Improve Intelligence Analysis for National Security, National Academy of Sciences, Committee on Behavioral and Social Science Research, May 15, 2009.
2. Walter Pincus, "DNI Cites $75 Billion Intelligence Tab," *Washington Post*, September 17, 2009.
3. James Bamford, "Who's in Big Brother's Database?" *New York Review of Books* 56(17), November 5, 2009.
4. Transcript of Senate confirmation hearings for David Gompert, October 13, 2009. Also see Noah Shachtman, "Rogue Satellite's Rotten, $10 Billion Legacy," *Wired Magazine Online*, February 20, 2008.
5. Robert Jervis, "The Iraq WMD Intelligence Failure: What Everyone Knows Is Wrong," remarks at University of Toronto, February 2007. His sponsored study report has more detail, but this speech is more revealing.
6. William Nolte, "Thinking about Rethinking: Reform in Other Professions," *Studies in Intelligence* 52(2),: 22, June 2008.
7. Massimo Calabresi, "Wikipedia for Spies: The CIA Discovers Web 2.0," *Time Magazine*, April 8, 2009.
8. Army intelligence explicitly separates themselves from the program. See humanterrainsystem.army.mil/faqs.html.
9. National Intelligence Council, *Global Trends 2025: A Transformed World*, 2008, accessed at http://www.dni.gov/nic/NIC_2025_project.html.
10. Vision 2015: www.dni.gov/Vision_2015.pdf.
11. David Muller, "Improving Futures Intelligence," *International Journal of Intelligence and Counterintelligence* 22(3), 382–395, 2009. This critique takes a focused practice perspective but suggests some workable compromises.
12. Orton's statements are from an oral presentation he made at the Seminar on Reflexive Systems, George Washington University, October 20, 2009.
13. PNSR Conference Proceedings, July 25–26, 2007, p. 14 (italics in original).
14. Andrew Van de Ven, "Structuring Cooperative Relationships between Organizations," *Strategic Management Journal* 13, 1992.

15. Center for Strategic and International Studies coordinated the Smart Power discussion, http://csis.org/program/smart-power-initiative.
16. Edward Luttwak, *The Grand Strategy of the Byzantine Empire* (Boston, MA: Harvard University Press, 2009).
17. Alvin Toffler, *War and Anti-War* (New York: Grand Central Publishing, 1995).
18. Public Intelligence Blog, www.phibetaiota.org. All of Robert Steele's work can be searched on this site.
19. See, for example, how the Interactivity Foundation promotes "staff work" for citizens: http://www.interactivityfoundation.org/Vision.html.
20. Public Intelligence Blog, www.phibetaiota.org.
21. The technologies are described in Andrew J. Cowell, Deborah L. McGuinness, Carrie F. Varley, David A. Thurman, "Knowledge-Worker Requirements for Next Generation Query Answering and Explanation Systems. In *Proceedings of International Conference on Intelligent User Interfaces* (IUI 2006), Sydney, Australia.
22. John Bodnar, *Warning Analysis for the Information Age: Rethinking the Intelligence Process*, Joint Military Intelligence College, December 2003, p. 180.

## 5 Economy for Good

1. John K. Galbraith, *The Culture of Contentment* (New York: Houghton Mifflin, 1992).
2. Ibid., pp. 6, 10, 12, 48.
3. Alan Greenspan, *The Age of Turbulence: Adventures in a New World* (New York: Penguin, 2008). For a criticism of Greenspan's thinking, see William Fleckenstein, Frederick Sheehan, *Greenspan's Bubbles: The Age of Ignorance* (New York: McGraw-Hill, 2008).
4. The following comments are based on "The Warning," *PBS Frontline* (first broadcast Oct. 20, 2009), http://www.pbs.org/wgbh/pages/frontline/warning/.
5. Waxman committee testimony, October 23, 2008.
6. Steve Denning, "Why We Have a Financial Crisis; Radical Transparency vs. the Age of Bullshit; the Exemplary Manager, Robert S. McNamara," www.stevedenning.com/High-Performance-Teams/radical-transparency.aspx.
7. Harry G. Frankfurt, *On Bullshit* (Princeton, NJ: Princeton University Press, 2005).
8. David Apgar, *Relevance: Hitting Your Goals by Knowing What Matters* (San Francisco, CA: Jossey-Bass, 2008).
9. Lisa D. Ordóñez, Maurice E. Schweitzer, Adam D. Galinsky, Max H. Bazerman, "Goals Gone Wild: The Systematic Side Effects of Over-Prescribing Goal Setting," working paper, *Harvard Business Review*, February 2009.
10. Wendell Potter interview, "Profits Before Patients," *Bill Moyers Now*, July 10, 2008, *http://www.pbs.org/moyers/journal/07102009/profile.html*.

11. See a thoughtful treatment of ownership options in William Greider, *The Soul of Capitalism: Opening Paths to a Moral Economy* (New York: Simon & Schuster, 2003). On employee ownership techniques, see Jeff Gates, *The Ownership Solution: Toward a Shared Capitalism for the 21st Century* (New York: Basic Books, 1999).
12. Herman Daly, John Cobb, *For the Common Good* (Boston, MA: Beacon Press, 1994).
13. Willis Harman interview, "Transformation of Business," www.context.org.
14. Jeffrey D. Sachs, "A Bridge for the Carmakers, The Future Is in Sight, They Just Need Help Getting There," *Washington Post*, November 17, 2008.
15. Storm Cunningham, *ReWealth!: Stake Your Claim in the $2 Trillion Investment Development Trend That's Renewing the World* (New York: McGraw Hill, 2008).
16. He has continued to modify his approach with every publication. His recent lectures have many updates and are the source for our commentary. "George Soros Lectures," October 26–30, 2009, *www.ft.com/cms*.
17. Paul Hawken, *Blessed Unrest: How the Largest Social Movement in History Is Restoring Grace, Justice, and Beauty to the World* (New York: Penguin, 2008).

# 6 Economy, Environment, Energy: Worlds Apart, or Three Perspectives on the Same World

1. F. Emery, E. Trist, "The Causal Texture of Organizational Environments," *Human Relations* 18: 21–32, 1965. Fluid dynamics is the field from which the turbulence concept was taken. Professors who must teach this subject say that the phenomenon of turbulence is too unpredictable and difficult to research, study, or teach.
2. Earlier articulation of what this means can be seen in D. Hawk and M. Takala, "Fluid Management in an Open Society: On Organizational Forms and Their Ability to Retain Fluids," Proceedings of the World Congress 2000, In P. Corning, ed., *Understanding Complexity: The Systems Sciences in the New Millennium*, Palo Alto, CA: Institute for the Study of Complex Systems, 2000.
3. In 1986 Gunnar Hedlund and I described what humans might do if they couldn't use hierarchy as their key organizing principle. This appeared in an unpublished paper for the International Society for the Systems Sciences (ISSS) meeting in St. Louis. His proposal was for the now widely accepted "heterarchy" form, e.g., small, temporary hierarchies. I, unfortunately, argued for the Greek idea of anarchy (human management of self). The disrepute and misunderstanding of this continues large.
4. M. Kosits, D. Hawk, D. Ing, "Relationship Alignment: Reducing Friction, Realizing Value," IBM corporate publication for the IBM Relationship Alignment Solutions Practice, 2004.
5. There are many presentations of the argument for why the Second Law of Thermodynamics matters to human affairs but perhaps the most

illuminating, and largest generator of consternation for optimists, comes from Nicholas Georgescu-Roegen's work: *The Entropy Law and Economic Process* (Cambridge, MA: Harvard University Press, 1971).
6. Found in the reference, *Dictionary of the History of Ideas* (New York: Charles Scribner & Sons, 1968, p. 670), the design argument poses a fundamental human presupposition: human design can only exist if there be teleology; i.e., the freedom to chose, to change your mind, or to learn. As such, predestination is disallowed.
7. Illich, Ivan, *Disabling Professions* (London: Calder and Boyers, Ltd., 1977).
8. bid., p. 22.
9. Workshop held at IBM. BEA Systems, Inc., was a participant.
10. David Hawk, "Environmental Protection: Analytic Solutions in Search of Synthetic Problems," Stockholm, Sweden: Stockholm School of Economics and Institute of International Business Publications, Volumes 1, 2, 3, 1977. Funded by Swedish Parliament and used by the Ministry to convince OECD countries not to duplicate the U.S. approach to environmental protection. It was initially to be jointly funded by the U.S. EPA but on the first day they withdrew saying it was found to be too comprehensive and made too much use of companies to examine themselves.
11. Complex, in our usage here, means too complicated to understand, and that this occurs because subdivision of the issue ensures that it cannot be understood. To make it understandable, and thereby less complex, a context including economics and environment is added.
12. While the article of 1965 was seen as very interesting at the time, it grew into one of the "classics of organizational literature" during the next ten years. Twenty years later it was dropped from the reprint of the "classics," and younger authors were given the early credit for spotting the importance of environmental scanning, awareness, and characteristics. Just now these original authors seem to be making a comeback in that all the later interpretations offered weakness in their stretch for an easier clarity.
13. These are the machines that, once they begin to work, they need no further energy to keep them in motion.
14. In one New Jersey Executive MBA class the students were asked if their firms predominately rely on "carrots" or "sticks" to manage their employees. One responder said, "First we beat them with carrots. If that doesn't work we use sticks." During the break he said, "I wasn't kidding."
15. Annaleena Parhankangas, David Ing, David L. Hawk, Gosia Dane, Marianne Kosits, "Negotiated Order and Network Form Organizations," *Systems Research and Behavioral Science* 22:1–22, 2005.
16. In this 4,000 square foot house summer air conditioning bills never exceeded $70/month for a 70 degree setting. Comparable houses required from $300 and $500 per month with limited thermal comfort. Little has happened to change industry practices except to market new systems as more efficient. When asked in 1998 as to why things have not changed installers pointed out that it was a cash flow issue. If change were introduced, they would end up selling smaller equipment, it would last longer, and there would be fewer service calls.

17. During 1994 meetings on this topic with EPA directors asked us to move ahead with speed. When discussions were held with installers and sales people the difficulties emerged. Marketing people pointed out that, "What the American consumer really wants is size. We thus asked for manufacture of a very large box. Customers bought many of them, even though its internal capacity was not increased."
18. This approach to Prisoner's Dilemma comes from the work of Anatol Rapoport, with his emphasis on how cooperation overcomes conflict to improve human conditions.

# 7 National Environmental Policy Act as a Reflexive Setting

1. Stephen Lansing, *Priests and Programmers: Technologies of Power in the Engineered Landscape of Bali* (Princeton, NJ: Princeton University Press, 1991).
2. Thomas F. King., *Our Unprotected Heritage: Whitewashing the Destruction of Our Cultural and Natural Environment* (Walnut Creek, CA: Left Coast Press, 2009).
3. National Highway Transportation Safety Administration (NHTSA), *Corporate Average Fuel Economy Standards, Passenger Cars and Light Trucks, Model Year 2011* , 2009. See *Federal Register* 74(59):14195–14244, March 30, 2009, Rules and Regulations. Also available at *Federal Register Online* via GPO Access, *wais.access.gpo.gov [DOCID: fr30mr09-12]*.
4. Pierre Bordieu, *Outline of a Theory of Practice* (Cambridge: Cambridge University Press, 1997).
5. John Stephenson, *Climate Change: Observations on Federal Efforts to Adapt to a Changing Environment* (Washington, DC: Government Accounting Office GAO-09-534T, 2009).
6. Herman Daly, John Cobb, *For the Common Good: Redirecting the Economy Toward Community, the Environment, and a Sustainable Future* (Boston, MA: Beacon Press, 1994), p. 382ff.
7. Karl A. Wittfogel, *Oriental Despotism: A Comparative Study of Total Power* (New Haven, CT: Yale University Press, 1957).
8. King, *Our Unprotected Heritage.*

# 8 Reflexive Personality

1. A. Neuringer, "Reinforced Variability in Animals and People: Implications for Adaptive Action," *American Psychologist* 59(9): 891–906, 2004.
2. Brian Holmes, "The Flexible Personality: For a New Cultural Critique," 2001, http://transform.eipcp.net/transversal/1106/holmes/en.
3. R. Burton, *On Being Certain* (New York: St. Martin's Press, 2008).
4. C. Tavris, E. Aronson, *Mistakes Were Made but Not by Me: Why We Justify Foolish Beliefs, Bad Decision, and Hurtful Acts* (Orlando, FL: Harcourt Books, 2007).

5. Dan Ariely, *Predictably Irrational: The Hidden Forces that Shape Our Decisions*, revised and expanded version (New York: Harper Collins, 2009).
6. R. McCrae, P. Costa, "Personality Trait Structure as a Human Universal," *American Psychologist* 52: 509–516, 1997. P. Costa, R. McCrae, *NEO PI-R Professional Manual* (Lutz, FL: Psychological Assessment Resources, Inc., 1992).
7. Pearson Assessments, WAIS-IV, 2008.
8. International Personality Inventory Project, www.ipip.org.
9. I. Myers, M. McCauley, W. Quenk, A. Hammer, *Myers Briggs Type Indicator Manual: A Guide to Development and Uses of the Myers Briggs Type Indicator*, third ed. (Palo Alto, CA: Consulting Psychologists Press, 1998).
10. B. Lahey, "Public Health Significance of Neuroticism," *American Psychologist* 64(4):241–256, 2009.
11. M. Baas, C. DeDreu, B. Nijstad, "A Meta-Analysis of 25 Years of Mood-Creativity Research: Hedonic Tone, Activation, or Regulatory Focus?" *Psychological Bulletin* 134(6):779–806, 2008.
12. E. Hirt, E. Devers, S. McCrea, "I Want to Be Creative: Exploring the Role of Hedonic Contingency Theory in the Positive Mood-Cognitive Flexibility Link," *Journal of Personality and Social Psychology* 94(2): 214–230, 2008.
13. J. P. Shanley, *Doubt: A Parable* (New York: Dramatists Play Service, Inc., 2005).
14. Ibid., p. 46.
15. Robert Kegan, Lisa Lahey, *Immunity to Change: How to Overcome It and Unlock the Potential in Yourself and Your Organization* (Boston, MA: Harvard Business School Press, 2009).
16. Robert Beyster with P. Economy, *The SAIC Solution: How We Built an $8 Billion Employee-Owned Technology Company* (Hoboken, NJ: Wiley, 2007).
17. Scott Wilson, "Bruised by Stimulus Battle, Obama Changed His Approach to Washington," *Washington Post*, April 29, 2009, p. A5.
18. A. Waterman, "On the Importance of Distinguishing Hedonia and Eudaimonia when Contemplating the Hedonic Treadmill," *American Psychologist* 62: 612–613, 2007.
19. J.W.G. Lang, P. Bliese, "General Mental Ability and Two Types of Adaptation to Unforeseen Change: Applying Discontinuous Growth Models to the Task-Change Paradigm." *Journal of Applied Psychology* 94(2): 411–428, 2009.
20. Tavris & Aronson, *Mistakes Were Made but Not by Me*.
21. N. Midgley, "Editorial: Improvers, adapters and rejecters—the link between "evidence-based practice" and "evidence-based practitioners." *Clinical Child Psychology and Psychiatry* 4(3): 323–327, 2009.
22. Lang and Bliese, "General Mental Ability."
23. R. Mueller-Hanson, S. White, D. Dorsey, E. Pulakos, *Training Adaptable Leaders: Lessons from Research and Practice* (Arlington, VA: U.S. Army Research Institute for the Behavioral and Social Sciences, 2005).
24. T. Krynski, J. Tenenbaum, "The Role of Causality in Judgment under Uncertainty," *Journal of Experimental Psychology: General* 136(3): 430–450, 2007.

25. B. Bell, S. Kozlowski, "Active Learning: Effects of Core Training Design Elements on Self-Regulatory Processes, Learning, and Adaptability," *Journal of Applied Psychology* 93(2): 296–316, 2008.
26. Richard Kilburg, *Executive Coaching: Developing Managerial Wisdom in a World of Chaos* (Washington, DC: American Psychological Association, 2000).

## 9  Reflexive Practice on the Global Scene

1. Matthew Green, *The Wizard of the Nile: The Hunt for Africa's Most Wanted* (Ithaca, NY: Olive Branch Press, 2008).
2. "Country Programme Plan" (internal working document), Save the Children, Kampala, Uganda, 2009.
3. Concerned Parents Association (Information Leaflet), Kampala, Uganda, 2008.
4. S. Kruse, K. Forss, "An Evaluation of the Norwegian Save the Children Association," Commissioned by Norad, Oslo, 2009.
5. Kim Forss, S. Hansen, L. McNeill, "Operational Review of CICCED Phase III," an evaluation commissioned by the Canadian Office of CICCED, Sida and the Norwegian Ministry of Foreign Affairs, Beijing, Oslo, and Stockholm, 2006.
6. "Forward Plan Document," MAMTA, New Delhi, 2003.
7. Uttar Pradesh, Bihar, West Bengal, Andhra Pradesh, Maharashtra, Gujarat, Rajasthan. See Kim Forss, M. Larsson, T. Sharma, "Rights and Responsibilities; The Environment of Young Peoples' Sexual and Reproductive Health," An Evaluation Commissioned by Sida, Stockholm, 2009.
8. "EPOPA Phase II 5th Annual Country Report 2006," Kampala, Uganda, 2006.
9. Russell Ackoff, *The Art of Problem Solving* (New York: Wiley, 1978).

## 10  Building Reflexive Practice in Graduate Education

1. Russell L. Ackoff, Sheldon Rovin, *Redesigning Society* (Palo Alto, CA: Stanford Business Books, 2003), p. 83.
2. Fred E. Emery, Eric L. Trist, *Towards a Social Ecology* (New York: Plenum, 1973).
3. S. Crainer, D. Dearlove, *Gravy Training: Inside the Business of Business Schools* (San Francisco: Jossey-Bass, 1999).
4. P.C. Schlechty, *Creating Great Schools: Six Critical Systems at the Heart of Educational Innovation* (San Francisco: Jossey-Bass, 2005). C. Christensen, C.W. Johnson, M.B. Horn, *Disrupting Class: How Disruptive Innovation Will Change the Way the World Learns* (London: Reed Elsevier, 2008). Russell L. Ackoff, D. Greenberg, *Turning Learning Right Side Up: Putting Education Back on Track* (Philadelphia, PA: Wharton School of Publishing, 2008).

5. Russell L. Ackoff, *Redesigning the Future: A Systems Approach to Societal Problems* (New York: John Wiley & Sons, 1974).
6. James T. Ziegenfuss, "America—the Beautiful Future? A Vision and Connected Strategies Needed," *USA Today* [*Journal of Education Society*] 123:22–24, November 1994.
7. James T. Ziegenfuss, "Building Country and Community Health Systems: The Futures and Systems Redesign Approach," International Congress of the Center for Latin American Development Administration (Caracas, Venezuela), presented in Madrid, Spain, October 1998.
8. Ackoff and Rovin, *Redesigning Society*, p. 63.
9. Russell L. Ackoff, Jason Magidson, Herbert J. Addison, *Idealized Design: Creating an Organization's Future* (Upper Saddle River, NJ: Wharton School of Publishing, 2006).
10. James T. Ziegenfuss, "A Methodology for Use of Systems Thinking and Redesign in Graduate Health Care Management Education," In Wojciech W. Gasparski, Marek K. Mlicki, Bela H. Banathy, eds. *Social Agency: Dilemmas and Education Praxiology* (New Brunswick, NJ: Transaction Publishers, 1996). James T. Ziegenfuss, "Designing the Health System's Future: An Academic Medical Center Course," Presented at the Nineteenth International Conference on Systems Research, Informatics and Cybernetics, IIAS, Baden Baden, 2007.
11. J.M. Shafritz, J.S. Ott, Y.S. Jang, *Classics of Organization Theory*, sixth ed. (New York: Wadsworth, 2006). Gareth Morgan, *Images of Organization* (Thousand Oaks, CA: Sage Books, 2006).
12. James T. Ziegenfuss, "Do Your Managers Think in Organizational 3-D?" *Sloan Management Review* 24(1):55–59, 1982. James T. Ziegenfuss, *Organization and Management Problem Solving: A Systems and Consulting Approach* (Thousand Oaks, CA: Sage Books, 2002).
13. Susan R. Myers, "Evaluation of Strategic Leader Cognitive Development Through Distance Education," doctoral dissertation, Pennsylvania State University, 2007. Susan R. Myers, "Senior Leader Cognitive Development through Distance Education," *American Journal of Distance Education*, April–June 2008.
14. G.J. Woods, "Organizational Change: Its Impact on Identity, Commitment, Inter-organizational Perceptions and Behavior," doctoral dissertation, Pennsylvania State University, 2008.
15. James T. Ziegenfuss, *Creating America's Future: Stopping Decay with Citizens, Students & Strategies* (New York: Rowman & Littlefield/ University Press, 2008).
16. Thomas Jefferson, "Letter to William Charles Jarvis," September 28, 1820.

## 11  A Behind-the-Scenes Scenario with Reflexive Practitioners

1. Mark Z. Jacobson, Mark A. Delucchi, "A Plan to Power 100 Percent of the Planet with Renewables," *Scientific American*, October 26, 2009.

2. Harold E. Klein, "Designing Scenarios for Planning and Decision-Making," Eighth Electric Utility Forecasting Symposium, EPRI, 1991. Also see Harold E. Klein, M. D'Esposito, "Neurocognitive Inefficacy of the Strategy Process," *Annals of the New York Academy of Science*, 1118:163–185, 2007.
3. Lester Brown, *Plan B 4.0: Mobilizing to Save Civilization* (New York: W.W. Norton & Co., 2009).
4. *Global Trends 2025*, National Intelligence Council, www.dni.gov/nic/NIC_2025_project.html.
5. Storm Cunningham, *ReWealth!* (New York: McGraw-Hill, 2008).
6. Climate Game Report, SAIC report under contract, 2007.
7. Amory Lovins, "Getting Off Oil: Recent Leaps and Next Steps," Rocky Mountain Institute, 2009, www.rmi.org.
8. Jerome Bruner, *Actual Minds, Possible Worlds* (Cambridge, MA: Harvard University Press, 1986), pp. 11ff.
9. Denning's site has a good list of story resources: www.stevedenning.com. A similar account initiates Russell Ackoff, *Ackoff's Fables: Irreverent Reflections on Business and Bureaucracy* (New York: Wiley, 1991). For a methodological justification, see Barbara Czarniawska, *A Narrative Approach to Organization Studies* (Newbury Park, CA: Sage, 1997).
10. Raphael Ramirez, John W. Selsky, Kees Van der Heijden, eds., *Business Planning for Turbulent Times: New Methods for Applying Scenarios* (Sterling, VA: Earthscan, 2008).
11. Harrison Owen, *Wave Rider: Leadership for High Performance in a Self-Organizing World* (Buchanan, NY: Readhowyouwant, 2009).
12. Thomas Hardy, *Tess of the d'Urbervilles* (New York: Penguin, 2003).
13. The dispute is chronicled in Elizabeth Kolbert, "Hosed: Is There a Quick Fix for the Climate?" *New Yorker*, November 16, 2009, p75–77. The original proposal is in Steven D. Levitt, Stephen J. Dubner, *SuperFreakonomics: Global Cooling, Patriotic Prostitutes, and Why Suicide Bombers Should Buy Life Insurance* (New York: William Morrow, 2009). The response by Raymond T. Pierrehumbert, plus many other comments and Levin's counter-response, are on www.RealClimate.org, October 29, 2009.

# Bibliography

Ackoff, Russell L. *Redesigning the Future: A Systems Approach to Societal Problems.* New York: John Wiley and Sons, 1974.
———. *The Art of Problem Solving,* New York: Wiley, 1978.
———. *Ackoff's Fables: Irreverent Reflections on Business and Bureaucracy.* New York: Wiley, 1991.
Ackoff, Russell L. and D. Greenberg. *Turning Learning Right Side Up: Putting Education Back on Track.* Philadelphia, PA: Wharton School Publishing, 2008.
Ackoff, Russell L. and Sheldon Rovin. *Redesigning Society.* Palo Alto, CA: Stanford Business Books, 2003.
Ackoff, Russell L., Jason Magidson, and Herbert J. Addison. *Idealized Design: Creating an Organization's Future.* Upper Saddle River, NJ: Wharton School Publishing, 2006.
Ariely, Dan. *Predictably Irrational: The Hidden Forces that Shape our Decisions,* revised and expanded version. New York: Harper Collins, 2009.
Baas, M., C. DeDreu, and B. Nijstad. "A Meta-Analysis of 25 Years of Mood-Creativity Research: Hedonic Tone, Activation, or Regulatory Focus?" *Psychological Bulletin,* 134(6), 779–806, 2008.
Becker, Ernst. *Denial of Death.* New York: Free Press, 1973.
Bell, B. and S. Kozlowski. "Active Learning: Effects of Core Training Design Elements on Self-Regulatory Processes, Learning, and Adaptability." *Journal of Applied Psychology,* 93(2), 296–316, 2008.
Beyster, Robert with P. Economy. *The SAIC Solution: How We Built an $8 billion Employee-Owned Technology Company.* Hoboken, NJ: Wiley, 2007.
Bodnar, John. *Warning Analysis for the Information Age: Rethinking the Intelligence Process.* Washington, DC: Joint Military Intelligence College, December 2003.
Bourdieu, Pierre and Loic Wacquant. *An Invitation to Reflexive Sociology.* Chicago: University of Chicago Press, 1992.
———. *Outline of a Theory of Practice.* New York: Cambridge University Press, 1997.
———. *Practical Reason: On the Theory of Action.* Palo Alto, CA: Stanford University Press, 1998.
Brown, Lester. *Plan B 4.0: Mobilizing to Save Civilization.* New York: W.W. Norton & Co., 2009.

Bruner, Jerome. *Actual Minds, Possible Worlds.* Cambridge, MA: Harvard University Press, 1986.
Burton, Robert. *On Being Certain.* New York: St. Martins Press, 2008.
Carr, Nicholas G. "IT Doesn't Matter." *Harvard Business Review,* May 2003.
Carse, James P. *Finite and Infinite Games.* New York: Ballentine, 1987.
Christensen, C., C.W. Johnson, and M.B. Horn. *Disrupting Class: How Disruptive Innovation Will Change the Way the World Learns.* London: Reed Elsevier, 2008.
Crainer, S. and D. Dearlove. *Gravy Training: Inside the Business of Business Schools.* San Francisco: Jossey-Bass, 1999.
Csikszentmihalyi, Mihaly. *Finding Flow: The Psychology of Engagement with Everyday Life.* New York: Basic Books, 1997.
Cunningham, Storm. *ReWealth!: Stake Your Claim in the $2 Trillion Investment Development Trend That's Renewing the World.* New York: McGraw Hill, 2008.
Czarniawska, Barbara. *A Narrative Approach to Organization Studies.* Newbury Park, CA: Sage, 1997.
Daly, Herman and John Cobb. *For the Common Good: Redirecting the Economy Toward Community, the Environment, and a Sustainable Future.* Boston, MA: Beacon Press, 1994.
Davenport, Thomas H. "The Fad that Forgot People." *Fast Company,* December 2007.
Emery, Fred E. and Eric L. Trist. "The Causal Texture of Organizational Environments," *Human Relations* 18, 21–32, 1965.
———. *Toward a Social Ecology.* New York: Plenum, 1973.
Fisher, Roger and Daniel Shapiro. *Beyond Reason: Using Emotions as You Negotiate.* New York: Penguin, 2006.
Fleckenstein, William, and Frederick Sheehan. *Greenspan's Bubbles: The Age of Ignorance.* New York: McGraw-Hill, 2008.
Florida, Richard. *The Rise of the Creative Class, and How It's Transforming Work.* New York: Basic Books, 2003.
Flyvbjerg, Bent. *Making Social Science Matter: Why Social Inquiry Fails and How It Can Succeed Again.* New York: Cambridge University Press, 2001.
Franfurt, Harry G. *On Bullshit.* Princeton, NJ: Princeton University Press, 2005.
Galbraith, John K. *The Culture of Contentment.* New York: Houghton Mifflin, 1992.
Gates, Jeff. *The Ownership Solution: Toward a Shared Capitalism for the 21st Century.* New York: Basic Books, 1999.
Georgescu-Roegen, Nicholas. *The Entropy Law and Economic Process.* Boston, MA: Harvard University Press, 1971.
*Global Trends 2025,* National Intelligence Council. www.dni.gov/nic/NIC_2025_project.html
Green, Matthew. *The Wizard of the Nile: The Hunt for Africa's Most Wanted.* Ithaca, NY: Olive Branch Press, 2008.
Greenspan, Alan. *The Age of Turbulence: Adventures in a New World.* New York: Penguin, 2008.

Greider, William. *The Soul of Capitalism: Opening Paths to a Moral Economy.* New York: Simon & Schuster, 2003.

Hawk, David. "Environmental Protection: Analytic Solutions in Search of Synthetic Problems." Stockholm, Sweden: Stockholm School of Economics and Institute of International Business Publications, 1977.

Hawk, David and M. Takala. "Fluid Management in an Open Society: On Organizational Forms and Their Ability to Retain Fluids." In P. Corning, ed. *Understanding Complexity: The Systems Sciences in the New Millennium.* Palo Alto, CA: Institute for the Study of Complex Systems, 2000.

Hawken, Paul. *Blessed Unrest: How the Largest Social Movement in History Is Restoring Grace, Justice, and Beauty to the World.* New York: Penguin, 2008.

Hirt, E., E.Devers and S. McCrea. "I Want to Be Creative: Exploring the Role of Hedonic Contingency Theory in the Positive Mood-Cognitive Flexibility Link." *Journal of Personality and Social Psychology* 94(2), 214–230, 2008.

Holt, Robert R. "Can Psychology Meet Einstein's Challenge?" *Political Psychology* 5(2), 1984.

Illich, Ivan. *Disabling Professions.* London: Calder and Boyers, Ltd., 1977.

Jacobson, Mark Z. and Mark A. Delucchi. "A Plan to Power 100 Percent of the Planet with Renewables," *Scientific American*, October 26, 2009.

Katsenelinboigen, Aron. *Indeterministic Economics.* New York: Praeger, 1991.

Kilburg, Richard. *Executive Coaching: Developing Managerial Wisdom in a World of Chaos.* Washington, DC: American Psychological Association, 2000.

King, Thomas F. *Our Unprotected Heritage: Whitewashing the Destruction of Our Cultural and Natural Environment.* Walnut Creek, CA: Left Coast Press, 2009.

Klein, Harold E. "Designing Scenarios for Planning & Decision-Making," Eighth Electric Utility Forecasting Symposium, EPRI, 1991.

Klein, Harold E. and M. D'Esposito, "Neurocognitive Inefficacy of the Strategy Process." *Annals New York Academy of Science* 1118, 163–185, 2007.

Kolbert, Elizabeth. "The Sixth Extinction?" *New Yorker*, May 25, 2009.

———. "Hosed: Is There A Quick Fix for the Climate?" *New Yorker*, November 16, 2009, 75–77.

Kosits, Marianne, David Hawk, and David Ing. "Relationship Alignment: Reducing Friction, Realizing Value." *IBM Journal*, 2004.

Krynski, T. and J. Tenenbaum. "The Role of Causality in Judgment Under Uncertainty." *Journal of Experimental Psychology: General*, 136 (3) (2007): 430–450.

Lahey, B. "Public health significance of neuroticism," *American Psychologist*, 64(4), 241–256, 2009.

Lakoff, George. *The Political Mind: Why You Can't Understand 21st Century American Politics with an 18th Century Brain.* New York: Viking, 2008.

Lang, J.W.G. and P. Bliese. "General Mental Ability and Two Types of Adaptation to Unforeseen Change: Applying Discontinuous Growth Models to the Task-Change Paradigm." *Journal of Applied Psychology.* 94(2), 411–428, 2009.

Lansing, Stephen. *Priests and Programmers: Technologies of Power in the Engineered Landscape of Bali.* Princeton, NJ: Princeton University Press, 1991.

Light, Paul C. *The Four Pillars of High Performance: How Robust Organizations Achieve Extraordinary Results.* New York: McGraw-Hill, 2005.

Lovins, Amory. "Getting Off Oil: Recent Leaps and Next Steps." Rocky Mountain Institute, 2009, www.rmi.org.

Luttwak, Edward. *The Grand Strategy of the Byzantine Empire.* Boston, MA: Harvard University Press, 2009.

Mannheim, Karl. *Ideology and Utopia: An Introduction to the Sociology of Knowledge.* New York: Harcourt Brace, 1955.

McCrae R. and P. Costa. "Personality Trait Structure as a Human Universal." *American Psychologist* 52, 509–516, 1997.

Moore, James S. *The Death of Competition: Leadership & Strategy in the Age of Business Ecosystems.* New York: Wiley, 1999.

Morgan, Gareth. *Images of Organization* (updated edition). Thousand Oaks, CA: Sage Books, 2006.

Mueller-Hanson, R., S. White, D. Dorsey, and E. Pulakos. *Training Adaptable Leaders: Lessons from Research and Practice.* Arlington, VA: U.S. Army Research Institute for the Behavioral and Social Sciences, 2005.

National Intelligence Council, *Global Trends 2025: A Transformed World,* 2008. http://www.dni.gov/nic/NIC_2025_project.html

Neuringer, A. "Reinforced Variability in Animals and People: Implications for Adaptive Action." *American Psychologist* 59(9), 891–906, 2004.

Nonaka, Ikujiro. *Manging Flow: A Process Theory of the Knowledge-Based Firm.* Palgrave Macmillan, 2008.

[Ogburn, William F.] *William F. Ogburn on Culture and Social Change, Selected Papers.* Chicago: University of Chicago Press, 1964.

Olson, Mancur. *Power and Prosperity: Outgrowing Communist and Capitalist Dictatorships.* New York: Basic Books, 2000.

Ordóñez, Lisa D, Maurice E. Schweitzer, Adam D. Galinsky, and Max H. Bazerman. "Goals Gone Wild: The Systematic Side Effects of Over-Prescribing Goal Setting" (working paper). *Harvard Business Review,* February 2009.

Owen, Harrison. *Wave Rider: Leadership for High Performance in a Self-Organizing World.* Buchanan, NY: Readhowyouwant, 2009.

Parhankangas, Annaleena, David Ing, David L. Hawk, Gosia Dane and Marianne Kosits. "Negotiated Order and Network Form Organizations," *Systems Research and Behavioral Science* 22, 1–22, 2005.

Potter, Wendell. "Profits Before Patients." (interview) *Bill Moyers Now,* July 10, 2008.

Ramirez, Raphael, John W. Selsky, and Kees Van der Heijden, eds. *Business Planning for Turbulent Times: New Methods for Applying Scenarios.* Sterling, VA: Earthscan, 2008.

Rapoport, Anatol. "Prisoner's Dilemma: Reflections and Recollections." *Simulation and Gaming,* 26(4), 489–503, 1995.

Ray, Paul. *The Cultural Creatives.* New York: Three Rivers Press, 2001.

Sakaiya, Taiichi. *The Knowledge-Value Revolution, or A History of the Future.* New York: Kodansha, 1991.

Schlechty, P.C. *Creating Great Schools: Six Critical Systems at the Heart of Educational Innovation.* San Francisco, CA: Jossey-Bass, 2005.

Schon, Donald. *Beyond the Stable State.* New York: Norton, 1973.

———. *The Reflective Practitioner: How Professionals Think in Action.* New York: Basic Books, 1983.

———. *Educating the Reflective Practitioner: Toward a New Design for Teaching and Learning in the Professions.* San Francisco: Jossey-Bass, 1986.

Schon, Donald and Marin Rein. *Frame Reflection: Toward the Resolution of Intractable Policy Controversies.* New York: Basic Books, 1994.

Shafritz, J.M., J.S. Ott, and Y.S. Jang. *Classics of Organization Theory* (sixth edition). New York: Wadsworth, 2006.

Shanley, J. *Doubt: A Parable.* New York: Dramatists Play Service, Inc., 2005.

Snowden, David J. and C.F. Kurtz. "The New Dynamics of Strategy: Sense-Making in a Complex and Complicated World." *IBM Systems Journal* 42(3), 2003.

Snowden, David J. and Mary Boone. "A Leader's Framework for Decision Making." *Harvard Business Review,* November 2007.

Soros, George. "George Soros Lectures," October 26–30, 2009, www.ft.com/cms.

Stacey, Ralph. *Complexity and Creativity in Organizations.* San Francisco: Berrett-Koehler, 1996.

Steiner, George. *After Babel: Aspects of Language and Translation.* New York: Oxford University Press, 1998.

Stephenson, John. Climate Change: Observations on Federal Efforts to Adapt to a Changing Environment. Government Accounting Office GAO-09–534T, 2009.

Tannen, Deborah. *The Argument Culture: Moving from Debate to Dialogue.* New York: Random House, 1999.

Tavris C. and E. Aronson. *Mistakes Were Made but Not by Me: Why We Justify Foolish Beliefs, Bad Decision, and Hurtful Acts.* Orlando, FL: Harcourt Books, 2007.

Thaler, Richard, and Cass Sunstein. *Nudge: Improving Decisions about Health, Wealth, and Happiness.* New York: Penguin, 2009.

"The Warning," *PBS Frontline,* October 20, 2009.

Toffler, Alvin. *Future Shock.* New York: Random House, 1970.

———. *War and Anti-War: Survival at the Dawn of the 21st Century.* New York: Grand Central Publishing, 1995.

Waterman, A. "On the Importance of Distinguishing Hedonia and Eudaimonia When Contemplating the Hedonic Treadmill." *American Psychologist,* 612–613, 2007.

Weick, Karl. *Sensemaking in Organizations.* Thousand Oaks, CA: Sage, 1995.

Wittfogel, Karl A. *Oriental Despotism: A Comparative Study of Total Power.* New Haven, CT: Yale University Press, 1957.

Woods, G.J. "Organizational Change: Its Impact on Identity, Commitment, Inter-organizational Perceptions and Behavior," Doctoral Dissertation. Pennsylvania State University, 2008.

Ziegenfuss, James T. "Do Your Managers Think in Organizational 3-D?" *Sloan Management Review* 24 (1), 55–59, 1982.

———. *Organization and Management Problem Solving: A Systems and Consulting Approach.* Thousand Oaks, CA: Sage Books, 2002.

———. *Creating America's Future: Stopping Decay with Citizens, Students & Strategies,* New York: Rowman & Littlefield/University Press, 2008.

# Index

3M Corporation, 32

Ackoff, Russell, 7, 34–35, 96, 164, 189, 192, 193
adaptation, 12, 16, 20, 26, 44, 75, 111, 130
  management, 197
  psychology, 165, 168, 169
alignment, 29–30
appreciation, 118, 195, 209
  appreciative inquiry, 32, 214
Ariely, Daniel, 151
Army War College, 196
at-risk practice (combining rational, focused, principled, interested), 39, 41–59, 60, 62–63, 155, 156, 165, 171, 204, 213

Bell & Kozlowski, 169
Beyster, Robert, 96–98, 159
Bodnar, John, 86–88
Boyd, John, 16–17
Bruner, Jerome, 212
Burton, Robert, 148–149
Business Process Reengineering (BPR), 48–52

Carse, James, 15
China (environment), 177–180
cognition, 203
common good, 24–26, 124, 188, 210
conflict tolerance, 160
Corporate Average Fuel Economy (CAFE), 141
crisis, 11–12
Csikszentmihalyi, Mihaly, 33
C-SPAN (Washington Journal), 35, 217
culture, change of, 3–16, 120, 121
Cunningham, Storm, 99
Customs and Border Protection (CBP), 135–137

Daly & Cobb, 98, 143
Davenport, Thomas, 48, 52
Denning, Stephen, 93, 212
Drucker, Peter, 30

Earth Game, 209
education for practitioners, 108, 110, 189–198, 212
Einstein, Albert, xi
elaborate, 31–33, 63, 206
emotional stability, 154
Energy Star program, 112, 118, 122

Fisher, Roger, 23
Five Factor Model, 152
flow, 33
Flyvbjerg, Bent, 38
Focused practice, 46–52, 60, 219
  model, 47
Fuller, Buckminster, 209

Gabel, Medard, 209
Galbraith, John K., 89–91

Index

games, 15, 26, 34, 63–64, 124
  see also simulation
Genoa project, 79
Gerson, Michael, 59
Google, 32
Grameen Bank, 206
Greenspan, Alan, 91–92

Hammer, Michael, 48
happiness, 162
Hardy, Thomas, 214
Harman, Willis, 99
Hawken, Paul, 103–106
health care, 195
Holmes, 147
Holt, Robert, xiii
Human Terrain System, 75

Illich, Ivan, 109
India (reproduction), 180–182
Interested practice, 55–59, 60, 221

Jervis, Robert, 72

Katsenelinboigen, Aron, 29
Kegan & Lahey, 158
King, Tom, 143–144
Klein, Gary, 22, 23
Kolbert, Elizabeth, 215
Krynski & Tenenbaum, 168

Lackoff, George, 22–23
Lang & Bliese, 164–165
leadership, 173, 188
learning process, 202, 204, 209
  see also Education, 189–98, 212
Levi-Strauss, Claude, 6
Levitt, Steven, 215
Light, Paul, 27–29
Luttwak, Edward, 80–82

Mannheim, Karl, 10, 52
McNamara, Robert, 93
Morgan, Gareth, 37–38
Mueller-Hanson, R., 168

Myers-Briggs Personality Inventory (MBTI), 153

National Academy of Sciences, 67, 119
National Counterterrorism Center (NCTC), 73–74
National Environmental Policy Act (NEPA), 126–144
National Intelligence Council, 75, 205, 209
National Intelligence Estimate process, 69
negotiation, 23, 116–117, 124
networks, 103, 110, 188
Next Generation Air Transportation System, 135
Nolte, William, 73
Nonaka, Ikujiro, 23, 38
nudges, 34, 203

Obama, Barack, 59, 161
Odom, William, 71
Ogburn, William, 8
Olson, Mancur, 33
Open Society Institute, 102, 103, 204
open space, 214
openmindedness, 158
organization, lack of, 188
organizational learning, 187
Orton, James D., 77–79
Owen, Harrison, 214

perspectives, see reframing
Peters, Tom, 33
phronesis, 23, 25, 38, 103
Pierrehumbert, Raymond, 215
potential or potentiate, 24–30, 185, 200, 208
  compared to robust, resilient, 26–28
  values of, 204
Potter, Wendell, 94–95
Practices/ practitioner, xiv, 10, 13–16

generic model of practitioner cognition, 152
see also Focused practice, Interested practice, Principled practice, professionals, 12–17, Rational practice, Reflexive practice
Principled practice, 52–55, 60, 220
professionals, xi, 12–17, 63, 110
  cognition, model of, 16–17
  see also practices
Project on National Security Reform (PNSR), 77–79
President's Daily Briefing (PDB), 68, 74, 76, 208
prune, 33–34, 102

RAND Corporation, 27
Rational practice, 44–46, 60, 118, 218
Reflexive practice, 19–40, 59–64, 210, 220, 223–226
  definition, 19–20
  education in, 189–196
  learning to be reflexive, 167–172
  model of, 21
  personality characteristics, 155
  weaknesses of, 38–40, 155 (table)
reframing, 22–24, 109, 131, 165–166, 192, 195–196, 203, 213
relatedness, 157
resilient, see potential
restoration economy, 207
robust, see potential
Rocky Mountain Institute, 210

Sachs, Jeffrey, 99
SAIC, 96–98, 159
Sakaiya, Taichi, 6
scan, 30–1, 75–77, 201–205
Schon, Donald, 4, 5, 6–8, 23, 56
Scowcroft, Brent, 67
self-organizing, 21, 214
sensemaking, 23, 75, 79, 204, 211
simulation, 208
Snowden, Dave, 36–38, 79
Soros, George, 100–103, 213
Spire modeling, 200–205, 207
Stacey, Ralph, 36–38
Steele, Robert, 82–86
story telling, 211
strategy (lack of), 159, 188, 200, 214
Summers, Larry, 92–93
systems thinking, 34–35, 109, 192

Tannen, Deborah, 57
Tavris & Aronson, 150, 166
Thaler & Sunstein, 34
Tofler, Alvin, 4–5, 7–8, 82, 198
Trist, Eric, 3, 7, 9, 115, 120
turbulence, 3–16, 42, 107

Uganda, 174–76, 183–87
uncertainty, see turbulence
United Nations, 173

Waterman, 162–163
Wechsler ability test, 152
Weick, Karl, 23
Woods, Tiger, 14
whole of government policy, 210